MW00843997

ALSO BY NICHOLAS CARR

Utopia Is Creepy

The Glass Cage: Automation and Us

The Shallows: What the Internet Is Doing to Our Brains

The Big Switch: Rewiring the World, from Edison to Google

Does IT Matter?

Superbloom

**HOW TECHNOLOGIES
OF CONNECTION
TEAR US APART**

Superbloom

Nicholas Carr

W. W. NORTON & COMPANY

Independent Publishers Since 1923

For information about permission to reproduce selections from this book,
write to Permissions, W. W. Norton & Company, Inc.,
500 Fifth Avenue, New York, NY 10110

For information about special discounts for bulk purchases, please contact
W. W. Norton Special Sales at specialsales@wwnorton.com or 800-233-4830

Manufacturing by Sheridan Chelsea
Book design by Chrissy Kurpeski
Production manager: Anna Oler

ISBN 978-1-324-06461-9

W. W. Norton & Company, Inc.
500 Fifth Avenue, New York, NY 10110
www.wwnorton.com

W. W. Norton & Company Ltd.
15 Carlisle Street, London W1D 3BS

1 2 3 4 5 6 7 8 9 0

To Ann

Society not only continues to exist by transmission, by communication, but it may fairly be said to exist *in* transmission, *in* communication.

—JOHN DEWEY

And when we come to the modern era, especially, we can understand nothing rightly unless we perceive the manner in which the revolution in communication has made a new world for us.

—CHARLES HORTON COOLEY

Pour me out another phone.

—DAVID BOWIE

CONTENTS

Superbloom

Poppies

THE POPPIES COME OUT EVERY MARCH IN WALKER CANYON, an environmentally sensitive spot in the Temescal Mountains seventy miles southeast of Los Angeles, but the show they put on in early 2019 was something special. Thanks to a wet winter in the normally arid region, seeds that had long lain dormant germinated, and the poppies appeared in numbers not seen in years. The flowers covered the canyon's slopes in carpets of vivid, almost fluorescent orange— the shade you get on hunters' vests and caps. On social media, word of the so-called superbloom spread quickly.

First on the scene were the influencers. On March 1, Jaci Marie Smith, a photogenic twenty-four-year-old Arizonan with four hundred thousand Instagram followers and a popular YouTube lifestyle vlog, posted a picture of herself sitting among the blossoms. She wore orange overalls, an orange pullover, and a creamy wool fedora, a flower in her mouth. "You'll never influence the world by trying to be like it," ran the photo's caption. The post earned tens of thousands of likes, as did a subsequent one featuring a photo of her clutching a bouquet of freshly plucked poppies with a caption promoting the brand of press-on nails she was wearing—"Neon pink nails for a fun change!"—and a link to buy them.

As the hashtag #superbloom proliferated—it would appear on Instagram a hundred thousand times over the next two weeks—hordes of other, less distinguished selfie-seekers followed the influencers into Walker Canyon. Cars clogged roads and highways. Police struggled to maintain order. The nearby town of Lake Elsinore declared a public-safety emergency. Many of the visitors, angling for the perfect shot, went off the canyon's marked trails and trampled the delicate flowers. Others, following Jaci Marie's lead, pulled the blossoms up by the fistful. After a traffic officer was hit by a car, the Lake Elsinore town council closed the main trailhead in an attempt to tame the crowd. The order was rescinded the next day when people started parking haphazardly along access roads and bushwhacking up the hillsides, phones in hand. "Flowergeddon," the press called it.

The backlash was swift and brutal. The early comments on the #superbloom posts had been uniformly sunny—"OMG so cute!" "Adorable!" "I love this!!!!"—punctuated with every imaginable variation of the heart emoji. But as news of the Instagrammers' plundering spread, the comments darkened. "Stop ruining the flowers for your selfish selfies," read a typical one. "Fuck you, you selfish asshole," went another. Scolding hashtags like #horribleperson, #publiclandshateyou, and #flowerdestroyer were affixed to the poppy posts as badges of shame. The influencers, sensing a threat to their meticulously cultivated auras of bubbly geniality, rushed to update their posts with excuses or apologies. Some deleted their messages altogether. In an internet minute, a semblance of joy had turned to a semblance of remorse.

As it played out in the poppy field and through millions of social media feeds, the affair in Walker Canyon offered a portrait in miniature of our frenzied, farcical, information-saturated time. There was the excitement of communal discovery and the noxiousness of mob action. There was the democratization of media production, with everyone churning out content and competing for the symbolic applause of the like button. There was the hurried, hieroglyphic language of hashtag, emoji, and exclamation mark. There were the influencers, with their cavalier blurring of commerce and conversation, and the followers, reveling in a pageant of mass mimicry. There were the trolls and their cruel, often misogynistic barbs. There were the virtue vigilantes, eager to pillory anyone straying outside prescribed lines of speech and behavior. And, everywhere, there were the phoneheads, so obsessed with their busy little screens that they could neither see their surroundings nor hear the voice of common sense.

As well as a portrait, it offered a metaphor. We live today in a perpetual superbloom—not of flowers but of messages. Our phones have turned us into human transceivers, nodes on a communication network of unprecedented scope and speed. Whatever else we may be doing, we are always receiving and emitting signals, many of which we're conscious of (words, images, sounds) and others of which we're not (data on our location, behavior, mood). When we first hooked ourselves up to the network, we did so with excitement and optimism. Being connected to so much information and so many people was thrilling, and it seemed obvious that all those connections would broaden our minds, enlarge our sympathies, and make the world a nicer place. More communication would mean more understanding.

It hasn't turned out that way. The excitement may still be there—if Instagram doesn't get you going, TikTok will; if TikTok seems stale, there's Discord or BeReal or whatever's next—but the optimism has turned to foreboding. We find ourselves facing a raft of unintended and unforeseen consequences—all the social pathologies on display in Walker Canyon as well as other, darker ones—and like the Lake Elsinore town council we're frustrated by our inability to address them. We spend our days sharing information, connected as never before, but the more we communicate, the worse things seem to get. Poppies are lush, vibrant, and entrancing. They're also garish, invasive, and narcotic.

PART ONE

COLLAPSE

Here come the line-gang pioneering by.
They throw a forest down less cut than broken.
They plant dead trees for living, and the dead
They string together with a living thread.

—ROBERT FROST

CHAPTER 1

A More Perfect Liquefaction

An Unlikely Guide

It's hard to imagine a man less suited to the banter and bluster of social media than Charles Horton Cooley. Born in 1864 to a blue-blood midwestern family—his father was an eminent jurist—Cooley grew up a sickly, solitary child, plagued by vague but debilitating stomach ailments. Moving his bowels was a trial. "Sometimes I think I am fit for nothing but a cloister," he wrote in his journal. In social situations, he went on, "I feel exiled from myself."[1] He remained reclusive as an adult. A professor at the University of Michigan, initially in economics, then as the founding member of the school's sociology department, he rarely collaborated with colleagues and seldom conversed with anyone outside a small set of family and friends. He spent most of his time alone in his Ann Arbor office, reading and thinking, with the occasional sojourn to a secluded lakeside cabin he'd built in the northern Michigan woods. "Rarely can a modern American," a relative would recall after Cooley's death in 1929, "have lived so withdrawn from the harassments of our times."[2]

Despite his shy, monastic ways, Cooley proved an incisive and original thinker about social relations. What he had trouble experiencing firsthand he was able to explore in the quiet spaces of his mind. Writing when sociology was still an infant discipline struggling to distinguish itself from economics and political science, he came to reject the orthodox view of society as a collection of individuals pursuing, through competition or cooperation, their own interests. To his eye, the opposite seemed nearer the truth. Society shapes the individual more than the other way around. "Self and society are twin-born," he wrote, "and the notion of a separate and independent ego is an illusion."[3] He believed in the existence of a "social mind" that's more than the sum of its parts, and he came to see that the way people exchange information determines the workings of that collective intelligence. It was Cooley in fact who coined the term *social media*—in a remarkable 1897 article called "The Process of Social Change."[4]

Published in the prestigious *Political Science Quarterly*, the article begins unsteadily. In its first few pages, Cooley speculates about whether the "Darwinian idea of change by survival" might help explain how societies evolve. He offers a series of observations about "race elements" and "unwholesome influences" that now come off as at best fatuous and at worst repugnant. But then he switches course. He dismisses natural selection and heredity as forces of social change. They work too slowly, too haphazardly. What really matters, he suggests, is communication. Because we humans are "imitative and sympathetic" creatures who adjust our attitudes and behavior in response to social cues, the way we communicate determines, in large measure, the way we think and act. Whenever the "mechanisms of communication" change, society changes. And the faster the mechanisms change, the faster society changes.

The two things that must always coöperate are human nature and the mechanism of communication. The first is a relatively permanent factor; but the second is highly variable, and is for that reason of peculiar interest and importance. Its variations have generally been in the direction of greater efficiency, and it is largely because of this fact that the history of the past two thousand years is a record of rapid and accelerating social change.

In his stress on the means of communication, rather than the content, Cooley anticipates the work of the celebrated media theorists of the second half of the twentieth century—scholars such as Harold Innis, Marshall McLuhan, and Neil Postman—who are now seen as the founders of contemporary communication studies. Cooley was, like them, a media ecologist. He recognized that communication technologies are much more than tools that people use to throw their voices and ideas across distances. Every new medium creates a new environment. As we adapt to the environment, it shapes our perceptions and thoughts, our relationships with others, even our sense of self. The Yale professor John Durham Peters points out that a crucial line in Cooley's article—"social influences act through a mechanism; and the character of their action depends upon the character of the mechanism"—could have been written by McLuhan. It means something very similar to the later writer's famous dictum "the medium is the message." Both men saw that how we communicate is even more important than what we communicate. Both found in the technology of communication an "engine of history," as Peters puts it.[5]

But Cooley's emphasis was different from McLuhan's. McLuhan was primarily interested in how communication technologies mold individual consciousness by altering sense perceptions and patterns of cognition. Cooley's interest lay in how the technologies shape the social mind by changing the way influence flows and associations form among people. A communication medium, for Cooley, is not just a conduit for information. It is an instrument for regulating group behavior and belief. By means of its media a society promotes values and sets norms, allocates praise and censure, promulgates models of conduct and character, motivates and coordinates action, and establishes hierarchies and other structures of power and status. Human nature may be largely fixed, but human behavior is always susceptible to social influence. "Association may not change nature, but it usually controls conduct," Cooley observes. And association is itself governed by communication.

Spheres of Influence

Early humans communicated with their bodies—through facial expressions and hand gestures, grunts and growls. When language at last emerged in the species, some two hundred thousand years ago according to the best current estimates, it greatly expanded the scope and precision of communication. More could be said, more could be shared, more could be known. But speech remained tied to the body. Like grunts and growls, words went directly from the mouth of the speaker to the ear of the listener. Our ancestors could communicate only with those in their immediate vicinity—within earshot or eyeshot. It was possible for ideas to travel through time and space, by being transferred from one speaker to another to another, but such chains of oral transmission are precarious. They're slow, easily disrupted, and prone to the distortions of hearing and memory. Anyone who's played the game of telephone knows how quickly messages get garbled when passed from person to person.

It wasn't until the invention of writing, just a few thousand years ago, that speech broke free of mouth and ear and became suitable for transmission by technological means. Once inscribed on papyrus or paper, words could travel across expanses of space and time with little or no distortion. While the spoken word "perishes instantly without material trace," observed the English novelist and critic Samuel Butler in an 1895 lecture, the written word "extends infinitely, as regards time and space, the range within which one mind can communicate with another." Writing grants to the thoughts and observations of a writer "a life limited by the duration of ink, paper, and readers, as against that of his flesh and blood body."[6] By tying speech to toolmaking and in turn commerce—by *technologizing* it—writing also ensured that the efficiency of communication would advance steadily and at an accelerating rate. Human ingenuity guaranteed that there would be books, printing presses, newspapers, telegraphs, fax machines, and computer networks. And the desire for money and prestige guaranteed that the competition to invent and improve such tools would be fierce.

Every communication medium is political, a conduit of power as much as thought. In extending the range of speech, writing widened the scope of personal and institutional influence. A written word had the potential to shape the thinking and behavior of far more people, around the globe and down the ages, than a spoken one ever could. The expansion of spheres of influence had profound social consequences. It gave central authorities such as churches, governments, and despots more levers of control. They could project their power through the circulation of laws, doctrines, and edicts, and they could protect their power by preventing others from gaining access to communication systems. Tools of communication also served as tools of empire.[7]

But in broadening spheres of influence, writing had another, countervailing effect. It gave people, at least those who could read, far greater exposure to the thoughts of others. Once printing presses began making books commonplace, every literate person could, as Cooley writes, "form his own environment by retaining what suits him from a variety of materials, and by opening communication with congenial minds in remote times and places." By freeing the reader from his physical surroundings and local social group, the written word not only hastened the spread of knowledge; it fueled the rise of individualism. The reader, withdrawing into the solitary act of reading, could chart the path of his own intellectual growth. The book may have been "the first product of mass production," as McLuhan wrote, but it "isolated the reader in silence and helped create the Western 'I.' "[8]

As written works—books but also journals and letters, newspapers and magazines—proliferated through the centuries, individuals gained ever greater exposure to thinkers and ideas. They could associate with others on the basis of affinity rather than just proximity. Even as writing extended the influential reach of central authorities, it decentralized both the power of influence and the power of association. The tension between centralized and decentralized communication would grow stronger as new, ever more capacious media emerged. In 1517, not long after the invention of the printing press, a small-town German priest named Martin Luther became one of the first persons to turn the tension to his advantage. By circulating thousands of printed copies of his subversive Ninety-Five Theses, he challenged the authority of the mighty Catholic Church, ignited the Protestant Reformation, and turned himself into the world's first media star.[9] He used decentralized media to establish himself as a center of influence. The interests of today's online influencers may lean more toward fashion accessories than articles of faith, but in using a new medium to bypass traditional intermediaries and reach an audience directly, they are Luther's heirs.

When Cooley invokes the term *social media* in his article, he uses it to describe the new groups that coalesced around ideas, interests, and personalities once communication was freed from its bodily constraints. Each group itself became a medium for circulating information and opinions among its members.

> There are as many social media as there are specialized groups of sympathetic and communicating individuals, and in choosing his environment a man chooses what groups he will belong to. Each of these groups or media is subject to movements more or less peculiar to itself; it has in some measure its own opinions, institutions and traditions.

As people with "like natures" became better able to find one another and form their own communities of interest, independent of where or even when they lived, society grew more dynamic, more change-able, and more unsettled.

Epiphany

Cooley lived at a pivotal moment in the history of communication, a time as tumultuous as our own. He was born in the decade (the 1860s) that saw the completion of the first transcontinental telegraph line and the development of the first telephone prototype, and he died in the decade (the 1920s) that saw the establishment of the first commercial radio station and the invention of television. He was an eyewitness to the many upheavals that happened when information began to move at the speed of electric current.

When he wrote "The Process of Social Change," he was very much aware of how new media technologies—he points to "tele-graphs, telephones, photography and the marvels of the daily newspaper"—would continue to accelerate the pace of social trans-formation. Political ideas, religious tenets, scientific discoveries, fashions in music and clothing: all would become "quicker in trans-mission and more general in their incidence, accessible at a greater distance and to a larger proportion of the people." More groups would form around common interests and beliefs, and as those inter-ests and beliefs became more specialized or more extreme, the new groups would splinter into still more groups. Authority and control would be even more subject to the opposing forces of concentration and centralization on the one hand and fragmentation and diffusion on the other. The consequences could not be predicted, but Cooley saw they would be momentous. "So far as concerns the general char-acter of social change," he concluded, "the effect may be described as a more perfect liquefaction of the social medium." As communica-tion speeds up, once-stable social structures and relations become as malleable as water.

Cooley's insights into the way mechanisms of communication change society by altering flows of influence and forms of association are instructive. As we'll see, they explain a great deal about how mass media reshaped society in the twentieth century and how social media is transforming society in our own time. But Cooley's analysis was incomplete. At the moment of his great epiphany—that striking vision of society liquefying in a welter of contending influences—his powers of prophecy failed him. He turned his eyes away from the more ominous implications of his argument. Unable to appreciate the blurriness of the lines that separate influence from manipulation, association from tribalism, he remained blind to the possibility that, by giving people ever greater power to filter information and form groups on the basis of personal whim or partisan passion, more efficient communication might breed factionalism, authoritarianism, and strife. It might destabilize or even fracture society.

Maybe as a result of his isolation from everyday "harassments," Cooley held to a sentimental view of human nature. When given the freedom to choose their own influences and associations, to create their own environment, people would, he believed, make thoughtful, rational decisions. Exposed to more facts and opinions, they would become better informed and broader minded. They might at times act selfishly or come under the spell of pernicious ideas, but the social pressure of communication would eventually push their thoughts and behavior back into line. "It is the tendency of communication," he wrote toward the end of his article, "to give human nature a fair chance, levelling before it the barriers of ignorance, blind hostility and constraint of place, and permitting man to organize his higher sympathetic and aesthetic impulses." As the mechanisms of communication continued their inexorable advance, social and cultural progress would follow technological progress.

Cooley could sustain his idealism only by curbing his genius. He had to gloss over the conflicts inherent in his portrayal of social change, to assume the expansion of a society's communicative capacity would, as if by magic, conjure solidarity out of individualism and unity out of division. The proliferation of groups would not weaken the whole but strengthen it. Cooley's faith in the power of communication to create "a larger togetherness," the cultural critic Philip Rieff would write in a perceptive 1962 essay, "reflected a deeper disinclination to take into account the demonic in man."[10] In his misreading of human nature, the recluse would have plenty of company.

The Social Missionary

Mark Zuckerberg had reason to feel cocky at the start of 2012. His eight-year-old company, Facebook, had vanquished its major rival, MySpace, and now sat alone at the top of the burgeoning social media market. Some nine hundred million people were regular users of the network, more than double the number just two years earlier, and they were posting nearly three billion messages every day. Ad sales and profits were booming. The company's prospects, already bright, were about to get brighter still, as Zuckerberg was secretly negotiating a deal to acquire a buzzy photo-sharing start-up named Instagram. With Facebook on track to go public in a few months, in what was shaping up to be the biggest U.S. IPO ever, Zuckerberg was set to become one of the wealthiest persons on the planet.

But the young entrepreneur had grander aspirations. He was going to change the world. On the first day of February, he wrote a long, earnest letter to would-be shareholders explaining that Facebook had a higher calling than making money. It was pursuing a "social mission" to create a more perfect society by getting people to communicate more. "People sharing more," he wrote, "creates a more open culture and leads to a better understanding of the lives and perspectives of others." He took inspiration, he said, from the world-altering communication technologies of the past, notably printing and television: "By simply making communication more efficient, they led to a complete transformation of many important parts of society. They gave more people a voice. They encouraged progress. They changed the way society was organized. They brought us closer together."[11] Facebook would do the same, on an even larger scale.

Zuckerberg's riches continued to grow in the ensuing years, but his social mission foundered. Events rebuked his hopes, again and again. Society did not grow more harmonious. It grew more fractious, and much of the blame fell on social media. Facebook in particular faced fierce criticism for, among other alleged offenses, encouraging bullying and shaming, circulating hate speech and lies, spying on the public, polarizing the electorate, and monopolizing the dissemination of information. Social media was transforming society, but not in the way Zuckerberg had promised.

It all boiled over in 2016. The year began when a heavily armed man, a twenty-nine-year-old father of two, stormed a pizza parlor in Washington, D.C. He was intent on freeing children who, according to rumors circulating online, were imprisoned in the restaurant by a Democratic Party pedophile ring. Though he found no captives, he succeeded in terrifying plenty of kids out for pizza with their families. The year ended with the election to the presidency of the United States of a malevolent coxscomb with a tweeting habit. The campaign had been marked by the spread, through Facebook, YouTube, Instagram, and other platforms, of thousands of fake and often bizarre news stories from made-up publications, all aimed at misleading or confusing voters. Social media had become, to steal a line from an old Joan Didion essay, "the ganglia of the fantastic electronic pulsing that is life in the United States," and the neurons were misfiring.[12]

The controversies didn't seem to disturb the equilibrium of the Facebook founder and chief executive. He remained unchastened, his cockiness intact. On February 16, 2017, just three months after the contentious U.S. vote, he posted another public letter, this one nearly six thousand words long. Titled "Building Global Community," it expressed even more grandiose ambitions than the 2012 missive. Reporters termed it a manifesto. Facebook was, Zuckerberg announced, expanding its mission from "connecting friends and family" to building "a global community that works for everyone." The ultimate goal was to turn the already vast social network into a benevolent superstate "spanning cultures, nations and regions." Facebook would become the world's "social infrastructure."[13]

Charles Cooley's ideas echoed strongly, if unintentionally, through the letter. Zuckerberg suggested that the global community he envisioned would emerge organically, and inexorably, from the formation of "millions of smaller communities." The influence-sharing groups that Cooley had referred to as "social media" Zuckerberg called "mediating groups that bring us together and reinforce our values." Facebook's role, he declared, would be to provide new software tools to automate the establishment of such groups. He expressed particular excitement about using artificial intelligence techniques to make group formation more efficient. The company would use machine-learning algorithms to identify sets of people likely to share interests or opinions, introduce them to one another on Facebook, and encourage them to set up formal information-sharing groups on the platform.

Underpinning Zuckerberg's manifesto was a conception of society as a technological system with a structure analogous to that of the internet. Just as the net is a network of networks, so society, in the technocrat's mind, is a community of communities.* Given the right set of common communication protocols—the ones provided by Facebook, naturally—all the world's subcommunities would interconnect to form a seamless global community. Community would *scale*, to use a term beloved by the tech elite. With its earlier invention of the News Feed algorithm, Facebook had automated the flow of information and influence among people, achieving what Zuckerberg called frictionless sharing. Now it would use its software to automate group formation through frictionless association.

But the entrepreneur's vision of "a global community that works

---

* Zuckerberg had long held a mechanistic view of society. From Facebook's early days, he would refer to the social network as a "graph," a term of art borrowed from the mathematical discipline of network theory. One of the curiosities of the early twenty-first century is the way so much power over social relations came into the hands of young men with more interest in numbers than in people.

for everyone" was a fantasy. Human beings are not computers. The communities they form are not electronic networks. Society does not scale. What was missing from Zuckerberg's manifesto was any sense of people as individuals, with their own backgrounds and beliefs, personalities and motivations, quirks and biases. People join together into groups on the basis of shared interests or values not technical protocols. Oftentimes the interests or values of one group will be in tension or conflict with those of other groups. Sometimes a group's beliefs will be odious or intentionally abrasive. A group of white nationalists is not going to interconnect with a group of Antifa protesters, at least not in a way that breeds understanding and harmony. A community of incels is not going to interconnect with a community of women software programmers to form a larger community. Networked computers communicate with a cold and predictable precision. People communicate with love, anger, passion, resentment, joy, and fear, among innumerable other emotions.

The Gift

The cosmos, the opening verses of the Bible tell us, was spoken into being: "God said, 'Let there be light'; and there was light." The original act of creation was an act of communication. Five days later, after God had spoken into being the sky and the stars, the land and the sea, trees and fish and mammals and bugs, we humans were in our turn spoken into being, with a special, sacred dispensation: "God said, 'Let us make humankind in our image, according to our likeness.'"

To be fashioned in God's image is to share his ability to speak. Our facility with language, the scriptures suggest, separates us from and elevates us above the other animals of Earth, all those grunting, growling beasts. When we speak, we express the divinity within us. We express as well our powers of creation, another of our godlike qualities. What we create with our words, before all else, is ourselves. The voice of consciousness that's forever talking inside our head— that weird hybrid of monologue and dialogue that makes speaker and listener one—is the sculptor of the self. Language, writes Karen Armstrong, a religion scholar and former nun, "is not only a vital means of communication, but it helps us to articulate and clarify the incoherent turbulence of our inner world."[14] Even the most ineffable experiences are quickly translated into words by the mind. Moment by moment, we speak ourselves into being. And then, turning our voices outward, we join with others in common pursuits. We use words to coordinate thought, feeling, and action. Together, we speak our world into being.

The singularity of human speech has been given a secular blessing by science. Plenty of other animals exchange information, sometimes with subtleties we can only guess at, but nowhere in evolution's vast and branchy tree is there to be found another species that comes close to *Homo sapiens* in communicative prowess. Singular in itself, our skill with language springs from other singularities in our makeup—in our physiology, our cognition, our psychology, our sensorium, our memory. And it is by means of our verbal dexterity that we do extraordinary, distinctively human things: think complex thoughts (*The Critique of Pure Reason*, the theory of relativity), build complex objects (a cathedral, an atomic bomb), and live together in complex societies (cities, nation-states). Whether understood as providential gift or natural phenomenon, our fluency at communication is central to our sense of ourselves as exceptional beings at the pinnacle of life's hierarchy.

Charles Cooley and Mark Zuckerberg could hardly be more different as men, but in expressing a belief in the inherent goodness of communication both joined a venerable Western tradition of humanistic thought. It's a tradition most of the rest of us subscribe to as well. Communication, we tell ourselves, is not just what makes us special. It is the nearest thing we have to a universal remedy for personal and social ills. The sharing of information and opinion shrinks the world. It breeds empathy and understanding. It mends divisions and calms strife. It turns adversaries into allies, enemies into friends. Communication is a moral force.

And if communication is good, more of it must be better. Ever since the great Enlightenment philosophers started dreaming of a world-encompassing Republic of Letters, society has felt an obligation to encourage any and all attempts to increase the efficiency of communication—its speed, its volume, its reach. Advances in media technology came to seem integral to liberalism, pluralism, and democracy—to the entire project of modernity. The eighteenth-century German philosopher Johann Gottfried von Herder expressed the common wisdom well in his *Letters for the Advancement of Humanity*: "The more and the more easily messengers reach everywhere here, everywhere there, then the more the communication of thoughts is advanced, and no prince, no king will seek to hinder this who understands the infinite advantages of the mind-industry, of mind-culture, of the reciprocal communication of inventions, thoughts, suggestions, even of mistakes committed and weaknesses."[15] To stand in the way of communication is to stand in the way of progress.

The messengers von Herder had in mind were, of course, human beings—envoys, couriers, and postal agents who carried documents on foot, on horseback, or aboard ship. In the eighteenth century, as in preceding centuries, communication systems were transportation systems. Messages were cargo. The invention of writing may have liberated speech from the body of the speaker, but every written work, whether letter or contract, newspaper or book, still had to take a physical form. It could move only as quickly as a human being—or, on rare occasions, a homing pigeon—could carry it. Information had not yet changed its state. It was still a solid. It had substance and weight, and it was subject to all the frictions of the material world.

In the centuries after the invention of writing, there had been many attempts to speed up the transmission of information, most involving the use of auditory or visual signals in place of physical documents.[16] The ancient Greeks constructed a system of lookout towers and fire beacons to send bulletins across their empire. West Africans communicated through talking drums, using subtle alterations in the tone and rhythm of beats to transmit messages. In the late eighteenth century, the French started sending communiqués through an elaborate "optical telegraph" involving watchtowers, telescopes, and mechanical semaphores. Others exchanged messages with smoke signals, flags and pennants, mirrors, cannon blasts and gunshots. Paul Revere used lanterns in a church steeple. However ingenious, all these methods of conveying information had severe limitations. They could send only simple messages over short distances, their transmissions were subject to distortion and ambiguity, and they could be rendered useless by bad weather or the setting of the sun.

The Vital Cord

The next real revolution in communication efficiency, the electronic one still playing out today, didn't begin until the arrival of the telegraph in the nineteenth century. Once words could be translated into codes and sent over wires as electric pulses, human messengers began to be replaced by mechanical ones. Freed from another layer of physical constraint, the efficiency of information exchange took a great leap forward. Messages began to speed invisibly and almost instantaneously from place to place. The mystical-seeming transmissions captivated a public infatuated with the spectacles of industrial innovation. Technological enthusiasm became endemic, and it reinforced people's faith in communication as an unstoppable moral force.

As the telegraph network expanded in the middle years of the century, a utopia of universal understanding appeared within reach. "A new channel of blessing has been opened for the world," the prominent Boston minister Ezra Gannett told his congregation in an 1858 sermon on telegraphy. "It is an institution for the people. Its office is, to diffuse intelligence; its effect, to allay differences. Men who talk together daily cannot hate or disown one another." The system's "most remarkable" consequence, he went on, "will be the approach

to a practical unity of the human race; of which we have never yet
had a foreshadowing, except in the gospel of Christ."[17] Telegraphy
"binds together by a vital cord all the nations of the earth," wrote
the authors of *The Story of the Telegraph*, a best seller published that
same year. "It is impossible that old prejudices and hostilities should
longer exist."[18] The book took its epigraph from the Book of Psalms:

> Their line is gone out through all the earth,
> And their words to the end of the world.

The 1865 International Telegraph Conference, held in Paris,
declared itself "a veritable Peace Congress." All the misunderstand-
ings that once led to wars, the chairman of the gathering assured
attendees, would be eradicated by "this electric wire which con-
veys thoughts through space at lightning speed, providing a speedy
and unbroken link for the scattered members of the human race."[19]
The telegraph is an "annihilator of distance," proclaimed Germany's
postmaster general in an 1876 speech. By liberating communication
from "clod and hoof," it would initiate an era of international fellow-
ship. "We have received this wonderful force of nature as a gift from
the Creator."[20] The obligation to increase the efficiency of communication felt all the more pressing when progress—material, social, and
spiritual—was made visible in the stringing of telegraph wires over
city streets and along country roads.

In 1899, two years after Cooley's article appeared, the *New York
Times* ran an impassioned editorial celebrating the laying of trans-
atlantic communication cables and calling on Western Union, the
giant American telegraph monopoly, to cut the cost of international
dispatches. By making its rates more affordable, the paper argued,
the company would extend the privilege and pleasure of high-speed,
long-distance communication to the general public. And it would
accomplish something of even greater import. It would help spread
peace and goodwill throughout the world. "Nothing so fosters and
promotes a mutual understanding and a community of sentiment
and interests," the editorialist declared, "as cheap, speedy, and con-

venient communication."[21] The truth of the statement would have seemed obvious to readers.

The construction of large-scale communication networks required enormous capital and extensive managerial coordination. In the United States, media became big business, as the rise of Western Union signified. To inventors, entrepreneurs, and corporate executives—Mark Zuckerberg's forebears—the public's celebration of communication proved a boon. It not only reinforced their messianic sense of self-importance but also served their business interests. It guaranteed them eager customers, enthusiastic investors, and indulgent regulators. As the pace of technological progress quickened, each advance in media triggered a new burst of millenarian rhetoric. Nikola Tesla, in an 1898 interview about his plan to create a wireless telegraph, said that he would be "remembered as the inventor who succeeded in abolishing war."[22] Not to be outdone, his rival, Guglielmo Marconi, declared in 1912 that his invention of radio would "make war impossible."[23] AT&T's top engineer, J. J. Carty, predicted in 1923 that the telephone system would "join all the peoples of the earth in one brotherhood."[24] In 1932, the popular technology writer and future RCA vice president Orrin Dunlap said that television would "usher in a new era of friendly intercourse between the nations of the earth."[25]

Such cheery predictions were put to an early test in the summer of 1914. In the immediate aftermath of the June 28 assassination of Archduke Franz Ferdinand of Austria by a Serbian nationalist in Sarajevo, hundreds of urgent diplomatic messages raced between European capitals through recently strung telegraph and telephone wires. As the historian Stephen Kern has described, the rapid-fire dispatches quickly devolved into ultimatums and threats. Rather than calming the crisis, they inflamed it. "Communication technology imparted a breakneck speed to the usually slow pace of traditional diplomacy and seemed to obviate personal diplomacy," Kern writes. "Diplomats could not cope with the volume and speed of electronic communication."[26] Diplomacy, a communicative art, had been overwhelmed by communication. Even as they impeded negotiations, the new tele-communication systems enabled armies and navies to mobilize much faster than had been possible when military orders traveled by courier. By August, the First World War was under way.

"The moral qualities—prudence, foresight, intelligence, penetration, wisdom—of statesmen and nations have not kept pace [with the] rapidity of communication by telegraph and telephone," the distinguished British diplomat Ernest Satow wrote in 1917, the war's bleakest year. "These latter leave no time for reflection or consultation, and demand an immediate and often a hasty decision on matters of vital importance."[27] In a speech delivered thirty years later, at the end of an even deadlier world war, Harold Innis would express the seeming paradox more bluntly still: "Enormous improvements in communication have made understanding more difficult."[28] Despite the thrilling, relentless expansion of people's ability to exchange information, despite the world being wrapped in wires and awash in messages, despite the unprecedented opportunities for friendly intercourse between nations, the twentieth century turned out to be the bloodiest in history. We had been telling ourselves lies about communication—and about ourselves.

CHAPTER 2

Privacy and the Public Interest

Two Paths

Around two o'clock in the afternoon on October 30, 1973, a disk jockey at the New York City radio station WBAI played a track called "Filthy Words" from George Carlin's latest album, *Occupation: Foole*. "I was thinking one night about the words you couldn't say on the public airwaves," the comedian began. He then rattled off seven choice examples, starting with "shit," winding through "fuck" and "cunt," and ending with "tits," and proceeded to riff on their origin, usage, and relative offensiveness for the next ten minutes.

A Long Island man named John Douglas heard the program in his car as he was driving home from a college-scouting trip to Connecticut with his teenaged son. Douglas was president of CBS's publishing and education arm. He was also a top-ranking member of Morality in Media, a prominent anti-obscenity advocacy group. He fired off a complaint to the Federal Communications Commission. "Whereas I can perhaps understand an 'X-rated' phonograph record's being sold for private use, I certainly cannot understand the broadcast of same over the air that, supposedly, you control," he wrote. "Can you say this is a responsible radio station, that demonstrates a responsibility to the public for its license?"[1]

After a year-long investigation, the FCC came down on Douglas's side. It ruled that the station had violated a long-standing federal law prohibiting the broadcast of "obscene, indecent, or profane language." The kind of "obnoxious, gutter language" that Carlin used, the commissioners wrote, "has the effect of debasing and brutalizing human beings by reducing them to their mere bodily functions." They emphasized that, when it comes to the regulation of speech, broadcasters require "special treatment" because they operate "in the public interest."[2]

WBAI's parent company, the nonprofit, progressive radio network Pacifica Foundation, appealed the ruling, claiming Carlin's monologue was political satire protected by the First Amendment. In 1977, a federal appeals court issued a split decision agreeing with Pacifica and reversing the FCC action. While granting that the commission had the authority to regulate radio and TV programming, the appeals court argued that the commissioners' ruling in the Carlin matter went too far. It entered "into the forbidden realm of censorship" and could "inhibit the free and robust exchange of ideas on a wide range of issues."[3]

The FCC took the case to the Supreme Court. In a five-to-four decision issued in July of 1978, nearly five years after the offending program aired, the court sided with the commission. Writing for the majority, Justice John Paul Stevens observed that while "each medium of expression presents special First Amendment problems," broadcasting's "uniquely pervasive presence in the lives of all Americans"—a presence, he stressed, that extends beyond the public square and into the rooms of private homes—circumscribes its free-speech protections. An electronic broadcast reaching many persons is different from an electronic call between two persons, Stevens argued, and the two forms of communication deserve to be treated differently under the law. While the government can't police private conversations, it can impose constraints on the content of broadcasts to protect the public good.[4]

Today, mired as we are in partisan, bitter, and seemingly fruitless debates over the roles and responsibilities of social media companies, the controversy surrounding Carlin's naughty comedy bit feels distant and even quaint. But its very alienness is what makes it so illuminating as a backlight on our own situation. Just fifty years ago, the country was able, however haltingly, however imperfectly, to debate and resolve contentious issues arising from the transmission of information through new communication systems. Individual citizens had a voice, as did corporations; legislators could pass laws; regulators could make rules, render judgments, and impose penalties; and the judiciary could hash out disputes in a deliberate, open way, drawing on statute, precedent, and common sense. Even when that hottest of hot buttons, the First Amendment, was involved, it was possible to make reasonable compromises between individual rights and the public interest. Not everyone agreed with the rulings and decisions—some disagreed vehemently—but the differences of opinion did not paralyze the body politic.

Why were things so different then? The answer is complicated, but it begins in the distinctions drawn by Douglas in his complaint and Stevens in his opinion. Both men point to how different communication technologies serve different purposes, even when they're transmitting the same information. Playing an "X-rated" recording on a phonograph at home, Douglas allows, is different from broadcasting it over the airwaves. An individual has to make a deliberate choice to buy a record—it costs money, after all—and another deliberate choice to place it on a turntable and drop the needle on a track. When a radio station airs the same track, it sends the signal indiscriminately to any receiver in range. While people have to tune their radios to a particular frequency to listen to the station, they have no control over what gets played when. Their ears are at the mercy of the station's programmers. Such power should not be taken on, Douglas argues, without some sense of civic-mindedness.

Stevens draws a different but related contrast: between a public broadcast and a phone call. Saying something to an acquaintance on a call, he suggests, is fundamentally different from saying the same thing on the air. A private conversation remains a private conversation even when conducted over a vast, commercially run telecommunications system. People can say whatever they want in whatever words they choose. But a broadcast, thanks to the breadth of its reach and pervasiveness of its influence, is always a public matter. It's neither unreasonable nor unconstitutional, he says, for the public to expect a radio station to use discretion in its programming. If the station wants to air a comic rhapsody of dirty words, it can at least wait until nighttime, when the kids are in bed.

Stevens's distinction between interpersonal, or one-to-one, communication and mass, or one-to-many, communication was not new. He was reiterating a venerable legal and ethical principle that, throughout the twentieth century, served as the cornerstone of media governance and shaped the structure and operations of the communication industry. The principle reflected and was reenforced by a sharp divide in media technology itself: conversations went through one set of networks; broadcasts went through a different set. The divide was manifest in every home. If you wanted to chat with someone, you'd pick up the telephone. If you wanted to view or listen to a show, you'd switch on the TV or radio. A conversation was one thing. A broadcast was another.

Private Words

It wasn't long after the invention of writing that people started sending letters to each other, and it wasn't long after that that they began worrying about the confidentiality of those letters. The Roman statesman Cicero, an avid letter-writer, fretted constantly about the security of his correspondence. In a typical note, sent to his brother Quintus, he wrote, "How cautious I want you to be in what you write you may infer from the fact that in writing to you I don't mention even overt political disorders, for fear of the letters getting intercepted and giving offense in any quarter." To his friend Atticus, he cautioned, "I won't write to you what I am going to do, only what I have actually done. Every spy in the country seems to have an ear cocked to catch what I say."[5]

The common way to secure letters in the ancient world was to seal them shut, usually with a blob of clay or bitumen. As far back as 500 BC, officials of the Persian Empire would write messages on animal skins, carefully fold the skins, tie them with string, then seal the knots with clay before entrusting them to couriers.[6] In medieval times, beeswax became the sealing agent of choice. Because bees were thought to be favored by God, their wax was assumed to provide an especially strong shield against prying eyes. Politically sensitive letters, such as those sent by monarchs, ministers, or clerics, were often further secured through elaborate folding, cutting, tying, and stitching techniques, a practice known as letterlocking.[7] Later in the Middle Ages, letter writers started slipping their messages into handmade envelopes, providing an extra protective barrier.

None of the safeguards worked all that well—seals were broken, envelopes torn open, letters pilfered—but the continuing, dogged efforts to keep correspondence secure nonetheless made clear that people shared a common, deeply held belief: personal conversations are private. Whether whispered or written, messages exchanged by individuals deserve to be protected from others' eyes and ears. When national postal systems began to be set up in Europe in the sixteenth century, the belief became a tenet of common law, known as the secrecy-of-correspondence doctrine. Shortly after Charles II established Britain's post office in 1660, he issued a proclamation stating that "no postmaster or other person, except under the immediate warrant of our principal Secretary of State, shall presume to open letters or packets not directed unto themselves."[8] Using similar language, Parliament put the royal decree into the statutes with the Post Office Act of 1710. Many other countries also enshrined the secrecy-of-correspondence doctrine in their laws or constitutions.

For early Americans, the doctrine had special importance. In the years leading up to the War of Independence, British agents routinely intercepted and read letters sent between the colonies and England. (Britain's prohibition on opening other people's correspondence never applied to the Crown, which for decades ran an espionage unit in the post office dedicated to rifling the mail.[9]) Incensed, the colonists responded by establishing their own "constitutional post," with a strict requirement that mail be carried "under lock and key." Benjamin Franklin, appointed America's first postmaster general in 1775, was adamant that postal agents respect the sanctity of the letters entrusted to their care. He required all agents to swear an oath never to open any letter passing through their hands. At the moment of the country's birth, the secrecy of correspondence became a democratic ideal. As the legal scholar Anuj Desai writes, "the principle of confidentiality of the mail in the American postal network dates back to, and is intimately intertwined with, the revolutionary goals of those who sought independence."[10]

Although the privacy of correspondence wasn't explicitly mentioned in the Constitution—probably because it was already written into post office regulations—it did receive a constitutional imprimatur in 1878 when the Supreme Court, as part of its landmark ruling in the *Ex parte Jackson* case, extended Fourth Amendment protections to letters. "The constitutional guaranty of the right of the people to be secure in their papers against unreasonable searches and seizures extends to their papers, thus closed against inspection, wherever they may be," the court declared. The justices were careful to distinguish the legal standing of private letters, "intended to be kept free from inspection," from that of widely circulated documents like newspapers and magazines, "purposely left in a condition to be examined."[11] A hundred years before the Carlin case, the distinction between personal communication and mass communication had been written into constitutional law.

The postal system remained the chief technology for long-distance personal communication until the telegraph's arrival. The new system differed from the mail in obvious ways. Telegrams couldn't be kept "closed against inspection" in sealed envelopes, for one thing. They had to be read by the operators who translated them into and out of Morse code. And unlike the government-run post office, the telegraph was in private hands, largely those of Western Union, almost from the start. Because of such differences, the question whether telegrams should be granted the same privacy protections as letters remained a subject of debate for decades. Congress, worried about constraining its investigative powers, was wary of shielding telegrams from its subpoenas, and the courts, loath to set broad new precedents, struggled with how to fit the new system into established law. As is often the case, the speed of technological advance outpaced government's ability to respond.

Despite the legislative and judicial wrangling, the public never had any doubt that messages sent over wires should be as secure as letters carried in pouches. As the telegraph network was built out during the second half of the nineteenth century, most states passed laws making it a crime for telegraph operators to disclose the contents of messages. The operators themselves took pride in what they saw as a professional and moral duty to maintain the confidentiality of transmissions. One telegrapher wrote in 1860 of the "high sense of honor which every operator feels upon this point." Keeping telegrams secret, suggests the technology historian Thomas Jepsen, "came to be seen as a new form of 'privilege,' such as already existed under common law, similar to the privilege that protected the privacy of communication between a client and his lawyer, or between a physician and his patient."[12]

The telegraph companies, knowing that breaches of trust would lead to losses of business, took pains to assure customers that dispatches would remain inviolate. "All messages whatsoever," Western

Union's corporate rule book stated, "are strictly private and confidential, and must be thus treated by employees." The company's managers and operators routinely refused to hand subpoenaed telegrams over to the government, even when under the threat of arrest.[13] The company's record was far from perfect. Where there's information, there's intelligence, and where there's intelligence, there's snooping. During a congressional dispute in the impeachment trial of President Andrew Johnson in 1868, the manager of Western Union's D.C. office gave the House impeachment manager copies of several telegrams sent by senators who voted for acquittal. And during the contentious 1876 presidential election, the company leaked sensitive dispatches to the campaign of its preferred candidate, the probusiness Republican Rutherford B. Hayes. "Hayes might never have been president but for the fact that Western Union provided secret access to the telegrams sent by his rivals," writes Columbia law professor Tim Wu.[14] To the press and the public, such abuses, when they came to light, underscored the need for legislators and judges to act to protect telegraphic communication.

One of the first legal scholars to make the case that messages sent over wires deserve the same Fourth Amendment shield as those sent through the post was none other than Charles Horton Cooley's father, Thomas McIntyre Cooley. "The importance of public confidence in the inviolability of correspondence, through the post-office, cannot well be overrated," the elder Cooley wrote in a treatise on constitutional law published in 1868, when he was serving as chief justice of the Michigan Supreme Court. "The same may be said of private correspondence by telegraph." Violating the confidentiality of a person's telegram "would be equivalent to an unlawful and unjustifiable seizure of his papers,—such an 'unreasonable seizure' as is directly condemned by the Constitution."[15] The privacy of telegrams, like that of all personal correspondence, is "absolutely essential to the peace and comfort of society," Cooley would go on to write in a later paper, entitled "Inviolability of Telegraphic Correspondence."[16] New technologies may change how we converse, the judge understood, but they don't change our belief, grounded in a sense of personal liberty and dignity, that we should get to control who hears or sees our words.

For most of the public, the debate over the privacy of telecommunications felt remote until the building of the telephone network at the turn of the century. Because sending a telegram was expensive and required a trip to a Western Union office in a city, the telegraph was used mainly by the monied. "The rich man's mail," it was called.[17] The telephone domesticated electronic communication. It brought the wire into the home. In the United States, with its commitment to universal service, telephones soon became as commonplace as mailboxes—and just as sacrosanct. Once dedicated household lines replaced neighborhood party lines, Americans expected the same guarantee of privacy for their calls as for their letters.

The public's desire for secure phone lines grew more urgent as wiretapping techniques became more sophisticated and electrical eavesdropping more common. "By the 1920s," reports communication scholar Colin Agur, "the art of wiretapping had advanced to the point that those with the know-how—typically police, private investigators, and members of criminal organizations—had fairly easy access to the conversations of their targets."[18] Things came to a head with the U.S. Supreme Court's controversial *Olmstead* decision in 1928. In a case involving the use of police wiretaps to convict a Seattle man named Roy Olmstead for bootlegging, the court ruled that the Fourth Amendment didn't apply to the tapping of phone lines. Because phone calls, unlike letters, lack physical form, wiretapping involves "no searching" and "no seizure," argued Chief Justice William Howard Taft. The evidence against Olmstead "was secured by the use of the sense of hearing and that only." He went on to suggest that anyone "who installs in his house a telephone instrument with connecting wires intends to project his voice to those quite outside."[19]

Justice Louis Brandeis, in a famous dissent, chided the majority for failing to adapt to "a changing world." The distinction between tangible and intangible forms of communication was baseless, he suggested, echoing the earlier arguments of Thomas Cooley, and it threatened the individual liberties guaranteed by the Constitution. With advances in communication technology, "subtler and more far-reaching means of invading privacy have become available to the Government," Brandeis warned. "Discovery and invention have made it possible for the Government, by means far more effective than stretching upon the rack, to obtain disclosure in court of what is whispered in the closet."

The *Olmstead* decision sparked outrage in the press. The court "has now made universal snooping possible," declared the *New York Times* in an editorial headlined "Government Lawbreaking."[20] With public pressure mounting, Congress at last felt compelled to impose safeguards on telecommunications. In the sweeping Communications Act of 1934, it established broad legal protections for the privacy of telegrams and telephone calls, prohibiting communication companies from divulging the contents of messages and placing tight restrictions on wiretapping and other methods of surveillance.

Under the act, telecommunications companies were required to operate as "common carriers," a legal term borrowed from the transportation business. Early in the industrial age, countries recognized that shipping firms were economic linchpins—many other businesses depended on their services—and as a result wielded enormous power over commerce and trade. To ensure they didn't abuse that power by favoring certain businesses and discriminating against others, shippers were required to carry all goods under the same terms. The Communications Act imposed a similar requirement on telecommunications carriers. They had to treat all telegrams and phone calls the same, transmitting them without regard to the information they contained. The companies, it was understood, had no business with the contents of the messages they transmitted. The messages might be zipping invisibly through wires, but from a legal standpoint they were still cargo.

Pathways of the Ether

The mass media age began quietly on Christmas Eve in 1906, when a Canadian-born inventor named Reginald Fessenden aired a program of religious music and Bible readings from a makeshift radio studio he'd built on the Massachusetts coast a few miles north of Plymouth. When Marconi had invented radio eleven years earlier, he saw it as an extension of the telegraph; it would be used to send Morse messages to places wires couldn't reach, like ships at sea or offshore lighthouses. He failed to grasp that radio's larger value might lie in the transmission of voices and music. Fessenden, who had for years been obsessed with adapting Marconi's technology to the transmission of speech, saw the future more clearly. He became the first to use "the wireless" to broadcast what we would now call a show.[21]

No one seems to have actually heard Fessenden's show, other than a few bemused sailors on the Atlantic, but it was momentous nonetheless. When the telegraph arrived, it may have been "a new business in the world," as Thomas Cooley called it,[22] but it had an important precedent in the mail system. The same was true of the telephone. Radio broadcasting had no such precedent. Though newspapers and magazines often circulated widely, there was always a delay between their printing and their reading, and they reached only those who bought them. With radio, for the first time, a large, dispersed audience—anyone within range of the signal—could receive the same information at the same time and without delay from a single source.

As would be the case with the internet nearly a century later, the exotic new medium remained in the hands of tinkerers and hobbyists during its early years. Radio sets were easy and cheap to make—instructions could be found in the Boy Scout Manual—and because they were transceivers, they were able to transmit signals as well as receive them. Anyone with a radio could act as a broadcaster, beaming messages to other radio owners tuned to the same frequency. Every evening during the early decades of the century, the airwaves buzzed with the transmissions of tens of thousands of amateur operators.

The openness of the network felt liberating. The operators' ability to project their voice, or at least their code, across hundreds of miles gave them a feeling of freedom and independence. It inspired a sense of personal agency at a time when industrialization and urbanization were imposing conformity and regimentation. "The amateurs," writes historian Hugh Slotten, "tended to view the spectrum as a new, wide-open frontier, akin to the American West, where men could pursue individual interests free from repressive authoritarian and hierarchical institutions."[23]

The amateur operators—adolescent boys, many of them—played a crucial role in the development of radio. They didn't just "adopt" the new technology, explains media scholar Susan Douglas; "they built it, experimented with it, modified it, and sought to extend its range and performance. They made radio their own means of expression."[24] Most of the "radio bugs" used their sets responsibly. But some, in another foreshadowing of the net, were bent on mischief and mayhem. Shielded by the medium's anonymity, they would transmit rumors and lies, slurs and slanders. The U.S. Navy, which relied on radio to manage its fleet, was a prime target. Officers "complained bitterly," Slotten reports, "about amateurs sending out fake distress calls or posing as naval commanders and sending ships on fraudulent missions."[25] Particularly irksome to the brass was the fact that the amateurs' homemade radios were often more sophisticated than the military's expensive kits.

The nuisance became a crisis in the early-morning hours of April 15, 1912, when the *Titanic* sank after its fateful collision with an iceberg off the coast of Newfoundland. The ship's radio operator was able to issue a distress call quickly, highlighting the value of the new technology in emergencies. But efforts to rescue the passengers were hindered by an ensuing barrage of amateur radio messages. The chatter clogged the airwaves, making it hard for official transmissions to get through. Worse, some of the amateurs sent out what we would today call fake news, including a widely circulated rumor that the ocean liner remained seaworthy and was being towed to the nearby port of Halifax for repairs. The false reports sowed confusion among would-be rescuers. Fifteen hundred people died.

The chaos in the airwaves during the *Titanic* rescue was an unintended by-product of the American government's laissez-faire attitude toward radio traffic. Although European countries had begun restricting wireless transmissions as early as 1903, radio had been left unregulated in the United States. There were few controls over who could broadcast, which frequencies they could use, or what information they could transmit. Politicians and journalists, dazzled by the magical new technology, feared that bureaucratic meddling would stifle progress. Government intervention "would hamper the development of a great modern enterprise," the *New York Times* opined in an editorial published three weeks before the *Titanic*'s sinking. "The pathways of the ether should not be involved in red tape."[26]

The *Titanic* tragedy changed everything. The public was outraged, and the press demanded immediate government action. "The recent disaster to the *Titanic* points with terrible and fateful directness to the absolute necessity of a controlling power to regulate wireless telegraphy," declared the popular magazine *Electrical World* in an editorial. "No measures of repression are too severe."[27] Four months later, Congress passed the Radio Act of 1912. Among the law's provisions were requirements that all radio operators be licensed by the Department of Commerce, that senders of malicious messages be prosecuted and fined, and that transmissions by amateur operators be restricted to the less desirable shortwave band of the spectrum—an "ethereal ghetto," as one historian would describe it.[28] Radio's Wild West days were over.

Neither the tragedy nor the new law dampened Americans' love for radio. As sales of sets soared in the boom years after the First World War, large companies moved into the market, quickly filling the void left by the amateurs' banishment. In 1920, Westinghouse Electric founded the country's first commercial station, KDKA in

Pittsburgh. It was a sensation. The initial broadcast, heavily promoted by Westinghouse, came on election night, when announcers gave rapt listeners up-to-the-minute results of the presidential race between Warren Harding and James Cox. "Between announcements of the returns," reported the *Pittsburgh Gazette Times*, "radiophone music was transmitted, which added much to the entertainment."[29]

Within two years, more than five hundred commercial stations were operating across the country, and radios had become the new centerpieces of American living rooms. Their broadcasts gave daily testimony to the miracles of science and technology. "Even in an age of marvels," wrote one Ohioan, "there is something awe-inspiring about the radio. Through the radio the throbbing present may be brought home to us and the dead past made to live again."[30] Radio sets were changing, though. While hobbyists, or "hams," continued to buy or build transceivers, most of the models sold to the general public lacked the capacity to send out signals. They could only receive them. Radio, it was now clear, would be a centralized medium, its programs and its influence flowing out in a single direction: from the broadcaster to the masses, from the one to the many.

Public Callings

In a 1922 article in *Popular Science Monthly*, Herbert Hoover, then the secretary of commerce in the Harding administration, celebrated "the wildfire spread of radio," which he called "much more amazing than any other thing we have seen in our time." The future president was excited and optimistic about the new technology, seeing it as a tool for elevating the public mind. "We are witnessing," he wrote, "a dawn glowing with the promise of profound influence on public education and public welfare." Every home with a radio "may confidently look forward to the receipt from the air of an ever increasing quantity of important and interesting information from many sources that have never before been so accessible to the American public."[31]

But Hoover saw dangers as well. He understood that broadcasting's "uniquely pervasive presence," as Justice Stevens would describe it decades later, was fated to change society in deep and unpredictable ways. Radio stations, through their selection of what to broadcast and what not to broadcast, would hold considerable sway over listeners' thoughts, habits, and even votes. The wireless would shape the country's culture and its politics, for better or for worse. It was obvious to Hoover and to pretty much everyone else at the time that the public had an interest in broadcasting that went well beyond turning the tuning knob.

As with the secrecy-of-correspondence doctrine, the idea that certain businesses ought to be responsive to the public interest had a long heritage. It derived from a centuries-old distinction between companies that have strictly "private callings" and those that also have "public callings." The Supreme Court explained the distinction in an 1877 decision upholding the government's right to regulate grain-storage facilities. "Property does become clothed with a public interest when used in a manner to make it of public consequence and affect the community at large," the justices wrote. "When, therefore, one devotes his property to a use in which the public has an interest, he, in effect, grants to the public an interest in that use, and must submit to be controlled by the public for the common good."[32]

Broadcasting is not grain storage. Because it deals in the intangible goods that shape public opinion—facts and ideas, news and comment—it is inherently political. That broadcasting had a public calling may have been obvious in the 1920s, but the nature of the calling was not. Without any precedent to draw on, society had to figure out, more or less from scratch, how to accommodate the powerful new technology—how to tap its benefits while curbing its destructive potential. It was a complicated, daunting challenge, requiring that the interests of the "community at large" be balanced not just against the interests of private enterprise but also against the interests of individuals, including the right to freedom of expression. The broadcast spectrum's limited capacity made the challenge all the

more pressing. The government would have to decide which appli-
cants were worthy of a license and which weren't.

Beginning in 1922, Hoover's Commerce Department convened a
series of conferences aimed at bringing order to the increasingly con-
gested and chaotic airwaves. Attending were representatives of government, industry, the military, and the listening public, along with
prominent radio engineers and scientists. Much of the discussion
involved technical issues, such as establishing equipment standards
and reducing interference between stations. But political, economic,
and social questions were also on the agenda. What criteria should
be used in allocating spectrum? Should certain frequencies—"clear
channels"—be set aside for nationwide stations? Should local stations, at the time mainly operated by universities or civic groups, be
protected from large commercial networks? Should advertising be
permitted? Should a balance of viewpoints be required? What roles
should religious and educational programming play? Should political
candidates and government officials be allowed to speak on the air?
Even the question whether stations should be allowed to play recorded
music, rather than required to hire musicians to perform live, was a
matter of debate. The wide range of topics reflected Hoover's belief
that, as he put it in a speech at one of the sessions, "The ether is a public medium, and its use must be for public benefit."[33]

In 1926, not long after the fourth of Hoover's conferences, the regulatory framework established under the Radio Act of 1912 crumbled
when a federal judge ruled that the Department of Commerce had no
authority to issue wireless licenses. The already crowded airwaves
were soon overwhelmed by new and more powerful stations broadcasting overlapping signals. The cacophony infuriated the public.
Looking to establish a legally sound process for regulating the spectrum and building on the work of Hoover's conferences, Congress
passed a new Radio Act in 1927. Defining access to the airwaves as a
privilege, the legislation mandated that radio stations serve the "public interest, convenience, or necessity"—an awkward phrase that
would come to have a profound influence on the nation's communi-

cations policy. To enforce the public-interest standard, as it came to be known, the act established an independent regulatory agency, the Federal Radio Commission, and gave it broad oversight authority.

The FRC wielded that authority with vigor. In one famous case, the commission acted to stem the spread of medical misinformation over the airwaves. A doctor named John Brinkley, who had made a fortune transplanting goat testicles into men as a treatment for impotence,* was operating his own radio station, KFKB, in Kansas. He used the station, one of the country's most popular, to promote a variety of quack treatments and medications, often offering specious and dangerous on-air diagnoses to listeners. In 1930, the FRC refused to renew Brinkley's broadcasting license, ruling that his programming "is inimical to the public health and safety, and for that reason is not in the public interest." When the doctor appealed the decision, claiming censorship, the federal appeals court backed the commission. The FRC had not subjected Brinkley's "broadcasting matter to scrutiny prior to its release," the court wrote, but had "merely exercised its undoubted right to take note of appellant's past conduct, which is not censorship."[34]

Congress intended the FRC's extensive rule-making powers to be temporary. Legislators still assumed that once various technical issues were worked out, the nascent radio industry would be able to regulate itself. That hope proved vain. Controversies continued to swirl through the ether. With the even more expansive Communications Act of 1934, Congress replaced the FRC with a permanent body, the Federal Communications Commission, and widened the commission's purview to include the personal communication systems of telephony and telegraphy as well as, through subsequent amendments, the newly emerging broadcast medium of television.

---

* Among the well-known patients of the "goat gland doctor" were Harry Chandler, the wealthy publisher of the *Los Angeles Times*, and J. J. Tobias, the chancellor of the University of Chicago's law school. Both men praised the efficacy of the transplants.

By combining the mandate that telephone and telegraph pro-viders operate as common carriers with the mandate that broad-casters act in the public interest, the legislation formalized the two-pronged regulatory philosophy that would govern electronic communications in the country for most of the rest of the century. The common carriage standard imposed clear, consistent guide-lines on telecommunications companies. They had to transmit mes-sages without prejudice and without violating the confidentiality of their contents. The public-interest standard was fuzzier. Neither the Radio Act nor the Communications Act defined exactly what it meant for broadcasters to serve the "public interest, convenience, or necessity." The interpretation was left to the commission, subject to court review. Over the years, the standard's meaning was hashed out through dozens of cases, many involving years of deliberation. As the legal scholars Erwin Krasnow and Jack Goodman observed in a 1998 law review article, "Perhaps no single area of communi-cations policy has generated as much scholarly discourse, judicial analysis, and political debate over the course of the last seventy years as has that simple directive to regulate in the 'public inter-est.'"[35] The FCC itself, according to one of its former commission-ers, "oscillated wildly between enthusiasm for the public interest standard and distaste for it."[36]

Both the contentiousness and the flexibility of the rule-making process could be seen in the way regulators, along with judges and lawmakers, struggled to address what has always been one of media's most charged issues: what to do about political bias in broadcasting. From its founding, the Federal Radio Commission had been con-cerned that stations would use their shows to promote the opinions of their owners and ignore or denigrate conflicting views. Control over a station, the commissioners worried, could turn into a monop-oly over information. The public interest "requires ample play for the free and fair competition of opposing views," the FRC declared in a 1929 ruling.[37] The Federal Communications Commission went fur-ther in the 1940s. Responding to complaints that a station had used the airwaves for political lobbying, it prohibited broadcasters from promoting causes and candidates. "The broadcaster cannot be an advocate," the commission decreed.[38]

The rule was immediately controversial, with many arguing it violated station owners' free speech and free press rights. The National Association of Broadcasters launched what one observer termed an "all-out fight" against the FCC.[39] In response, the commission convened hearings on the issue in 1948, gathering the testimony of dozens of representatives from the broadcasting industry, the public, and various civic groups. The discussions led the FCC to establish what came to be known as the fairness doctrine. Under the new rule, stations were required to devote airtime to discussions of issues of interest to the local community, and while they could present their own opinions, they also had to allot time for other views. "It is this right of the public to be informed," the commission stressed, that forms "the foundation stone of the American system of broadcasting."[40] The fairness doctrine turned into another political battlefield. It was revisited and revised frequently over the years, and each update ignited new legal and political disputes.

As the doctrine's fraught history suggests, the public-interest standard is no magic bullet. Its amorphousness means that its interpretation will always be messy, combative, and provisional, as political processes tend to be in a democracy. Some legal scholars and pundits, particularly those with a libertarian bent, have argued that the standard's imprecision gives government regulators too much leeway. The standard, writes a typical critic, is "vague to the point of vacuousness, providing neither guidance nor constraint."[41] But that view, others argue, misses the point. The public-interest standard is more than a legal principle. It's an ethical principle. It ensures the people's right to have a say in the workings of the institutions and systems that shape their lives, a right fundamental to a true democracy and a just society. The vagueness of the standard is necessary for a simple reason: in a pluralistic society, the public interest changes as the public mind changes. As the economist Gerhard Colm observed, "without some controversy about the changing meaning of the public interest, democracy would not be alive."[42]

Mass Media and Mass Men

By the end of the 1930s, radio broadcasting in the United States had entered what's now called its golden age. The chaos of the early years had subsided. The governmental licensing regime had relieved congestion and interference, and technical advances in transmitters and receivers had greatly improved the quality of signals. The radio industry, dominated by large commercial networks such as NBC and CBS but also encompassing many local and nonprofit stations, produced a variety of entertaining and informative shows that captivated listeners. More than 80 percent of households owned at least one radio, and the typical American had the set turned on for upwards of four hours a day.

There was plenty to criticize about radio. Some popular shows, such as the notorious *Amos 'n' Andy*, perpetuated then-common racist and sexist stereotypes, and in granting broadcast licenses the FCC routinely discriminated against members of minority groups.* Intellectuals and moralists decried the mediocrity and vulgarity of commercial radio, with one prominent newspaper columnist, Robert Ruark, describing broadcasts as "corny, strident, boresome, florid, inane, repetitive, irritating, offensive, moronic, adolescent or nauseating."[43] But whatever radio's flaws, the vast majority of Americans, urban and rural, poor and wealthy, highbrow and low, loved it. They made their feelings known through fan mail. During a single month in 1936, NBC received more than a million letters lauding its programs, its performers, even its advertisers. "Last night our baby was born during the Victory Hour," wrote one particularly enthusiastic

---

* In the 1970s, the FCC shifted course, establishing a Minority Ownership Task Force and introducing tax incentives that led to a fivefold increase in minority ownership of stations.

listener, referring to a popular variety show starring Will Rogers and Al Jolson. "We are going to raise him on radio." Radio transmissions may have flowed in one direction only, but the postal network gave the audience a way to respond to the broadcasters. Fan mail formed a feedback loop. The networks used the incoming letters as market research, fine-tuning their programming (and their ads) to give listeners more of what they craved. "Far from objecting to the rising commercialism of the airwaves," reports cultural historian Alice Goldfarb Marquis, the public "enthusiastically embraced it."[44]

Franklin Roosevelt's popular fireside chats, heard by as many as two-thirds of U.S. adults, crystallized the essential role broadcasting had come to play in the country's culture and politics. The chats provoked their own flood of mail, with Americans sending the president thousands of letters a day, most expressing gratitude for his calming and optimistic words. Radio gave the nation a shared and generally hopeful soundtrack during the Depression, one of its darkest and most divisive times. Rather than rendering listeners inert and submissive, historians Lawrence and Cornelia Levine argue, the wireless "tended to *counter* passivity, to stimulate audiences to thought and action, and to give them a sense of participation and inclusion—often for the first time in their political lives."[45]

What radio did not do is bring peace, love, and understanding to the world. The medium spread darkness as well as light. If its effects in the United States and other Western democracies were generally benign, the picture was different in authoritarian states. Dictators found in the centralized medium, with its one-to-many channeling of information, a tool perfectly suited to thought control. In the Soviet Union, where tightly scripted broadcasts tended to be heard through public loudspeakers rather than private sets, the Bolshevik regime viewed radio as a means "to reset the mental horizons of its population," in the words of historian Stephen Lovell.[46] There was no feedback loop; what the audience wanted didn't matter.

In Germany, the Nazis seized control of the state radio network the moment Hitler was appointed chancellor in January of 1933. Soon after, the Reich's communication chief, Joseph Goebbels, spear-headed an effort to build and distribute a cheap plastic radio, the *Volksempfänger*, with a tuning mechanism designed to pick up only German stations. Within a few years, most Germans owned one of the sets, through which poured, in addition to the Führer's interminable speeches, a steady stream of nationalistic and antisemitic propaganda. Schoolchildren were often quizzed on the content of the broadcasts to ensure they and their families were listening. "It would not have been possible for us to take power or to use it in the ways we have without the radio," Goebbels said in a speech at a Berlin radio conference in the summer of 1933. Radio made it possible to carry out "a principled transformation in the worldview of our entire society, a revolution of the greatest possible extent."[47] To control a nation's soundtrack was to be always inside its citizens' heads.

That the spread of mass media was accompanied by the rise of Nazism and other totalitarian movements seemed like more than a coincidence to many observers. Broadcasting's centralized design, with its concentration of power and its tight control of information, seemed to mirror the political structure of the authoritarian state. In the United States and Europe, sociologists, anthropologists, and psychologists, along with journalists and policy analysts, began to suspect that radio and other systems of mass communication could, in the words of Stanford cultural historian Fred Turner, "turn the individual personality and, with it, the structure of society as a whole in a totalitarian direction." Mass media might create "mass men."[48] Think tanks with names like the Institute for Propaganda Analysis were set up to study the issue.

With the outbreak of World War II, the fears intensified. Nazi sympathizers in the United States began to use the airwaves to spread fascist ideas. The weekly broadcasts of the rabble-rousing, pro-Hitler "radio priest," Charles Coughlin, drew tens of millions of listeners. As the country prepared to enter the conflict, Turner reports, policy makers grappled with two questions: "First, how could they convince democratic Americans to go to war without turning them into the sort of unthinking authoritarians they would be trying to defeat? And second, what kinds of media could they use to do it?" The questions inspired a few dozen prominent intellectuals, including anthropologist Margaret Mead, psychologists Gordon Allport and Erich Fromm, pollster George Gallup, and art historian Arthur Upham Pope, to form, with the Roosevelt administration's backing, the Committee for National Morale. The goal was to examine the connections between communication, individual personality, and national character, with a view to undertaking a radical restructuring of media to make it less likely to serve as an arm of tyranny. If existing mass media, built on the one-to-many model, tended to produce an "authoritarian personality," couldn't a new form of mass media, built on a many-to-many model, produce a "democratic personality"?[49]

During the war, members of the committee, notably Mead and her third husband, Gregory Bateson, a British anthropologist who had a sideline as an American spy, began to sketch out what such a communication system might look like. They imagined an immersive, interactive multimedia environment. Information in all forms—text, image, sound, motion picture—would be presented to an active, engaged audience of citizens. No traditional editors or producers, no government bureaucrats or propagandists, would script the experience; people would be free to choose what to look at and listen to at any given moment. Most important, the medium would erase the divide between creators and consumers. People wouldn't have to resort to the mail to make their feelings known. Everyone would have the tools and the network access needed to express themselves through the system. Everyone would have a voice. Information would flow in all directions at once. The Committee for National Morale shared Charles Cooley's faith in the rationality and goodwill of the public. An unconstrained, decentralized flow of information would open people's minds and arouse, as Cooley had put it, their "higher sympathetic and aesthetic impulses."

The vision of a decentralized, democratized media informed two expansive exhibitions staged at New York's Museum of Modern Art to support the war effort: 1942's renowned *Road to Victory* and its 1943 sequel, *Airways to Peace*. After the war, the vision, fusing the political and the aesthetic, continued to inspire intellectuals and avant-garde artists. It infused Edward Steichen's vast, enveloping photography exhibit, *The Family of Man*, which debuted at MOMA in 1955 and, with funding from the U.S. Information Agency, traveled to dozens of other countries. In the late fifties and throughout the sixties, the vision took partial if fleeting form in the psychedelic, multimedia be-ins and happenings of the beats and hippies. It also informed the counterculture's political aspirations. The Students for a Democratic Society, in its 1962 Port Huron Statement, demanded that "society be organized to encourage independence in men and provide the media for their common participation."[50] Writing in the *New Left Review* in 1970, the influential German intellectual Hans Magnus Enzensberger predicted that, as communication technology advanced, all forms of media would come together in "a universal system" that would be "egalitarian in structure," giving the masses the means to mobilize to overthrow "bourgeois culture."[51]

Beyond the high-toned museum exhibits, the dope-stoked festivals, and the radical theorizing, the ideal barely registered with the public. People were more devoted than ever to the one-to-many broadcasts coming out of their radios and TVs. The simple fact was that the technology required to create an interactive, many-to-many communication system that could reach into private homes did not exist. The kind of democratic medium imagined by Mead and others lay outside the realm of the possible. But in Washington, D.C., a small group of computer scientists and network engineers, working for the Pentagon's Advanced Research Projects Agency, or ARPA, was about to fix that.

CHAPTER 3

The Feed

Mixed Media

If you were to travel back in time to 1978, the year the Supreme Court decided the Carlin case, and walk through the front door of a typical middle-class American home, you might think you had entered a media museum. The entire modern history of communication technology would be on display. There'd be bookcases with hardcovers and paperbacks. The morning paper would be spread out on the kitchen table. Magazines would be lying about, their titles—*Time, Money, Life*—testifying to the publishing industry's bygone swagger. You'd see envelopes and postage stamps, library cards, film cameras and photo albums, a typewriter, radios of various sizes. Mounted on the kitchen wall would be a communal telephone, and there might be another phone or two on bedside tables in the bedrooms. In the living room, you'd find a bulky color TV, a wire snaking out the back and up to an aerial on the roof. There'd be a stereo—turntable and receiver, eight-track or cassette deck, speakers—and records and tapes to play on it. There might even be, if there were teenagers in the house, a newfangled Atari 2600 video-game console.

We remember the mass media era as a time of uniformity— everyone saw the same hit movies and TV shows, listened to the same Top 40 songs, read the same wire-service news reports—but what we forget is that it was also a time of great formal variety in the tools and artifacts of communication. Media spoke in many voices, through devices designed to suit particular modes of expression. There was a constant press to come up with new methods to record, store, and transmit information, and because different kinds of information took different physical forms, those methods branched out in many directions. Communication devices were specialized—like hand tools or kitchen gadgets. You couldn't record an orchestra on a type-writer, or take a photograph with a telephone, or mail a letter through a radio. And while, technically, you could broadcast the text of a novel through a TV or project it onto a movie screen, no one wanted to read it that way. The technologies overlapped in places—words and pictures could be printed with the same machine onto the same sheet of paper; radio programs could be distributed to stations through phone lines; tape recorders could make copies of vinyl records—but that just added to the diversity of what we retrospectively call "analog media." (Back then it was just "media." No one had cause to use the adjective *analog* until the adjective *digital* came along.) The businesses that coalesced around the different methods of communication were specialized as well, with different capital and labor requirements, patterns of competition, and regulatory regimes. You didn't get your news and your music and your shows from the same company.

Within each general category of content—text, sound, image, motion picture—came further differentiation and specialization. Text took many forms. Personal letters, handwritten or typed, were sent through the mail. Telegrams were transmitted over wires and delivered by courier. Newspapers were printed on rolls of cheap newsprint, cut and folded into tabloid or broadsheet format, and distributed by newsagents and paperboys. Magazines were printed on glossier paper and mailed to subscribers or sold by the issue in shops. Books were printed on still more durable stock, glued or stitched into bindings, and sold in bookstores or through book clubs. And then there were catalogs, greeting cards, comic books, memoranda, faxes, and on and on.

Sound media were nearly as various. Telephones converted voices into electric signals and transmitted them, at first with the aid of operators, then automatically, through an intricate network of wires and switches. Calls could be local, long distance, or international, each involving different carriers and billing schemes. Songs, symphonies, speeches, and jokes were etched into the grooves of vinyl disks or magnetized onto tapes and sold through record stores and department stores or loaded into jukeboxes. The same recordings were played over the radio, along with live shows, news reports, advertisements, and the patter of announcers and DJs. Images, still or moving, circulated in myriad forms, too—some printed or photocopied, some projected onto screens in theaters, some broadcast to home TVs, some slipped into children's View-Masters.

Taming the Flood

The distinctions between media were not just technical, industrial, and legal. They were semantic, cultural, and aesthetic. With distinctions in form came distinctions in meaning. Think of the various media used for interpersonal communication. If you wanted to correspond or converse with someone, you had a lot of options. You could mail a handwritten or typed letter or a postcard, you could make a phone call, you could send a wire or a fax. Each medium entailed a different style of expression, a different degree of timeliness, a different level of intimacy, and a different set of social norms and expectations. When you chose a medium, you also chose a way of speaking. The medium was part of the conversation.

Or think of news and its many formats. Delivered daily, a newspaper had immediacy and breadth, with a stress on getting the facts about important events out as quickly as possible. There were well-delineated sections—local, domestic, international, sports, business, arts, weather—to give coherency to the reports and aid the reader in navigating them. Weekly newsmagazines provided more perspective and context, filtering out lesser stories and adding reportorial depth to more salient ones. Monthlies, or "slicks," added still more color and personality, with immaculately reproduced photographs and long, thematic "think pieces" that tied events and ideas together.

Broadcasters built up their own news organizations, a legacy of the fairness doctrine's requirement that they cover "public issues." On television, half-hour news programs, aired around dinner time, provided fast-paced, visual summaries of the day's events. Talk shows such as *60 Minutes* and *Meet the Press* offered longer reports on topics and controversies of the moment, often including interviews with public figures. TV bulletins were reserved for momentous events—an assassination, an airliner crash. Radio news offered a bit of everything, with some stations broadcasting news all day, others giving brief reports on the hour, and still others giving longer round-ups in the evening. While the content of the various news media overlapped, their reports were complementary, entailing different journalistic methods, levels of detail, and political perspectives. The news formats all had their shortcomings. They rarely gave voice to opinions outside the bounds of the mainstream, and they tended to be slow to challenge the status quo. But they also had important strengths—in checking facts, in investigating fraud and corruption, in putting hard questions to politicians—and in combination they gave people a shared understanding of contemporary events that was essential to a productive public sphere.

When new media artifacts came along, they often opened new realms of expression, even if they were developed for commercial reasons. During the 1940s, big record companies, looking to attract new customers and counter competition from broadcast music, invested in creating a higher-quality replacement for 78s, the heavy, noisy shellac records that had dominated the market for decades.

RCA came up with the seven-inch single, a lightweight vinyl disk that spun at 45 revolutions per minute and, like the 78, held one song on each side. Columbia Records took a bolder approach. Ted Wallerstein, the label's president and a classical music buff, pushed his engineers to expand the capacity of records so that a single disk could hold an entire symphony. After much trial and error, they came up with the twelve-inch long player, or LP, a flexible vinyl disk that turned at a leisurely 33⅓ rpm and could accommodate twenty minutes of audio per side.[1]

The near simultaneous arrival of the two incompatible formats set off a brief standards war, called the battle of the speeds, that ended in a happy compromise: new record players came with a speed switch that allowed either format to be played. The introduction of the LP boosted record sales, as intended, but it also gave recording artists a new, larger canvas to work on. It inspired songwriters and musicians to create, in addition to catchy singles, carefully sequenced suites of songs that fit the expansive LP form. By the middle of the sixties, albums like John Coltrane's *A Love Supreme*, The Beatles' *Sgt. Pepper's Lonely Hearts Club Band*, and Love's *Forever Changes* were expanding the artistic possibilities of popular music—and giving listeners new aural experiences.

We saw in the last chapter how society, moving in fits and starts, getting some things right and some things wrong, developed a legal and regulatory framework for controlling the thrilling but unpredictable forces unleashed by electronic communication. Here we see the personal side of the story, the one that played out in living rooms, kitchens, and bedrooms. It's easy today to look back at the twentieth-century world of analog media and see an inefficient, fragmented mess—a mess that digitization would clean up—but the inefficiency and fragmentation served important social, intellectual, and artistic purposes. By imposing what Mark Zuckerberg disdainfully calls friction on the processes of information production, distribution, and retrieval, the specialization of media networks and devices also imposed order on the welter of information that was suddenly pouring into people's homes. The specialized technology served as a means to sort and segregate information and regulate the pace and timing of its delivery. A philosopher might say the specialized tools formed an epistemic architecture, one that aided understanding by helping people distinguish the trivial from the important, the fleeting from the enduring, the personal from the political, the factual from the fictive. Like the legal and regulatory system that surrounded it, the analog media system was imperfect, but its very messiness helped maintain communication's human scale. Its physicality and fragmentation prevented the speed and volume of electronic networks from overwhelming people's sense-making capacities.

Equally important, the analog system imposed discipline on and encouraged discretion in reading, viewing, and listening habits, giving people a sense of control over the media products that were proliferating so quickly. An individual had to make a conscious decision to pick up a magazine or switch on a TV or stick a dime in a jukebox. It was impossible to do everything all at once, and no one would have wanted to. The friction—the cost, the effort, the act of choosing—was part of the pleasure. "Drop the coin right into the slot," sang Chuck Berry in "School Days," his ecstatic 1957 single. "You gotta hear something that's really hot."

Mechanism and Meaning

"The fundamental problem of communication," wrote Bell Labs engineer Claude Shannon in "A Mathematical Theory of Communication," an article published in 1948 in the *Bell System Technical Journal*, "is that of reproducing at one point either exactly or approximately a message selected at another point." He added, as an aside: "Frequently the messages have *meaning*; that is they refer to or are correlated according to some system with certain physical or conceptual entities." And then he added, as a clarification: "These semantic aspects of communication are irrelevant to the engineering problem."[22] Eighty pages long and dense with arcane equations and diagrams, Shannon's article went unnoticed by the public. But as the science journalist James Gleick would later write, with only slight exaggeration, it was "a fulcrum around which the world began to turn."[3]

Shannon was not suggesting that meaning doesn't matter. He just wanted to make clear that the "semantic aspects" of a message are immaterial to the technical aspects of its transmission. Meaning is separate from mechanism. In one sense, he was restating the old idea underlying common carriage. When a postal courier or other shipping agent took possession of a personal letter in the eighteenth century, he was concerned about its transport, not its content. He wanted to plot the fastest route, keep the cost of the shipment low, and temper the risk of the letter being damaged, lost, or stolen along the way. What the letter said was of no concern to him. It mattered only to the correspondents (who, unless a problem arose, remained happily oblivious to the details of the letter's transport). A letter was two different things: a message with meaning and a piece of cargo. A similar duality would characterize telegrams and telephone calls, though as information shed its material form a carrier's technical concerns became less about navigating the world and more about processing signals and symbols.

Shannon's theory of communication was esoteric, involving entropy, uncertainty, and probability, but it was aimed at solving a practical and pressing problem for his employer: how to squeeze the maximum number of phone calls through the wires of its network. Information, Shannon realized, always travels through a medium in coded form. That's true even of spoken words that go through nothing but air. The speaker's throat and mouth turn the words into sound waves (the code), and the ear of the listener decodes the waves back into words. With documents sent through the mail, speech is encoded in the letters of the alphabet. With telegrams, there's a succession of encodings: strings of alphabetic characters are converted into strings of dots and dashes, which are then converted into an analogous, or analog, pattern of electrical pulses. With the telephone, a vibrating metal diaphragm converts the sound waves of speech into a continuous (and, again, analog) electric signal and, at the receiving end, a small loudspeaker converts the signal back into sound waves and directs them toward the listener's eardrum.

Shannon further saw that every communication channel has a certain calculable capacity (its bandwidth, we now say) and a certain calculable susceptibility to distortion, or noise. By manipulating transmission codes to compress messages and by adding error-correction codes to counter the effects of noise, Bell System carriers could use their equipment to its fullest possible capacity. They could avoid unnecessary capital investments and turn a heftier profit. Shannon provided the math to accomplish such optimization. Before his paper, network management involved guesswork and rules of thumb. After his paper, it was a science. Industrial objectives—efficiency, standardization, automation—could now be rigorously applied to human speech.

Shannon intended his theory to apply to communication of all sorts, but the reason it came to have such epochal importance is that it arrived at the same time as a new kind of machine for manipulating information: the digital computer. In his article, he introduced the word *bit*—a contraction of *binary digit*—to describe the smallest, most basic unit of information: the amount required to distinguish between two mutually exclusive and equally probable alternatives. The outcome of a coin toss, for instance, contains a single bit of information; it can be communicated with one of two digits: 0 for heads, 1 for tails. The same is true of the state of an electric switch: 0 for off, 1 for on. Because a digital computer is built of switches, binary code is ideally suited to serve as its native language, the numerical "machine code" that regulates its operations and expresses its logic.

Shannon also saw that any information capable of being stored or transmitted by a communication mechanism, including a digital computer, can be translated into binary code. The information, whatever its original or ultimate form, can be expressed in zeroes and ones. It can be broken down, for purposes of transmission or storage, into its most elemental units—units without any meaning, at least not to human beings. Such encoding, moreover, provides crucial advantages over other coding schemes. In addition to its flexibility, binary code offers resiliency and efficiency. Because it involves only two discrete symbols, it isn't subject to much ambiguity. It resists distortion. Static or other noise that would render human speech unintelligible is unlikely to interfere with the interpretation of a simple binary signal. The code's simplicity and clarity also make it easy to copy, endlessly and perfectly. And, using Shannon's algorithms or their descendants, computers can automatically compress the code, pruning away redundant or inessential bits, to get the most out of a network's available bandwidth. More information can be transmitted more speedily.

Though no one, not even its creator, understood the full ramifications at the time, Shannon's theory sealed media's fate. The language of computer networks would become the language of media networks. If all information can be represented by zeroes and ones, then all information can be transmitted through digital computers. And if binary code is the most efficient way to transmit information, then it's only logical that all information *should* be transmitted through computers. Given sufficient bandwidth, a computer network would become the universal medium. All those household media gadgets would be replaced by software. With the appearance of Shannon's paper, the intricate, rickety architecture of analog media began to tremble.

In 1950, two years after his article came out, Shannon spoke at one of the Macy Conferences on Cybernetics, a celebrated series of interdisciplinary symposia on communication and computing held at a Park Avenue hotel in New York. His theory was now famous among the mathematicians and information scientists in attendance, luminaries like John von Neumann, Norbert Wiener, and J. C. R. Licklider. In discussing his ideas, Shannon again emphasized the separation of the meaning of a message from the mechanism of its communication. Also at the conference was Margaret Mead. As the discussions continued, she began to grow uneasy with what she was hearing. Having spent years studying how groups of people make meaning through shared rituals and beliefs, through language and gesture, she wasn't quite so sure that the division between mechanism and meaning was as clean as it was being made out to be. She wondered whether the mathematical optimization of communication might not introduce a new kind of distortion, one that would skew the sense of messages or strip away nuance. "If you are trying to communicate the fact that somebody is angry," she said, struggling to put her concern into the right words, "what order of distortion might be introduced to take the anger out of a message that otherwise will carry exactly the same words?"[4] As mechanisms of communication are made more efficient, would subtleties of meaning get lost or garbled? Would the signal, not the noise, turn out to be the more dangerous source of distortion?

There was an irony to the anthropologist's worries. It was the computer network, after all, that would come to fulfill her dream of an immersive, interactive multimedia environment. In questioning the ideal of mathematically optimized communication, she was questioning her own ideal of a truly democratic medium. But she could not have known that in 1950, any more than Shannon or the other pioneers of digital computing could. The commercial production of computers was just starting up. Housed in large cabinets that gave them their name—mainframes—the new calculating machines were as big as dumpsters, cost millions of dollars, and couldn't communicate with each other. No one, other than maybe a few science-fiction fantasists, could have imagined that by the century's end they'd shrink to the size of toaster ovens and be used to watch TV shows, listen to music, and exchange endearments and insults.

The Atari 2600, a toy, would be the unlikely harbinger of the new era. With a cheap eight-bit microprocessor that generated silly sounds and images, it was the first popular digital-media device to find a place in the home, a combination stalking horse and Trojan horse. The most beloved of its early cartridges was Pac-Man, and like that game's eponymous hero, digital media would soon be gobbling up everything in its path.

Content Collapse

In 1962, the Defense Department recruited J. C. R. Licklider to over-see ARPA's research program on information processing. In the years since the 1950 Macy conference, the affable and ambitious Licklider, known to all as "Lick," had become an evangelist for what he called "man-computer symbiosis." He heralded a future in which "human brains and computing machines will be coupled together very tightly."[5] At ARPA, he faced a more immediate challenge: get-ting the machines themselves coupled together. The various data-processing systems used by the agency's researchers were incompat-ible; they couldn't share programs or data. In 1963, he wrote a long memo to his colleagues proposing an effort to build what he termed, only half jokingly, an "intergalactic computer network."[6] Although he would soon leave the agency to become an IBM consultant, his project took off. By decade's end, the Pentagon had the first general-purpose, wide-area computer network—the Arpanet—up and run-ning. Twenty years later, having slipped free of military control, the network morphed into the internet. What had been designed as a geeky academic research hub turned into a vast library-cum-agora, open to anyone with a modem and a web browser.

In a replay of the early radio boom, Americans rushed online. The experience was exhilarating—another new frontier had opened—and frustrating. Connecting to the net from home meant dialing in to a distant server through a noisy, low-bandwidth telephone line. Even with the fastest modem available, downloading a song took ten minutes. Downloading a movie might tie up the family phone line for a day. Sound and picture quality were cruddy; browsers, glitchy; streaming, inconceivable. At the turn of the century, fewer than one in twenty Americans had a broadband link at home. But over the next few years that number shot up as phone and cable companies upgraded their equipment and pitched affordable internet plans to their customers. By 2007, half of Americans had home broadband. By 2010, two-thirds did.[7]

When personal computers first entered the home, they were stand-alone, multipurpose data-processing machines, high-tech Leatherman tools. You loaded a program into memory to do something useful or entertaining—write a letter, manage the family budget, play Oregon Trail with the kids—and then loaded another to do something else. All your files and data remained within the machine or on floppy disks you owned. Once connected to a broadband network, computers turned into something very different. They became media devices, home transceivers with capabilities infinitely more advanced than those of early radio sets. Unlike the specialized analog devices they replaced, computers were generalists; they could do everything. All forms of content were digitized, compressed with Shannon's formulas, and uploaded to the net. With broadband, surfing the web suddenly felt effortless—a series of clicks and taps, a fine-motor choreography of summoning and dismissal, everything always at hand. Fast, efficient, rationalized "new media" vanquished slow, inefficient, cluttered "old media."

From a technological standpoint, the triumph of digital media may have been inevitable, but it didn't happen in a vacuum. It was hastened by political changes. In the early 1970s, economists and politicians began to sour on industrial regulation, viewing it as a cause of the "stagflation" then crippling the economy. An unfettered free market seemed the best guarantor of growth and prosperity. Government controls on many business sectors, including telecommunications and broadcasting, began to be lifted. The Nixon administration exempted cable television from the public-interest standard and other programming restrictions. The Carter administration followed by deregulating radio, with the FCC declaring that the public interest would best be served by eliminating "unnecessarily burdensome regulations."[8] With Ronald Reagan's landslide election in 1980, the deregulation push gained overwhelming force. The FCC lifted programming controls from broadcast television and rescinded the fairness doctrine. Although the public-interest standard remained in the statutes, it had lost its teeth. For the FCC, defending the public interest now meant little more than expanding consumer choice.

The free-market spirit permeated the sweeping Telecommunications Act of 1996. Promoted with great enthusiasm by President Bill Clinton and his technophilic vice president, Al Gore, the legislation stripped away most of the market strictures that had defined the structure of the media industry since the Communications Act of 1934. It erased the boundaries between different media markets and services, freeing phone companies, cable companies, broadcasting networks, and internet start-ups to compete wherever they liked. The convergence of media technology was soon mirrored by a convergence of markets, as traditional telecommunications and broadcasting firms battled tech giants and internet newcomers for dominance in digital communications.

The combination of deregulation and digitization erased the legal and ethical distinction between interpersonal communication and broadcast communication that had governed media in the twentieth century. When Google introduced its Gmail service in 2004, it announced, with an almost imperial air of entitlement, that it would scan the contents of all messages and use the resulting data for any purpose it wanted. Our new mailman would read all our mail. The public, in thrall to Google and eager for free email accounts, barely flinched. The centuries-old secrecy-of-correspondence doctrine was tossed aside just as personal correspondence and conversation were moving online. On the internet, the wiretap wouldn't be a bug; it would be a feature.

Internet companies were also freed of the obligation to take account of the public good. The Telecommunications Act included broad safe-harbor provisions—the now notorious "Section 230"—that shielded internet companies from legal liability for the third-party content they disseminated. Though businesses like Google and Facebook would soon be broadcasting into homes far more information than radio or TV stations ever did, little in the way of civic responsibility would be demanded of them. Without the constraints of either the secrecy-of-correspondence doctrine or the public-interest standard, online media gained important marketing and legal advantages to go along with its technological edge. The government, having bankrolled the building of the internet, now guaranteed its hegemony over all aspects of communication.

The Telecommunications Act did impose one constraint on internet firms. It made it a crime to use the net to circulate to minors any content that "depicts or describes, in terms patently offensive as measured by contemporary community standards, sexual or excretory activities or organs." Immediately challenged by the American Civil Liberties Union as an infringement on free-speech rights, the anti-obscenity provision was thrown out by a federal district court in Pennsylvania. The Justice Department, under Attorney General Janet Reno, appealed the ruling to the Supreme Court, and it again fell to John Paul Stevens to write the high court's opinion. This time, Stevens rejected the government's argument. Drawing an explicit distinction with his ruling in the Carlin case, he argued that the internet was fundamentally different from traditional broadcast networks. Whereas radio listeners might accidentally be exposed to obscene speech when tuned to a station, internet users "seldom encounter such content accidentally." Finding information on the net "requires a series of affirmative steps more deliberate and directed than merely turning a dial." Minors, Stevens went on to say, lack the "sophistication" necessary to "retrieve material" from the web without the help of adults.[9] As it turned out, children would prove to have a considerably more sophisticated understanding of the net's workings than the justice did.

Today, the remnants of the analog world lie scattered around us—some of its artifacts, such as film cameras and vinyl records, have even become fetish objects—but the old media system has been dismantled. The convergence of media technology hasn't just destroyed the bipartite regulatory framework and the divisions between media businesses. It has blurred the distinctions between categories of information—distinctions of form, register, sense, and importance—

that the epistemic architecture of the analog era preserved and even accentuated. Content has collapsed, as our adoption of the drab, generic term *content* to refer to all forms of expression testifies. Everything now has to fit the internet's conventions and protocols, with their stress on immediacy, novelty, multiplicity, interconnectedness, and above all efficiency. The brakes that were imposed, by necessity more than design, on electronic communication during the last century are gone. With digitization, communication has lost its human scale.

The Algorithmic Editor

The internet's original design metaphors—domain, site, page—came from the material world. They provided a sense or at least an illusion of continuity with the stability and fixity of physical media. The connection was severed during the first decade of the twenty-first century when social media platforms began experimenting with more dynamic ways to distribute information. The design metaphors that soon emerged—feed, stream, loop, scroll—stressed flux and fluidity. Nothing lasts, they suggested. Nothing has more than passing interest.

Facebook's introduction of the News Feed in the early-morning hours of September 5, 2006, crystallized the changes. Before the feed, Facebook looked and worked like a traditional website. Modeled on the class directories that colleges used to hand out to incoming freshmen, it consisted of a series of pages, each containing a user profile. On entering the site, members would land on their own profile page and then click one by one through their friends' pages, picking and choosing what to look at. The News Feed unstitched Facebook's metaphorical bindings. Each member now saw a continuous, customized stream of posts and updates automatically chosen by a content-filtering algorithm written by the company's coders.

The News Feed was the product of an intensive yearlong project, by far the most complex programming effort the young company had ever attempted. It was inspired by Mark Zuckerberg's frustration with the inefficiency, the friction, of online communication, which to his mind stemmed from the involvement of human beings in the process of evaluating, selecting, and sharing information. Whereas computers were fast, predictable, and programmable, people were slow, capricious, and difficult to control. As Ruchi Sanghvi, the Zuckerberg lieutenant who led the News Feed project, would later put it, the company's reliance on individuals to seek out information on their own—to go "to one person's profile and then another and then another"—was "hugely inefficient."[10] The feed removed human deliberation and judgment from the process. It replaced personal agency with machine agency.

Although Claude Shannon might have bristled at the association, the News Feed was the logical conclusion of his mathematical theory of communication. When Facebook's algorithm evaluated, ranked, and organized information, it did so without regard to the information's meaning. The "semantic aspects" of communication were irrelevant to its calculations. But whereas Shannon and his Bell System employer were concerned only with the transmission of information—the transport function—the Facebook algorithm made editorial decisions. It selected what people would see or not see through a statistical analysis of their past behavior as well as the behavior of people like them. The algorithm delivered whatever pattern of zeroes and ones it calculated to have the highest probability of grabbing and holding people's attention, as measured by the time they'd spend looking at or responding to a post. If judged from a semantic perspective, the perspective of, say, a human editor, the resulting stream of content appeared random. It was just one thing after another: a video of a laughing baby, a news headline about a school shooting, a photo of a friend on vacation, an ad for a toenail fungus remedy, a contouring tip from a Kardashian, a story about microplastics in the ocean. Everything in the feed was given the same semantic weight, which was no weight. Everything had the same semantic context, which was no context.

Zuckerberg explained the News Feed's rationale to his staff in a memorable sentence: "A squirrel dying in front of your house may be more relevant to your interests right now than people dying in Africa."[11] The statement is grotesque not because it's false—it's altogether true—but because it invokes a category error. It yokes together in an obscene comparison two events of radically different scale and import. And yet, in his callous way, Zuckerberg articulated the essence of content collapse. Social media renders category errors obsolete because it renders categories obsolete. All information belongs to a single category—it's all "content"—and it pours through a single channel with a single objective: maximizing "engagement." News, entertainment, conversation, and all other forms of human expression would from now on be in direct competition, angling for both the consumer's fleeting attention and the algorithm's blessing.

When Facebook members came face to face with the News Feed for the first time on the morning of September 5, they rebelled. Having their posts and updates circulated to other people automatically felt like a violation of privacy and trust. Many of them realized, for the first time, that everything they did on the site was being monitored by the company. "You pretty much are being tracked with every movement you make on Facebook," one user complained. "It's like someone peeking in on my conversations."[12] Hundreds of thousands of members protested the change, posting and reposting angry comments on the site and joining Facebook groups with names like Students against Facebook News Feed, I Hate Facebook, and Ruchi Is the Devil. *Time* declared it social media's "first official revolution."[13] Within a few hours, Zuckerberg had rushed out a sorry-not-sorry apology, in the form of a Facebook post with the title "Calm down. Breathe. We hear you." He expressed regret for sparking the fury but at the same time defended the feed: "We agree, stalking isn't cool; but being able to know what's going on in your friends' lives is."[14]

What Zuckerberg didn't mention is that the company's traffic measures were already showing that the feed was a huge success. It was doing exactly what it was designed to do. The journalist Steven

Levy later reported on the scene playing out inside Facebook's head-quarters while the users were fuming:

> Sanghvi and her team were looking at the logs and finding some-thing amazing. Even as hundreds of thousands of users expressed their disapproval of News Feed, their behavior indicated that they felt otherwise. Users were spending more time on Facebook than ever before. It was a validation of the entire concept.[15]

The protests themselves, as they swept back and forth across the net-work, growing in size and intensity, proved how effective a content-filtering algorithm could be in galvanizing people's attention, stir-ring their emotions, and encouraging them to post, comment, and share. Outrage, anger, and mob action: all were signals of extraordi-narily high engagement. And after the protests faded—the students soon realized that they liked the convenience of getting all content of interest through a single automated stream rather than having to traipse across pages—the engagement remained. All those zeroes and ones had come into perfect alignment.

Responsive Chords

A few pages into Tony Schwartz's 1973 best seller, *The Responsive Chord*, there appears a black-and-white photograph of a factory, its smokestacks silhouetted against the sky. The image, Schwartz com-ments, will provoke different but equally visceral reactions depend-ing on who's looking at it. To some it will say "progress." It will conjure up positive feelings related to technological innovation, good jobs, attractive new products, and prosperity. To others it will say "pollu-tion." It will conjure up negative feelings related to industrial exploi-tation, corporate rapacity, greed, and ecological disaster. The photo expresses no fixed meaning, Schwartz stresses. Its meaning is cre-ated by the "responsive chord" it strikes in the mind of the viewer.

Born in New York City in 1923, Schwartz was a media polymath.

As a boy, he was a ham radio enthusiast and displayed a talent for drawing and design. During World War II, having earned a degree in graphic design from the Pratt Institute, he served as an artist for the U.S. Navy, creating posters promoting the war effort. After the war, he worked on Madison Avenue as an art director for several advertising agencies before starting his own shop, the Wexton Company. He had a sideline as an audio engineer, recording albums, producing radio shows, and designing Broadway soundscapes. He acted as a media adviser to captains of industry, celebrities, and politicians. He taught courses on communication and design at top universities, appeared regularly on television as a commentator, and wrote widely discussed books and articles. He was also an agoraphobe—a recluse, like Charles Cooley, but more so. Fearful of encountering people on the street, he spent most of his time and did most of his work in his Manhattan studio on the ground floor of what had once been a Pentecostal church. His reliance on communication technologies in his day-to-day life made him a particularly sensitive interpreter of media's uses and effects.

Schwartz is largely forgotten now, but his best-known work—the "Daisy" advertisement he created for Lyndon Johnson in his presidential campaign against Barry Goldwater in 1964—remains a cultural touchstone. The stark one-minute spot, aired on television only once, two months before the vote, makes no mention of Goldwater. It shows a freckle-faced little girl standing in a field of daisies, plucking petals from one of the flowers. As she gets down to the last petal, the image freezes, and the camera slowly zooms in on her face. We hear a man's voice in the middle of a countdown: "ten, nine, eight, seven . . . " When he reaches zero, the girl's image is replaced by one of an atomic bomb exploding. A mushroom cloud takes shape, and Johnson, in a solemn voiceover, says, "These are the stakes: to make a world in which all of God's children can live, or to go into the dark."

The ad embodied Schwartz's "resonance theory" of communication. In an age of mass media, he posited, people have more information than they can handle. To seize their attention and influence their thoughts and behavior, you don't need to give them more stuff to think about. You need to activate the information and attendant emotions already present in their memory. "In communicating at electronic speed," he wrote, "we no longer direct information into an audience, but try to evoke stored information out of them, in a patterned way." A successful message doesn't deliver meaning; it calls forth meaning. "That which we put into the communication has no meaning in itself. The meaning of our communication is what a listener or viewer *gets out* of his experience with the communicator's stimuli." The Daisy ad presented a series of simple audiovisual stimuli—an innocent girl, a meadow full of flowers, a countdown, a mushroom cloud—intended to trigger responses latent in the minds of a targeted subset of the audience, in order to increase the odds they'd get out and vote for LBJ. It worked.

Though Schwartz was probably unaware of it—he was in his eighties when it happened—Facebook's introduction of the News Feed put his ideas at the very core of media. The resonance theory helps us understand why mindless machines, through a statistical analysis of behavioral variables, can so thoroughly command people's attention. The power of the feed algorithm doesn't lie in the meaning of the messages it delivers—the algorithm knows nothing of meaning—but rather in its ability to match messages to individuals' emotional triggers. It automates the striking of responsive chords. It gives everyone a custom stream of Daisy ads.

For Claude Shannon, the fundamental problem of communication had been getting a message from one place to another as quickly as possible without distortion. For Mark Zuckerberg and his Silicon Valley mates, the fundamental problem of communication was putting the most resonant message in front of an individual at the most opportune moment. The essential function of the mechanism of communication wasn't transport anymore. It was manipulation—manipulation of information and by extension manipulation of those receiving the information. Before the feed, it was possible to argue that Facebook was a common carrier, a dumb network that transmitted messages without regard to their content. After the feed, Facebook was a different beast—part broadcaster, part wiretapper, part propagandist.

Sin Eaters

It was also, to the great discomfort of the company and its CEO, part censor. On the Saturday after Christmas in 2008, a dozen members of the Mothers International Lactation Campaign, or MILC, gathered outside Facebook's headquarters in Palo Alto to breast-feed their babies. They were protesting the company's practice of removing photographs of nursing women from its site. One of the "lactivists" explained to a reporter that she had recently uploaded a picture of herself suckling her nine-month-old and Facebook had deleted it, with a warning that if she continued to post such photos she risked banishment from the network. The MILC demonstration gained wide and sympathetic coverage in the press, and it echoed through Facebook itself. More than eighty thousand users joined a group named Hey Facebook, Breastfeeding Is Not Obscene! The company rushed out a spokesman to make an official statement. "We agree that breastfeeding is natural and beautiful," he cheerily began, then went on to stress that "photos containing a fully exposed breast—as defined by showing the nipple or areola—do violate [our] terms on obscene, pornographic, or sexually explicit material."[16]

As the clumsy response suggests, Facebook was taken off guard by the protest. At the time, two years after the News Feed's debut, the company had yet to establish a formal process for dealing with controversial content. A small team of low-level, largely untrained employees had been assigned the job of reviewing users' complaints about other users' posts and pictures. They followed, as Dave Willner, the company's first head of content policy, would later describe it, a set of vague guidelines, written on a single sheet of paper, that took the form of "a list of things you should delete: so it was things like Hitler and naked people." Their rule of thumb, as another Facebook employee would recall, was subjective in the extreme: "if it makes you feel bad in your gut, then go ahead and take it down."[17]

Because it had been founded as a site for college kids, with each member required to have a verified .edu email account, Facebook in its early years was insulated from the dark content that was showing up in ever greater quantities elsewhere on the web. Other social networks weren't so lucky. After Google bought YouTube in October of 2006, the search giant immediately faced difficult decisions about disturbing videos posted to the site, often by anonymous users. In December, two videos of Saddam Hussein's execution appeared. One showed his hanging; the other, his corpse. Though both seemed to violate a company policy prohibiting graphic violence, YouTube's content-moderation team, led by one of Google's top corporate lawyers, decided to allow the video of the hanging, deeming it of historical importance, even as it removed the video of the body. Not long after, a mysterious, grainy video of a man being severely beaten by several other men was uploaded to the site. The moderators quickly took down the clip and then, just as quickly, put it back up. They had learned in the interim that the video had been filmed by an Egyptian human rights activist and apparently showed the beating of a detainee in a police interrogation cell.[18] The depiction of violence was intended to document state oppression, not titillate sadists.

Facebook, as it pursued rapid growth to satisfy its early investors, soon found itself grappling with the same kinds of uncomfortable choices. At the end of 2006, the company lifted its restrictions on membership, opening its virtual doors to everyone. In early 2007, it began allowing users to upload videos. In 2008, it released its first mobile app, turning smartphones and their cameras into powerful and ubiquitous media-production tools. As millions, then billions, of people joined the network, the News Feed became much more than a conduit for chatter, gossip, and selfies. It became a primary source of news, entertainment, and advertising for pretty much everybody everywhere. It also became a primary outlet for the demonic in man.

Images of Hitler and naked people were the least of it. Facebook found itself broadcasting videos of rapes and murders, photographs of child abuse and animal torture, racist and sexist screeds, revenge porn, recruitment pitches by terrorist organizations, and threats of violence against individuals and groups.

Weeding out the bad stuff proved, to the company's frustration, resistant to automation. Thanks to their pattern-matching capabilities, computers were able to block images that had previously been identified as, say, child pornography, but their obliviousness to meaning rendered them useless when it came to evaluating most suspect content. As YouTube's struggles had made clear, interpreting words and pictures demands more than the application of a set of explicit rules. It can't be reduced to a statistical analysis of patterns of digits. It entails subtle judgments about context, a sensitivity to cultural norms, an appreciation of linguistic and visual ambiguity, and an ability to judge intent and weigh contending interests. Figuring out whether a video of a hanging is newsworthy or purely malicious requires an understanding of who's being killed and why, the historical and political background of the event, and the motivations of the person doing the recording, as well as a familiarity with journalistic ethics, local laws, and social norms. It requires a worldly perspective. It requires human beings.

As controversies over content mounted during 2009, Facebook rushed to set up a formal moderation program. Its small, ad hoc team ballooned into a vast, worldwide bureaucracy, encompassing thousands of workers and reams of guidelines and checklists. Today, the company reportedly has upwards of fifteen thousand moderators, most of whom are recruited and managed by big outsourcing firms such as Accenture and Cognizant.[19] Whenever a user or an algorithm flags a potentially offending piece of content—something that happens a few million times a day—a moderator reviews it on a screen and decides whether to remove it or not. The rules the moderators follow can be at once disturbingly detailed and bafflingly abstruse, as was revealed in 2012 when a disgruntled former moderator leaked to the press a confidential guidebook used by contractors in reviewing content. The document, which Facebook called "a snapshot" of its moderation standards at the time, bans images of "internal organs, bone, muscle, tendons, etc." but allows images of "crushed heads, limbs, etc." and "deep flesh wounds."[20]

What's rarely heard in the outrage over the ugly content that pervades social media is an acknowledgment of the public's role in its spread. The vast, shadowy infrastructure of moderation is necessary because feed algorithms promote the bad stuff, and the algorithms promote the bad stuff for the same reason they promote any content: because people are drawn to it. The algorithms are adept at reading the human id and satisfying its desires, however twisted. For two years beginning in 2015, a West Virginia couple ran a YouTube channel called DaddyOFive that featured videos of them performing cruel pranks on their young children, often reducing the kids to tears. The channel was "hugely popular and generated millions of hits," according to a contemporary report in the *Guardian* newspaper. It formed "a core part of YouTube's content aimed at children."[21] After the pair were arrested for child neglect in 2017, the mother told a reporter, by way of explanation, that her family "would get excited when they got a lot of views."[22] Gruesome or perverse images and words are extreme examples of the clickbait and trolling that have grabbed eyeballs online since people first connected to bulletin-board systems through dial-up modems. Algorithmic feedback loops amplify a signal that's always been there.

That's little comfort to the moderators. Their work, described by the *Wall Street Journal* as "the worst job in technology," is grueling and distressing. A typical moderator, well educated but working for low pay with little job security, will review as many as eight thousand flagged posts a day, often witnessing acts of unimaginable depravity. In describing the job, one former moderator told the *Journal*, "I was watching the content of deranged psychos in the woods somewhere who don't have a conscience for the texture or feel of human connection."[23] Many of the moderators end up traumatized, some suffering psychological problems long after they quit the work. One woman in the field compared herself and her colleagues to the "sin eaters" of the seventeenth century, desperate paupers who would be given a little money to eat bread at funerals in order to assume the sins of the deceased.[24]

Social media firms have gone to great lengths to keep the grim modern ritual of content moderation hidden from the public. The work conflicts with the upbeat image they like to promote. It also grates against their political ideals. Like other internet entrepreneurs, the founders of the major social networks lean toward libertarianism. They're free-speech absolutists who celebrate radical "openness" and "transparency" and find any form of censorship repellent, especially when it occurs on the net. Given the choice, most of them would not have gotten into the content-moderation business at all. But as executives beholden to shareholders, they had no choice. They couldn't risk repelling users and advertisers. As the legal scholar Kate Klonick wrote in a 2018 *Harvard Law Review* article on content moderation, "the primary reason companies take down obscene and violent material is the threat that allowing such material poses to potential profits."[25]

While the companies may be motivated by private concerns, their moderation programs, like their filtering algorithms, have an enormous impact on public affairs. In addition to deciding the fate of obscene and violent material, moderators make decisions about speech in general, drawing lines, always subjective and often arbitrary, between what's permissible and what's not. In 2010, the law professor and First Amendment authority Jeffrey Rosen observed that "Facebook has more power in determining who can speak and who can be heard around the globe than any Supreme Court justice, any king or any president."[26] That power, now spread across many social platforms, is greater today. We may have stopped talking about the role of the public interest in governing decisions about what's published and broadcast, but the public interest is still being taken into account. It's just not happening out in the open, through established political and judicial procedures and institutions. The public interest is being interpreted in secret, by large corporations that see the public not as a polity but as a customer base. We've outsourced the stewardship of speech to Big Tech.

Oracles and Orphic Words

Thanks to its success in attracting and holding an audience, and despite the controversies surrounding the content it dishes out, Facebook's algorithmic News Feed quickly became the template for other social media platforms and then for traditional media companies as they shifted their offerings online. Everyone rushed into the business of information engineering (and, whether they wanted to or not, content moderation). When the smartphone displaced the laptop and desktop as the public's preferred personal computer, feeds, streams, loops, and scrolls proved ideally suited to the device's small, responsive touchscreen and its continually updated apps. Swiping became second nature to all of us—up, down; left, right. And because the combination of digitization and deregulation had removed the secrecy-of-correspondence doctrine as a legal barrier to corporate snooping, media outfits and other internet companies were free to track every touch and tap, using the data to further optimize their algorithms. An automated feedback loop, controlled by a few businesses, now governed the flow of information throughout society. We didn't have to write fan mail or otherwise voice our opinions to marketers. The medium itself was gathering our reactions.

That the News Feed was introduced almost exactly one hundred years after Reginald Fessenden's Christmas Eve radio broadcast may be a coincidence, but it helps put our current situation into historical perspective. Behind the rise of mass media during the past century, a less visible but even more fundamental shift was unfolding: the industrialization of communication. As media systems advanced from the electric to the electronic to the digital, the spirit of the Industrial Revolution, with its stress on measurement and productivity, expanded from factories and offices into the intellectual and political realms of conversation, discourse, and debate. The push to achieve ever greater efficiency in information exchange, guided by Shannon's equations and accelerated by business competition, became a major force shaping social relations.

The goal of optimizing human communication for efficiency was never controversial. It seemed like a logical extension of the widely held belief that the public square should operate as a marketplace of ideas. Just as free competition among manufacturers ensures that the best goods win out over inferior ones, the assumption goes, so free competition among thinkers serves to winnow good thoughts from bad, facts from falsehoods. In the battle for the public mind, the strongest ideas triumph. The belief had its origins in the Enlightenment. In *Areopagitica*, his radical 1644 treatise opposing censorship, John Milton declared that if "all the winds of doctrine were let loose to play upon the earth," truth would invariably win out. "Let her and Falsehood grapple; who ever knew Truth put to the worse in a free and open encounter?"[27] Thomas Jefferson, in his 1801 inaugural address, assured the public that "error of opinion may be tolerated" as long as "reason is left free to combat it."[28] The analogy to industrial competition was made explicit by Justice Oliver Wendell Holmes, Jr., in his famous dissent in the Supreme Court's 1919 First Amendment case *Abrams et al. v. United States.* The "ultimate good" is served by "free trade in ideas," he wrote. "The best test of truth is the power of the thought to get itself accepted in the competition of the market."[29] As industrial markets gain from efficiency, so too would their intellectual counterparts. The more efficient the mechanism of communication, the more freely and quickly the competition of ideas would play out.

Underlying the ideal of a marketplace of ideas is another ideal drawn from economics: that of the virtue of abundance. Traditional economic theory is built on the unhappy assumption that in a world of friction and constraint, physical goods are inherently subject to scarcity. When too many people desire a product in limited supply, the market works to curb demand through price increases. Sometimes the state has to step in to prevent so-called tragedies of the commons, where people or businesses rush to consume, exploit, or hoard important resources, to the detriment of the general good. Officials establish laws and regulations—allocating radio spectrum through licensing, for instance—to control demand. When it comes to informational products, however, the internet seemed to herald a new economy of abundance. Because digital goods can be copied endlessly at little or no cost, the public would enjoy limitless quantities of them. Over the past thirty years, the sense of an impending utopia of information abundance has carried an "aroma of awesomeness," as a group of legal scholars wrote in a 2022 journal article.[30] The aroma wafted through popular books with titles like *The Zero Marginal Cost Society, The Long Boom, Cognitive Surplus, Free*, and *Abundance: The Future Is Better Than You Think*. Naive as it turned out to be, the excitement convinced people that the laws and regulations that governed the old scarcity economy were no longer needed. Society could and should allow new communication technologies, and the industries built on them, to advance without restraint. You can't have too much of a good thing.

Facebook's News Feed culminated the industrialization of communication. It marked the moment when machines took command of media, when the programming of culture through software routines began to feel normal and even, given the unremitting flows of information, necessary. Once the amount of available content exceeded people's capacity to evaluate and sort it all, turning the epistemic work over to computers—automating it—seemed the obvious solution. And because the public had always welcomed the increasing speed and volume of information flows as a manifestation of technological and social progress, as a ratification of humanity's special destiny, no one questioned the wisdom of applying industrial standards to expressions of thought and emotion.

The way we've come to talk about information as a quantifiable resource reveals how thoroughly we've embraced the industrial view. In the 1980s, the Xerox Corporation, a pioneer of personal computing technology, announced that "72 billion new pieces of information are created for us every year and 75 per cent of all information in existence was created only in the past 20 years."[31] At a business conference in 2010, Google's then CEO Eric Schmidt mused about the "technology revolution" that the internet had set off. "There were five exabytes of information created by the entire world between the dawn of civilization and 2003," he observed. "Now that same amount is created every two days."[32] The audience reacted with wonder and pride. The Columbia University astrobiologist Caleb Scharf, in his 2021 book, *The Ascent of Information,* made a similar point: "The total number of words spoken by all humans that have ever lived, across all their lifetimes, comes to around 5 exabytes worth of data. In just one year we can now exceed that by a factor of 400."[33] It's one thing to discuss the storage capacity or throughput of an information network in terms of bits and bytes. It's another thing to reduce human thought and speech, the entire history of culture from "the dawn of civilization," to a number, as if one were weighing a shipment of coal or corn syrup.

Implicit in such calculations is a belief that the only information that counts is information that can be encoded and transmitted by machines. Speech and other forms of human expression are raw materials to be processed mechanically. That's exactly the view social media companies have come to take. Just as a potato chip or a cigarette is meticulously engineered to trigger certain biological reactions in the human body and mind—pleasure and craving, notably—so communication is now engineered to trigger similar reactions. What fills online feeds, research shows, is content that stirs strong emotions and provokes symptoms of "physiological arousal"—a quickened heart rate, tensed muscles, dilated pupils.[34] The nervous system is put on alert, primed to respond to incoming stimuli. We feel compelled to scroll more, see more, share more. We're drawn deeper into the feed. Whether we realize it or not, social media churns out information that's been highly processed to stimulate not just engagement but dependency.

Snack-food and tobacco companies long tried to distance them-selves from the social and medical consequences of their product engineering—maladies such as heart disease, obesity, and cancer. Social media companies have taken a similar tack in trying to dis-tance themselves from the problems arising from their information engineering. When, in a 2018 congressional hearing, Zuckerberg was asked if Facebook is a media company, he was quick to dismiss the idea. "I consider us to be a technology company," he said, "because the primary thing that we do is have engineers who write code and build products and services."[35] He was attempting, with a cynical echo of Shannon, to distinguish the processing of information from the mean-ing of information. Facebook had everything to do with the former and nothing to do with the latter. But in a world of computerized media, the distinction, whatever its engineering or public-relations benefits, is specious. Even if semantic considerations are irrelevant to their calcu-lations, the algorithms used to sort and channel information regulate what content is transmitted, the form it takes, and how it's interpreted. They influence meaning both directly (by selecting the information people see) and indirectly (by promoting certain forms of expression and discouraging others). Margaret Mead was right. The manipula-tion of information is always also the manipulation of meaning.

"People are not in general influenced by long books or discourses," the American poet John Jay Chapman wrote in an 1897 essay on Ralph Waldo Emerson, "but by odd fragments of observation which they overhear, sentences or head-lines which they read while turning over a book at random or while waiting for dinner to be announced. These are the oracles and orphic words that get lodged in the mind and bend a man's most stubborn will."[36] Social media is not success-ful because it goes against our instincts and desires. It's successful because it gives us what we want. As a machine for harvesting atten-tion, its productivity is unmatched. As a machine for bending the will, it is a triumph of efficiency. In engineering what we pay atten-tion to, it also engineers much else about us—how we talk, how we see other people, how we experience the world.

PART TWO

THE TRAGEDY OF COMMUNICATION

Words move quicker than meaning.

—JEAN BAUDRILLARD

CHAPTER 4

Fast Talking,
Fast Thinking

Marching Backwards

Something unexpected happened when engineers and mathematicians logged onto the Arpanet early in the 1970s. They started sending personal messages to each other. Although the system had been designed for sharing computer resources and exchanging software files, electronic mail became its killer app. No envelopes or stamps, no Wite-Out, no trek to the mailbox: sending someone a note suddenly seemed effortless. Messages bred messages. A system audit in 1974 found that email accounted for three-quarters of all Arpanet traffic.[1] When, a year later, the programmer John Vittal added reply and forward commands to the messaging program, obviating a lot of retyping, email's growth curve got even steeper.

"In the developmental history of the Arpanet, electronic message service was a sleeper," Licklider would recall in a 1978 paper written with the MIT computer scientist Albert Vezza. "It soon became obvious that the Arpanet was becoming a human-communication medium with very important advantages over normal U.S. mail."[2] The immediacy of email, he observed, encouraged a new style of written correspondence, more casual, more abrupt, and sloppier than that used in letters: "One could write tersely and type imperfectly, even to an older person in a superior position and even to a person one did not know very well, and the recipient took no offense. The formality and perfection that most people expect in a typed letter did not become associated with network messages, probably because the network was so much faster." Email conversations also had advantages, Licklider pointed out, over those conducted through telephone lines: "One could proceed immediately to the point without having to engage in small talk first." And since "the sender and receiver did not have to be available at the same time"—email messages, unlike phone calls, were asynchronous, to use the technical jargon—an email felt less intrusive than a call. People would hesitate before dialing a phone number; they'd hit send on an email without a second thought.

Email suited the needs of researchers and technologists. At once telegraphic and conversational, it allowed quick, productive exchanges of information while also promoting an unfussy, egalitarian collegiality. Customs and norms that slowed down traditional methods of long-distance communication—the expectation of pleasantries in a phone call, the obligation to proofread a letter before mailing it—could be dispensed with when talking through computers. Getting to the point was, as Licklider suggested, the point. And because it cost nothing to send an email, you could dash off as many notes as you pleased as quickly as your fingers could type. You could air a thought as soon as it entered your head. Why wait?

Email soon spread into businesses and universities, but it wouldn't become popular with the general public for another twenty years. When it did, with the arrival of AOL Mail, Hotmail, and Yahoo! Mail in the mid-1990s, people didn't immediately embrace the terse, utilitarian style of Arpanet exchanges. They wrote personal emails in pretty much the same way they had always written personal letters. Messages were lengthy, chatty, and composed with care. They opened with salutations and closed with compliments. In the 1998 romantic comedy *You've Got Mail*, a movie that signaled email's cultural ascendency, the messages exchanged between the online paramours played by Meg Ryan and Tom Hanks are expansive, heartfelt, and self-consciously writerly. "People are always telling you that change is a good thing," muses Shopgirl (Ryan) in a message to NY152 (Hanks). "But all they're really saying is that something you didn't want to happen at all has happened." She then proceeds, in a long, well-turned paragraph, to talk about her career, the death of her mother, and the unhappy state of the world. Though typed on a computer and transmitted through a digital network, Shopgirl's message would have met with the approval of the nineteenth-century etiquette expert Caroline Carlton, who in an 1868 guide offered advice to would-be epistolarians: "Letters of friendship, love, and affection are sacred things, and should be so imbued with the spirit of the writer as to render them worthy of the devoted attention they call for."[3]

Marshall McLuhan observed that whenever a new communication medium comes along, people initially use it as if it were an old medium, one they're accustomed to and comfortable with. "We march backwards into the future," he wrote. "We impose the form of the old on the content of the new."[4] In time, though, people adapt to the distinctive technical and economic characteristics of the new medium. They fit their pattern and style of speech to the technology. The process of adaptation may proceed slowly at first, but it tends to accelerate when younger people—those without much attachment to the old medium—begin to use the new system. Generational change hastens technological and cultural change.

So it went with email in the years before and after the turn of the century. To its early users, the email system, true to its name, felt like an updated version of the mail system, with speedier delivery and no need for postage. It seemed obvious that the content of electronic mail should be electronic letters. The sense of continuity was reinforced by the use in email applications of features drawn from paper correspondence, such as *cc* and *bcc* fields, signatures, and inboxes. "There was a feeling," Vittal explained, "that for user understandability we had to mimic traditional forms of communication—office memos, letters, postcards. Drawing parallels helped people understand what they could do."[5] Even the icons associated with email programs tended to employ skeuomorphic symbols borrowed from the world of letters: stamps, envelopes, pens, mail trucks.

As email use exploded, perceptions and habits changed. People felt mounting pressure to shift to a stripped-down style of writing. With new messages pinging into mailboxes every few minutes, each clamoring for attention, no one had time to write or read long, elegant missives. The discursive, carefully composed email fell out of fashion. To send one was an imposition; to receive one, an irritation. The curt style of the engineer and the mathematician became everyone's style.

"Many social norms just don't make sense to people drowning in digital communication," wrote the *New York Times* technology columnist Nick Bilton in 2013. He urged people to expunge "little courtesies" and "little niceties" from their messages and in general abandon "time-wasting forms of communication." He quoted a like-minded acquaintance: "I have decreasing amounts of tolerance for unnecessary communication because it is a burden and a cost."[6] Bilton's application of the language and method of cost-benefit analysis to personal correspondence struck many older *Times* readers as distasteful—an appalled sixty-two-year-old wrote in to call him "a sociopath"[7]—but it was revealing. It expressed, in fittingly graceless terms, the way most people had come to view online exchanges. A conversation conducted through computers was a series of transactions, best carried out quickly, without time-sapping frills or digressions.

Two years later, another *Times* columnist, Teddy Wayne, struck a very different note when he wrote a nostalgic "eulogy for the long, intimate email." He recalled that for about a decade after he'd signed up for his first email account in the late 1990s, he had "sent and received countless rambling letters to friends." Email back then was "a tool for substantive dialogue." But the "nonstop deluge" of digital messages put an end to that. Now his emails, like those of his friends, were clipped and to the point. Messages came and went in "choppy bursts"—easily skimmed, easily dismissed. No one had time for anything "reflective and lengthy."[8]

Please, Mr. Postman

In lamenting the end of what he termed the "golden age of the epistolary personal email," Wayne was really lamenting the passing of something larger from the culture: a form of correspondence—unhurried, thoughtful, elevated—that the mail system had brought into being. Though the exchange of letters by postal couriers dates to antiquity, as Cicero's voluminous correspondence demonstrates, letter writing and reading were for centuries restricted to society's elites—aristocrats, courtiers, diplomats, churchmen, merchants. They were the only ones who could afford the high price of postage (or avoid it altogether, with franking privileges), and they were the only ones who could read and write. For many members of this small, well-educated, prosperous set, the ritual of daily correspondence became indispensable to their social and even spiritual lives. They sensed something metaphysical in the post—the way it gave materiality to conversation and turned absence into presence. "Letters are friendship's sacraments," wrote the Elizabethan poet and cleric John Donne. "More than kisses, letters mingle souls."[9] A bit later in the seventeenth century, Johannes Vermeer expressed a similar sentiment in his extraordinary painting *Girl Reading a Letter at an Open Window*. The young woman stands before the large window, but she isn't looking through it. She's transfixed by the words on the luminous sheet of paper she holds in her hands. A letter, Vermeer implies, is itself a window, taking us out of our own narrow circumstances and into communion with a distant other.

As literacy advanced in the eighteenth century, the number of people who regularly sent and received letters increased. Still, letters remained luxuries. It wasn't until the middle of the nineteenth century that postal rates fell far enough to make letter writing a popular pursuit. In 1840, the British Parliament established the Uniform Penny Post, reducing the price of a stamp to a single penny for any personal letter sent within Great Britain and Ireland. The U.S. Congress soon followed suit, slashing the cost of domestic mail in 1845 and again in 1851. In 1840, when mailing a letter cost twenty-five cents, or about a third of an average laborer's daily wage, Americans sent 27 million letters, most of them for business or other administrative purposes. In 1860, when a letter could be posted for just three cents, Americans sent 161 million letters, a sixfold increase.[10] During the second half of the century, the number of letters carried through the mail grew sixteen times faster than the country's population.[11] A lot of the letters were perfunctory or transactional, but many were of the soul-mingling variety.

It would be hard to overstate how deeply people's lives were changed by access to the mail. In the latter half of the nineteenth century, a time of growing migration and mobility, not to mention the dislocations of war, "epistolary intimacy" became "a basic mode of social and familial interaction," writes historian David Henkin in his book *The Postal Age*. "Americans began to turn expectantly to the post, calibrating their perceptions of connectedness to the regular schedules of the U.S. mail."[12] Letter writers were not just able to converse with friends, lovers, and family members across great distances; they often found they could say things through the post that they found difficult or impossible to say in person. Letters sustained but also deepened relationships. And the care and attention devoted to a letter's composition and reading were themselves expressions of affection and respect. Once read, a letter often became a keepsake and, in time, an heirloom.

Beyond its social role, letter writing was for many persons an act of self-expression and, more deeply still, self-reflection and self-definition. Sitting down and composing a letter provided women and men with a rare opportunity to contemplate their daily lives and, through the careful arrangement of words and sentences, shape their experiences and emotions into a coherent and meaningful narrative. The slowness of the mail removed letter writing from life's everyday toing-and-froing. The delay between writing and reading cleared a space for introspection, for organizing one's thoughts without regard to society's demands for immediate reaction and response. If, as William Wordsworth suggested, the origin of poetry lies in "emotion recollected in tranquility," then the writing of a letter brought at least a little of the poetic sensibility into people's otherwise busy days. The reading of books and journals had given individuals a means of constructing a distinct intellectual self. The writing of letters gave them a means of constructing a distinct experiential self. Letters served as testaments as well as sacraments.

The rapid advances in telecommunications and broadcasting during the twentieth century gradually diminished the social importance of the mail, but letters continued to be seen as an indispensable means of staying in touch with far-off acquaintances. For most people, long-distance calls were too expensive to be used for frequent or leisurely chats; they were reserved for special occasions or emergencies. The phone, like the telegraph before it, served as a complement to the mail, not a replacement for it. Philip Larkin's great dark-night-of-the-soul poem "Aubade," published in 1977, testifies to the vital role that personal letters continued to play in maintaining social connections throughout most of the last century. When morning mercifully arrives at the poem's close, it brings to the poet a fleeting but redemptive vision: "Postmen like doctors go from house to house." Fifteen years earlier, the Marvelettes had hit number one with a catchier version of the sentiment:

Please, Mr. Postman, look and see,
Is there a letter, a letter for me?

It was email that pushed the personal letter to culture's periphery. The volume of first-class mail handled by the U.S. Post Office, after rising steadily throughout the nineteenth and twentieth centuries, collapsed after 2000. The decline was concentrated in personal letters. The number of pieces of what the post office calls "correspondence mail between households" fell by nearly 70 percent between 2001 and 2020.[13] In a survey conducted in 2021, half of all Americans confessed that they had neither written nor received a personal letter in the preceding five years; only about a third said they had received or sent one over the preceding twelve months. Nearly a quarter of adults under forty-five have never written a personal letter in their lives.[14] The handwritten letter, along with the deliberate, reflective practice of its composition, has been sacrificed to productivity.

The death was foretold by the German social critic Theodor Adorno. In his 1951 book, *Minima Moralia*, he wrote of his sense that the industrial "spirit of practicality" was expanding from the realm of business into that of everyday social relations. An efficiency-minded approach to communication was beginning to warp the way people spoke to each other:

If time is money, it seems moral to save time, above all one's own, and such parsimony is excused by consideration for others. One is straightforward. Every sheath interposed between men in their transactions is felt as a disturbance to the functioning of the apparatus, in which they are not only objectively incorporated but with which they proudly identify themselves.

The discursive, unhurried style of the personal letter, Adorno feared, was giving way to the blunt style of the bulletin. "The straight line is now regarded as the shortest distance between two people, as if they were points."[15]

The Children's Code

Electronic mail, for all its cultural import, would turn out to be a transitional technology, a hinge between analog and digital communication. Even as adults were navigating the shift to email, their children were busy inventing its successor, an even more condensed, even more casual style of writing that would come to be the primary language of online conversation. Beginning in the late 1990s, teens and tweens would commandeer the family PC after school and during the evening hours, ostensibly to do homework but actually to chat with friends through new instant-messaging programs such as ICQ and AOL Instant Messenger, or AIM. They would often carry on several conversations at once, clicking effortlessly from one small window to another like a chess master moving between boards at a simul. The ability to juggle many chats at once, combined with the privacy of on-screen exchanges, made instant messaging feel like a vast improvement over telephone calls for schoolkids looking to socialize while at home. That parents considered IM a strange and suspicious activity only added to its appeal.

Untethered to the traditions of the postal system, the young millennials (as they were coming to be called) quickly and instinctively developed a style of writing geared to the internet and the computer screen. They used all the characters available on the keyboard—letters, numbers, punctuation marks, accent marks, arithmetic and monetary symbols, logograms—as flexible semantic symbols. They smashed the phonetic alphabet and out of its pieces built something new. The fact that many American public schools had abandoned the teaching of phonics years earlier—replacing it with the "balanced literacy" approach favored by progressive educators[16]—may have made the creation of the new language easier. Because reading instruction had come to place more stress on recognizing words visually than sounding them out phonetically, teens and preteens likely had a diminished auditory sense of written language and a propensity to interpret written characters as visual symbols. They had been trained to read more by eye than by ear—a hindrance to book reading but a boon for screen reading.

IM became, as Kent State professor Pamela Takayoshi put it in 2008, "a separate language form from formal English," with its own "set of language features and standards."[17] In a study conducted with her colleague Christina Haas, Takayoshi reviewed thousands of instant messages sent by students and identified their salient features.[18] To speed up composition and reading, words were pruned of unnecessary letters (*how bout u let me know when u're ready*) or replaced by homophonic characters (*dont lie 2 me*); punctuation marks were omitted or used haphazardly (*yeah that's y im doing it over thanksgiving*); and common phrases were condensed into initialisms and acronyms (*lol, lmao*). To give messages a conversational tone, ellipses were used to indicate pauses (*i have some liquor . . . and some beer . . . but . . .*); capitalization was used for emphasis (*he just . . . LOOKED . . . at me*); letters were repeated to suggest excitement, exasperation, or sarcasm (*riiiight*); and typographic emoticons like ;-) and <3 were used to express affect or signal irony. Syntax was simplified. The rules and conventions of proper writing were ignored or happily subverted.

The resulting exchanges blurred traditional distinctions not only between talking and writing but also between text and image:

Bill: haha i don't know, it just sounds weird having you call me that
Bill: its too informal for my taste
Bill: haha
Sharon: WOW wut ru a fuckin teacher lol
Bill: hey we don't use the f bomb
Bill: i was just joking
Sharon: bitch please
Sharon: lol so wuz i
Sharon: =)

Slangy, flirty, and profane, IM conversations seemed on the surface like typical adolescent chatter. And they were that. But they were something more. They marked another cultural turning point. As Claude Shannon would have recognized, young people were creating, on the fly, a new communication code adapted to a new medium. Although instant messaging retained elements of traditional alphabetic writing—words were still involved; punctuation marks floated around—it incorporated visual and symbolic elements associated with older, pictorial forms of writing such as hieroglyphics and cuneiform. It was a linguistic mishmash, its grammar as much graphical as lexical.

Millennials were the first to sense that when communication becomes unremitting and chaotic, when content collapses, with messages from many sources vying constantly for recipients' attention, reading as traditionally practiced becomes untenable. It's too slow, too methodical, too reliant on a steady visual and mental focus. Messages streaming through a screen, one overlapping the other, need to be taken in at a glance, decoded by the eye with minimal cognitive effort or attentional drain. Reading becomes less a matter of following a line of thought and more a matter of recognizing a pattern. Writing shifts from the linear and literal to the visual and symbolic. What matters most, as the Dutch communication professor Lieke Verheijen has noted, "is efficiency: getting one's message across as rapidly, succinctly and effectively as possible, irrespective of standard language rules that are violated along the way."[19]

When Shannon had proposed using mathematical formulas to compress transmissions by removing redundant information, he had assumed that the compression would be accomplished mechanically, through technical procedures and protocols within the network. With IM, the communicators themselves—the kids—were doing their own compression. Many of their stylistic innovations served to trim redundancy from written English—*before* becomes *b4*; *talk to you later* becomes *ttyl*—in order to speed up writing and reading. Even the practice of repeating letters and punctuation marks (*yeeessssss!!!*) can be seen as a strategy for communicating tone and sense as speedily as possible. Tapping one key repeatedly takes much less time than hunting and pecking across a keyboard.

With the internet and its superbloom of messages, communication efficiency was no longer just a technological goal of network designers and operators. It was a social goal, to be pursued even when composing an intimate message for a close friend. Human beings were using the system, but they were also, as its transmitting and receiving nodes, acting as integral components of the system, as instruments of network optimization. They were playing roles reminiscent of the telegraph operators of old, but instead of employing an established code, they were inventing their own. As Adorno anticipated, they had been incorporated into the functioning of the apparatus.

The IMers even introduced simple, post hoc error-correction routines into their transmissions:

> **Annie:** i have to type up my academic awars
> **Ryan:** lol
> **Annie:** *awards

Rather than slow down exchanges by proofreading and editing messages before sending them, an IMer would clean up any confusing or embarrassing typo after the fact in a separate message, often using an asterisk to signal the change. As it turned out, error correction was rarely needed. As long as writers avoided syntactic complexity and semantic depth, as long as they kept it light, recipients had little problem deciphering the meaning of even the most typo-ridden messages. Ambiguity could usually be left unresolved. Precision in wording and phrasing was unnecessary. A concern for correct spelling and punctuation came to be seen as standoffish. Licklider had been right: sloppiness in online correspondence was acceptable from a social perspective and salutary from an efficiency perspective.

Riding the Waves

When mobile phones became cheap and commonplace during the first decade of the twenty-first century, they replaced home PCs as the favored communication tools of the young. The language of instant messaging turned into the language of texting. The transfer was seamless. Textspeak, as it was soon known, suited cell phones' tiny screens and keypads. It suited as well the thumb-typing required by the handheld devices' portability. And it suited the 160-character limit originally imposed on SMS text messages sent over cellular networks.

Because people carried their phones with them all day and because texting could be used for asynchronous as well as synchronous exchanges—correspondence and conversation alike—texting soon became an all-consuming habit for teens and twenty-somethings. By 2010, more than two trillion texts were being transmitted every year in the United States, most by the young.[20] The average American teenager was sending or receiving well over a hundred texts a day, equivalent to about seven or eight every waking hour.[21] (That was in addition to the messages, written in a similar style, that they were posting in rapidly growing numbers on social networks like MySpace, Facebook, and Tumblr.) By 2012, according to Pew Research, texting had become "the dominant daily mode of communication between teens and all those with whom they communicate"—far more prevalent than phone calls or even "face-to-face socializing."[22] The story was much the same in the rest of the world.

Even as textspeak became the young's favored language for interpersonal communication, it continued to be viewed with dismay and disdain by the old. Parents and teachers saw it not as an innovative form of speech geared to a new medium but as a debasement of standard written English. One college professor, writing for the *Guardian* in 2002, condemned textspeak as "bleak, bald, sad shorthand," a cover for "dyslexia, poor spelling and mental laziness."[23] Another ruffled elder, in a 2007 newspaper column, compared texters to "vandals who are doing to our language what Genghis Khan did to his neighbors eight hundred years ago. They are destroying it: pillaging our punctuation; savaging our sentences; raping our vocabulary."[24]

Even those who took a less agitated view of texting assumed it was a passing adolescent fad. In a 2008 paper, David Crystal, a British linguist who had written two well-received books about the internet's effect on language, predicted textspeak would soon go out of fashion: "The whole point of the style is to suit a particular technology where space is at a premium; and when that constraint is dropped, abbreviated language no longer has any purpose."[25] Crystal's assumption—shared by many others at the time—was that textspeak had developed in response to the limited bandwidth of nascent digital and cellular networks. Faced with slow transmission speeds and high data charges, IMers and then texters had had no choice but to strip their writing to its barest essentials. Once the network limits went away, the thinking went, the young would go back to writing full sentences and paragraphs. The old rules of spelling, punctuation, and grammar would come back into force.

That was a misreading of the phenomenon. It mistook a secondary cause for the primary cause. The development of textspeak, like the earlier development of email style, was prompted less by space constraints than by time constraints. As the earliest IMers had realized, keeping up with the torrents of conversation pouring through computer screens demanded quick reflexes, nonstop skimming, and constant shifts of focus. Every second spent on one message left one less second for all the rest. Speed in reading and terseness in writing were essential to staying afloat on the information flood, which in turn was essential to maintaining a robust social life. Brevity also offered another important social benefit: it raised the odds that your messages would actually be read. Research dating back to the early days of email had shown that, as message flow intensifies, recipients start to ignore long, involved messages while continuing to read short, snappy ones.[26]

Efficiency in expression—what the Columbia University linguistics professor John McWhorter has called texting's "cult of concision"[27]—was never really about conserving bandwidth. It was about conserving attention. As network capacity expanded, transmission costs fell, and message flows intensified, textspeak did not become obsolete. It became all the more indispensable, not just for kids but for adults. The growth in bandwidth also allowed a greatly expanded use of visual symbolism in messages, a trend that culminated with the arrival of the internet meme, textspeak's multimedia cousin. Memes are notoriously difficult to describe without recourse to examples,* but in general they employ a still or moving image, often a humorous one drawn from popular culture, that provides a logical template, or visual syntax, for a message. Captions are then overlaid on the image to customize the message. Because they're built on recognizable templates, memes are, at least to the initiated, easy to interpret quickly—they've been called "outsourced thoughts"—and because they take the form of a single image or GIF or even just a single written phrase, they're easy to share. At once a language and a social currency, they're a mode of expression ideally suited to social media.

With the coming of the smartphone and the mobile app at the end of the new century's first decade, technology, language, and commerce continued to evolve symbiotically, now at an even faster pace. Emoji replaced emoticons, and apps served up palettes of the tiny symbols, enabling users to insert them into posts, comments, and other messages with a tap. Ever more solicitous autocorrect and autocomplete functions automated the composition of messages. Like, heart, share, and other "social buttons," along with semantic symbols like hashtags and @ signs, further sped responses. Automatic linking tools allowed pictures and videos to be added to messages instantly. Touchscreens facilitated scrolling and swiping. Meme generators proliferated. Notifications kept everyone aware of incoming content. With people checking their phones scores or even hundreds of times

---

* As the often-memed *Lord of the Rings* character Boromir might say, "One does not simply . . . explain memes in words."

a day, digital communication, and the ethos of textspeak, began to pervade the general culture. A new communication medium had again created a new environment, but this one was more encompassing than any of its predecessors. We carried it with us wherever we went.

As textspeak in its various forms became indispensable to communication, it turned into a valuable business asset. The language may have been invented by teens, but its compressed, highly symbolic nature served the interests of social media companies. By speeding up the creation of messages, it provided the companies with endless streams of compelling content, all produced for free by the users themselves. By speeding up the consumption of messages, it gave the companies more opportunities to show advertisements and sponsored posts. And by incorporating an array of standardized affective symbols—markers of emotion—the language made it easier for the companies' computers to analyze users' preferences, intentions, and moods. It facilitated tracking, profiling, and personalization. The new communication code proved as suited to efficient machine reading as to efficient human reading. When the News Feed arrived, its *lingua franca* was waiting.

It's no surprise that when millennials came of age they had little patience for the electronic mail that so mesmerized their parents. Having spent their puberty instant-messaging and their adolescence texting, they found email slow and cumbersome, cluttered with spam and junk, and painfully archaic. Emails were something you had to "go through." Their younger, Gen Z siblings, most of whom had received their first smartphone by the time they turned twelve, developed an even greater antipathy toward the medium. Managing an inbox felt like work, and composing an email felt like a school assignment—full sentences were expected; errors were noted. Worst of all, writing an email required, if only for a moment, a retreat from the social whirl into the quiet of one's own thoughts. It was anxiety producing. "Every time I get an email, it is like getting stabbed," a college student explained to a reporter in 2021. "Another thing for me to do."[28] The system Licklider had celebrated for its speed and informality now seemed too slow and too formal.

In 1997, the year before *You've Got Mail* came out, the New England Confectionery Company, better known as Necco, added EMAIL ME to the messages printed on the tiny candy hearts it sells for Valentine's Day. Thirteen years later, in 2010, it retired EMAIL ME and replaced it with TXT ME. Though the email network isn't going away, at least not any time soon, it seems fated to function more and more as a conduit for business and administrative correspondence—bills, notices, solicitations, and other drab bureaucratic ephemera. Replaced by an even more compressed form of interpersonal correspondence, email is following the same route the post office has taken over the past few decades.

The Forever Conversation

Textspeak is worth celebrating. Ingenious and playful, it testifies to the strength of the human urge to communicate and the vigor of the human capacity to adapt to new media. It testifies as well to the irreverence and nerve of the young. Without any planning or expert guidance, without any parental oversight or permission, without even knowing what they were doing, schoolkids came up with an efficient (and fun) way to converse over computer networks, drawing on the entire history of communication, from grunt to glyph, to create a novel language. Turning a complex technological system to their own purposes, they learned to socialize in a new environment. Texting, as McWhorter put it in a 2013 TED talk, is "a miraculous thing."[29]

But miracles can be mixed blessings. In his talk, McWhorter described textspeak as "fingered speech." The oxymoron expressed what at the time was a common view of texting, at least among its defenders. Textspeak was seen as a written version of oral speech—a means to replicate on screens the easygoing style of friendly, face-to-face conversations. Its restricted vocabulary, syntactic minimalism, and offhand sloppiness were not flaws; they simply reflected the way people talk. "When we're speaking casually," McWhorter explained, "we speak in word packets of maybe seven to ten words." Compared with writing, "speech is much looser, it's much more telegraphic, it's much less reflective."

Before computers came along, gabbing through writing had been impossible. No medium existed that could mimic in textual transmissions the easy back-and-forth of spoken conversation. Speech couldn't be fingered. Written correspondence remained distinct, in style and tone, from talking. It was more formal and more ruminative, and it drew on a larger vocabulary and deployed, when needed, a more elaborate syntax. It was the language of exposition, analysis, and narrative. Conversation and correspondence complemented each other.

When connected to a computer or cellular network, people could for the first time exchange written messages in real time, without delays. A kid sitting alone in her bedroom or in the back seat of the family car could chat with her friends as if she were sitting with them around a lunch table in the school cafeteria. As Gretchen McCulloch, another linguist who champions textspeak, observes, "writing now comes in both formal and informal versions, just as speaking has for so long." Thanks to texting and its offspring, we're "surrounded by a vast sea of unedited, unfiltered words that once might have only been spoken."[30]

If that were the whole story, it would be easy to share McWhorter's and McCulloch's view of textspeak as a benign development in the history of communication, a welcome expansion of humankind's expressive capacities. But it's not the whole story. As the internet became the world's primary informational medium, the language developed for instant messaging and texting became a substitute not just for talking but for writing. It became the primary language for correspondence as well as conversation, the pressure of relentless communication having blurred the distinction between the two. And then, as all content collapsed onto the smartphone's screen, the distinction between private communication and public communication blurred as well. Textspeak's compressed, casual, often crude style came to define the great majority of the speech circulating through social media platforms. It infused the post, the reply, the comment, the caption, the chat. It entered the workplace through apps like Slack. As reporters and public figures flocked to Twitter and Facebook, the style seeped into journalism and politics. It "infiltrated," as Sophia McClennen, director of Penn State's Center for Global Studies, says, "more traditional news, broadcasting and other forms of what you might think of as more serious speech."[31] The spirit of textspeak permeated the public square.

That doesn't mean everything's been homogenized. The styles of writing that characterize popular social media platforms vary in their particulars, depending on the design of the platform and the audience it serves. Facebook posts are different from tweets. Tweets are different from Instagram captions. Instagram captions are different from TikTok comments. TikTok comments are different from WhatsApp messages. But they all share the fundamental characteristics of textspeak. They are all variations on a theme, and the theme is streamlined, easy-to-skim communication.

As McWhorter noted, when people talk casually they prune their vocabulary to a small set of common words, use sentence fragments instead of sentences, and keep their syntax simple. As much is said through gestures and expressions as through words. That allows the conversation to move at a fast clip while remaining animated, expressive, and engaging. Talking turns speech outward, toward others. It keeps things familiar. Reading and writing, when practiced with attentiveness and care, serve a different role. They slow the mind down, force it to grapple with the complex and the unfamiliar. In the words of the cultural critic Thomas de Zengotita, "reading and writing turn the mind inward, cultivate habits of rational reflection, encourage the imagination, the inner life in general—thus giving birth to a self in the modern sense."[32]

What we gain by substituting fingered speech for reading and writing is the ability to keep up with a conversation that swirls around us all the time. What we sacrifice are depth and rigor. Turned always outward, speech becomes less a way of sorting out our thoughts, of thinking for ourselves, and more a way of reacting to others. We rely on quick and often emotional judgments while eschewing slower, reflective ones. The language we use shapes not just how we express our thoughts; it shapes the form of our thoughts. It influences how we think as well as how we talk.

Many philosophers, from Aristotle to William James, have described the dualistic nature of human thought. One way we think is quick, intuitive, and largely unconscious. It draws on sensory impressions, instinct, and experience to recognize patterns in the world, and it often uses emotion as a means of interpreting phenomena. The other way is slow and deliberative, involving the conscious, step-by-step application of reason. In their influential 1975 article "Attention and Cognitive Control," Michael Posner and Charles Snyder labeled these two ways of thinking "automatic" and "conscious" and used them as the basis for their groundbreaking "dual-process model" of the human mind.[33] The late Nobel laureate Daniel Kahneman popularized the distinction in his best-selling 2011 book, *Thinking, Fast and Slow*. He referred to the automatic, unconscious form of thinking as System 1 and the controlled, deliberative form as System 2. The latter, he emphasized, requires sustained attention, while the former happens effortlessly. Both modes are valuable and can produce subtle insights—that chess master at the simul, having deep experience with the game, relies more on pattern recognition than reasoned analysis in making moves—but "only the slower System 2 can construct thoughts in an orderly series of steps."[34] You can grasp a great deal about the world through intuition, but to think critically you need to suppress your reflexive instincts and enter System 2 mode. You need to slow down and exert conscious control over your mind.

Textspeak, in its various forms, is both a reflection and an instrument of the System 1 mind. To be adept at social media, to successfully navigate the informational whitewater, is to rely on automatic thinking—on snap judgments and hot takes. The deliberativeness of System 2 thinking is ill suited to interpreting and reacting to a continuous stream of messages in real time. To put it another way, reasoned analysis requires the friction of hard mental work. And friction, as Zuckerberg and the other designers of social media platforms make clear, is the enemy of the efficient operation of digital communication networks. Quick, intuitive thinking is the lubricant that keeps the machine moving.

The consequences aren't limited to the favoring of reflex reactions over measured assessments. Open-ended, contemplative ways of thinking—the philosophical, the ruminative, the introspective—have also been marginalized. That's one of the reasons our culture has become so politicized in recent years. The screen's hegemony prevents us from experiencing art as, in Susan Sontag's words, a "form of mystification" aimed "at the completion of human consciousness, at transcendence."[35] It turns art, like all other forms of expression, into mere message. Sticking a painting or a novel into an ideological category is quicker and easier than engaging in the slow, pensive work of aesthetic appreciation.

Charles Cooley, in arguing that greater media efficiency widens our influences and broadens our minds, took it for granted that new communication technologies would make information more accessible without altering its expression or interpretation. As the mechanisms of communication gained speed and capacity, people would draw from a larger, more various set of works; they would think deeply about what they had read; and they would learn from the good and discard the bad. What he failed to anticipate was how media efficiency, when pushed to an extreme, so accelerates the flow of information that people no longer have the luxury of careful reading, methodical evaluation, and contemplative inquiry. The breezes of influence combine into a whirlwind. Attention splinters, understanding grows thin. Rather than leveling barriers to knowledge and sympathy, communication itself becomes a barrier.

CHAPTER 5

Antipathies

Environmental Spoiling

In 1976, the social psychologist Ebbe Ebbesen and two of his colleagues at the University of California at San Diego conducted a study of the residents of a large condominium complex in Irvine, south of Los Angeles. They wanted to find out how physical proximity influences the way people feel about each other. They interviewed some two hundred residents, asking about their interactions and relationships with their neighbors. Whom did they talk to? Whom did they avoid? Whom did they like? Whom didn't they? The nearer people lived to each other, the researchers found, the more likely they were to be friends. The odds were far higher that a person would bond with a next-door neighbor than with someone a hundred yards down the street. That finding was no surprise. Not only was it commonsensical; it was consistent with a well-established psychological principle called the proximity effect.

But the researchers also discovered that living close together often had the opposite result. It aroused not fondness but enmity.

While neighbors were much more likely to be friends, they were also much more likely to be enemies. In fact—and this was a surprise—proximity seemed to breed animosity more often than it did affection. "Proximity appeared to be even *more* important in disliking than in liking," the researchers reported in a 1976 article in the *Journal of Experimental Social Psychology*. "More disliked than liked individuals lived close to the subjects." Among close neighbors, enemies outnumbered friends.

The reason neighbors often become friends, previous research had shown, is simple: they run into each other a lot. They have frequent opportunities to meet and chat, and through such casual conversations they develop a familiarity that spawns mutual empathy, and the empathy fosters a sense of attachment. Neighbors become enemies, the condo researchers discovered, for a very different reason: "environmental spoiling." The closer you live to another person, the more exposed you are to his habits and opinions. If you find those habits and opinions irritating—he doesn't bring in his garbage cans, say, or he doesn't clean up after his dog, or he puts up political signs supporting candidates you loathe—you'll resent him for degrading your surroundings. And because his proximity guarantees his irritating habits and opinions remain always in view, your resentment, and your antipathy, will fester. Because of that antipathy, moreover, you'll take pains to avoid running into him when you're out and about. So the casual contacts that promote empathy and fondness never happen. Enmity, once provoked, becomes self-reinforcing.

It's difficult to imagine the condo study being conducted today. Concepts of distance and space, once rooted in the material world, have grown hazy, particularly when it comes to interpersonal relations. Thanks to the net, the link between social proximity and physical proximity has been severed. It's as easy to socialize through a computer or phone screen with someone a thousand miles away as it is to socialize in person with someone next door. It's easier, in fact, as the screen, unlike the neighbor, is always at hand. But the study's findings are, if anything, more illuminating than ever. They help explain why social media's effects have been so different from what we expected—why the technology of connection has produced more strife than harmony. Now that we're all virtual neighbors, we're all in one another's business all the time. We're exposed, routinely, to the opinions and habits of far more people, both acquaintances and strangers, than ever before. With an almost microscopic view of what everybody else is saying and doing—the screen turns us all into Peeping Toms—we have no end of opportunities to take offense. There may not be any garbage cans or dog turds in the virtual world, but there's plenty of environmental spoiling.

The Difference Engine

We humans are nothing if not optimistic when it comes to our social relationships. When we meet new people, or even anticipate meeting them, we have an inclination to like them, and we sense that our fondness for them will grow as we learn more about them.[2] We see communication on a personal level the same way we see it on a societal level: as a reliable way to form and strengthen bonds. We've all experienced the many ways interpersonal communication can go awry—the casual conversation that turns into a quarrel, the innocent word that gets taken the wrong way, the careless remark that poisons a friendship—but we discount them as anomalies. We don't let them shake our belief that the more information two people exchange, the more they'll understand each other and the closer they'll become. Like Zuckerberg, we trust that "people sharing more" leads to people getting along better.

It isn't hard to understand where the optimism comes from. We hang out with the people we like the best—our close friends, our work buddies, our romantic partners—and those are also the people we know the most about. Our intuition tells us that having more information about another person must be tied to liking that person. But our intuition is skewed. Whenever we decide we don't like someone— that neighbor with the dog, for instance—we start to avoid them and

so gather less information about them. But when we strike up a friendship with someone, we spend more time with them and learn more
about them. As we prune our acquaintances in this way, we end up
surrounded by a small and unrepresentative set of people whom we
both like a lot and know a lot about. Our personal experience distorts
our understanding. Knowing and liking may be strongly correlated
within groups of established friends, but that tells us nothing about
how people in general react to learning more about others.

In 2007, a group of Boston-area social psychologists, led by Harvard's Michael Norton, ran a series of experiments to discover what
really happens when we receive more information about others.
The researchers first conducted surveys to get a baseline reading on
people's attitudes. They found, as expected, that the vast majority
of people—between 80 and 90 percent—believe that the more they
get to know about another person, the more they'll like that person.
Then they tested that assumption. In two experiments, one involving college students and the other involving visitors to an online dating site, some four hundred subjects were given descriptions of a
fictional person. The descriptions took the form of sets of character
traits, randomly chosen and varying in number from one to ten. The
participants were asked to rate how much they thought they would
like the person described by the traits.

The results were striking. As the number of personality traits
given to participants increased, their liking for the individual
described decreased. More information consistently led to less liking. The study revealed, the researchers reported in an article in the
American Psychological Association's *Journal of Personality and
Social Psychology*, "that the relationship between knowledge and
liking within individuals is in fact negative: that more information
about any one person leads, on average, to less liking for that person." The melancholy upshot: "Although people believe that knowing leads to liking, knowing more means liking less."[3]

Norton and his colleagues conducted additional experiments to
figure out why that's so. The explanation, they found, lies in "dis-

similarity cascades." It has long been known that perceptions of similarity play a decisive role in determining whom we like and whom we don't. We have a bias to like people that seem similar to us and dislike those who seem different. What the experiments revealed is that the tendency toward disliking is even stronger than the tendency toward liking. As soon as the study participants were exposed to a character trait indicating that a person was unlike them in some way, they began to place more emphasis on evidence of dissimilarity than on evidence of similarity. Differences became more salient and commonalities less salient as the amount of personal information grew.[4] "Encountering one instance of dissimilarity causes subsequent information to be interpreted as further evidence of dissimilarity," the researchers explained. "The negative relationship between information and liking is caused by the fact that dissimilarity cascades as the amount of information increases." The study suggested something no one had suspected: that a communication network might serve as a vector of enmity even more than of friendship.

The research was controversial. The results seemed to contradict other psychological experiments, including studies of the proximity effect, which indicated that familiarity promotes affection.[5] An academic spat broke out in the pages of the *Journal of Personality and Social Psychology.* One prominent group of critics, while accepting the validity of the Norton team's findings, argued that the research was too narrow. It failed to account for the many different ways that people can socialize. They pointed in particular to research indicating that brief conversations between strangers tend to produce feelings of attraction.[6]

In a response to the criticism, Norton and his colleagues acknowledged that their study was not comprehensive and that the connection between interaction and affection or aversion will vary depending on the situation.[7] When two strangers chat, for example, they may indeed sense a liking for each other, but that could be because people are in general wary of disclosing a lot of personal information to someone they've just met. If no evidence of dissimilarity is divulged in a short conversation, strangers may continue to be influenced by their inclination to like new acquaintances. The dissimilarity cascade never starts rolling. That also helps explain why casual, neighborly interactions produce the proximity effect. If you have regular friendly chats about the weather or the local sports teams with a guy who lives nearby, your empathy for him will tend to grow, and you may well end up liking him a bit more. If he starts getting too personal—telling you about his political theories or bragging about how much money he has or detailing his sex life—your reaction might be very different. The more you're told, the more likely it is you'll hear something that offends or repels you. Self-disclosure gets riskier as it goes deeper.

Always on Display

The Norton group pointed out that trait-based experiments like the ones they conducted do a good job of replicating how we actually learn about people today. Rarely do we form impressions of others simply by chatting with them on a sidewalk or a stoop. We gather discrete bits of information about them from many sources through our phones and computers. We google them. We look at their social media profiles. We scan their posts and comments. We glance at their selfies and other photos. We check out their follower lists and their likes and shares. We parse their texts and other messages. Digital data-gathering is how we size up strangers and new acquaintances, and it's how we keep tabs on people we already know, including long-standing friends. We've gotten used to interpreting people as assemblages of traits, as patterns of data.

Our information gathering is usually productive. Studies dating back to the early days of instant messaging and texting show that strangers tend to disclose much more information about themselves when chatting through computers than when talking in person—a result of what psychologists call the online disinhibition effect.[8] The old taboo that checked our urge to talk about ourselves in public faded away when we found ourselves looking into a screen instead of another person's eyes. With the rise of social media, oversharing became the new norm. Facebook, Snapchat, X, and other platforms have been painstakingly designed to encourage self-expression. By emphasizing quantitative measures of social status—follower and friend counts, like and retweet tallies—the platforms reward people for broadcasting endless details about their lives and opinions through messages, posts, photos, and videos. In the physical world, we remain present even when we're quiet. In the virtual world, we don't. To shut up, even briefly, is to disappear. To confirm our existence, we have to keep posting. We have to keep repeating *Here I am!*

As all this personal information swirls around the net, people find a lot of evidence of what they have in common with others and a lot of evidence of what they don't. They see likenesses, and they see differences—and over time, as the Norton research suggests, they begin to place more weight on the differences. It's hard to imagine a communication mechanism more perfectly geared to the initiation and propagation of dissimilarity cascades than social media. The information that circulates through a social network can act as an attractant. More often, it's a repellent. That most gloomy of sayings is true: Familiarity breeds contempt.

It also breeds envy and rivalry. Just as social media's stimulation of self-disclosure triggers our instinct to dislike those we see as different from ourselves, it gives us ever more opportunity and ever greater cause to be envious of others and covetous of what they possess or represent. As with affection and enmity, envy is closely tied to feelings of proximity. We're much more likely to envy someone close to us—literally (nearby in space) or figuratively (having a similar background or social status)—than someone distant from us. "When there is no proximity, comparison is less likely to arise and the subject is less prone to feel inferior," explains Aaron Ben-Ze'ev, an Israeli philosophy professor and a pioneer in the study of human emotions. "When some proximity does exist, the element of the attainable becomes more dominant and the probability of envy arising increases, as does the intensity of that envy."[9] You might well envy a coworker who has a newer or more expensive car than you, but you're unlikely to envy a pop star who drives a Bentley.

At least that's how it worked in the past. Envy was circumscribed by location and class. Then, a century ago, mass media began extending the range of human envy by providing individuals with a close-up view of the lives of an ever greater number and variety of other people. Radio and particularly television gave listeners and viewers a sense of intimacy with people they previously would have considered too distant, physically or socially, to pay much attention to. Still, mass media imposed its own social boundary. Not everyone, after all, could appear on radio or TV. Social media has now erased even that line. By allowing everyone to display themselves on the same screen using the same forms of communication, it has gone much further than mass media ever did in eradicating the sense of distance that once limited feelings of envy. As the political scientist and author Alexandra Samuel has written, social media

> makes a wider range of outcomes, goods, and experiences feel like they're within our reach. We have at least the illusion of intimacy with a much wider range of people, so we're able to imagine not just what our lives would look like if they were 15% better, but what it would look like to have the wealth of a Kardashian, the influence of Elon Musk, and the talent of Rihanna.[10]

By turning us all into media personalities, social media has also turned us all into rivals.

Envy has its uses. For individuals, it can be a spur to ambition, achievement, and creativity. For society as a whole, it can play a role in raising awareness of inequities. "The passion that has given driving force to democratic theories is undoubtedly the passion of envy," wrote Bertrand Russell in *The Conquest of Happiness*. But envy is fundamentally a destructive emotion, personally and socially. As Russell went on to observe, "Of all the characteristics of ordinary human nature envy is the most unfortunate; not only does the envious person wish to inflict misfortune and do so whenever he can with impunity, but he is also himself rendered unhappy by envy. Instead of deriving pleasure from what he has, he derives pain from what others have."[11] Even as envy makes us less content with our own lives, it breeds resentment and animosity toward others. It makes differences stand out all the more sharply. "Thanks to social media," writes Samuel, "we're actually well on our way to dismantling all the social norms and structures that used to mitigate the risks envy posed to both personal and social well-being."[12]

If conversing online engendered empathy the way talking in person does, the negative effects of the explosion of self-disclosure would be ameliorated, at least to some degree. Through all those exchanges of messages, all those posts and replies, all those likes and hearts and fire emojis, we would, bit by bit, gain a greater appreciation of the feelings and perspectives of others. But talking through computers is not the same as talking in person. When we speak through screens, we don't experience the subtle physical cues—the gestures, the expressions, the glances—that often provide a clearer window onto the inner lives of others than do words alone. Nor do we give others the attention that we do when they're standing or sitting beside us. Indeed, the presence of a phone distances us even from those sitting right next to us.

Sherry Turkle, an MIT social psychologist who has been studying how people communicate through computers for decades, has described social media as an "anti-empathy machine." She argues that we suppress our capacity for empathy by "putting ourselves in environments where we're not looking at each other in the eye, not sticking with the other person long enough or hard enough to follow what they're feeling."[13] Over the long run, she says, a dependency on online communication can reduce people's ability to feel empathy in general, making them less empathetic even when they're not on their phone or computer. Even their self-awareness can be blunted.

"Research shows that those who use social media the most have difficulty reading human emotions, including their own."[14]

Empathy is what neuroscientists call a complex emotion. It requires, as Helen Reiss, a psychiatry professor at Harvard Medical School, puts it, an "exquisite interplay" of brain networks.[15] Unlike basic emotions such as anger and disgust, which arise almost instantaneously in response to stimuli, complex emotions take time to emerge in the mind. Like complex thoughts, they require attentiveness, a steady rather than a darting eye. Although we're quick to assume a direct correlation between communication and empathy— the more information we exchange, the more empathy we'll feel— empathy depends far more on the quality of our communication than its volume. It's another thing we sacrifice when we talk too much.

Sword and Shield

In the 1960s, Dalmas Taylor and Irwin Altman, two young psychology researchers at the Naval Medical Research Institute in Bethesda, Maryland, began a study of how relationships develop between people working in tight quarters under stressful conditions—in a submarine, say, or on the deck of a destroyer. They quickly discovered that surprisingly little research had been done on how relationships deepen, or fall apart, as time passes. There were lots of narrowly focused studies of different facets of human interaction but few attempts to develop an overarching model of how bonds strengthen or weaken. Through years of experiments, surveys, and fieldwork, the two developed such a model, which they came to call the social penetration theory. They laid out its details in *Social Penetration: The Development of Interpersonal Relationships*, a highly influential 1973 book that is still considered a central text in social psychology.[16]

Relationship building, as Taylor and Altman describe it, is a slow and delicate process, contingent on the pace, content, and reciprocity of communication. It proceeds through four stages. In the first, *orientation*, new acquaintances discuss fairly trivial matters, revealing only superficial information about themselves—the music they listen to, for instance, or their favorite movies. Wary of creating conflict when forming initial impressions, they speak cautiously and remain circumspect. If some affinity is established, they move on to the second stage, *exploratory affective exchange*. Now they talk more freely, letting more of their personality show, and they discuss more sensitive subjects, like their political views or their health. Still, they avoid revealing details about their inner lives, continuing to restrict their disclosures to what Taylor and Altman term "public areas." In the third stage of the penetration process, *affective exchange*, true friendships are established. The conversation shifts from exploration to revelation. The previously hidden private self comes into view, as the friends discuss intimate aspects of their upbringing, their emotions, and their beliefs. As they open up to each other, the tone of the conversation becomes more spontaneous and animated—less self-conscious, if not altogether unguarded. In the final and most intimate stage, *stable exchange*, conversations flow easily, without restraint or restriction. Mutual trust is established, allowing the most private personal information to be shared, including information that is a source of shame or sadness. The bond is implicit. For most people, few relationships reach this point. Stable exchange is reserved for lovers and the closest of friends and family members.

In their book, Taylor and Altman used the familiar trope of peeling an onion to explain their theory. As relationships progress, more layers of the self are peeled away. Exchanges of information grow steadily broader, as conversations extend to more and increasingly sensitive topics, and steadily deeper, as more private feelings and experiences are explored. The exchanges, the authors stress, consist of more than words. Gestures, expressions, and touches also matter, as do the way people orient themselves in the space they share and, when they're apart, think or fantasize about each other. The process is fragile. At any stage, conflicts can arise. One person may reveal something that repels the other. The tone of the conversation may turn abrasive or desultory. Or self-disclosure may become unbalanced, with one partner revealing intimate details of a sort the other withholds. Under such stresses, the relationship may revert to an earlier phase—close friends become casual acquaintances, maybe—or come to an acrimonious end. Communication becomes constrained or breaks down. The layers, to push the metaphor too far, go back on the onion.

Soon after the book's publication, Taylor shifted into the field of university administration, where he would go on to have a distinguished career. Altman continued his psychological research, and he kept circling back around the book's argument. He sensed that something was missing, that he and Taylor had told only part of the story. The social penetration theory explained how people form bonds by gradually opening themselves up to others. What it didn't address was people's conflicting desire to shield themselves from social penetration—to establish boundaries that limit communication and disclosure. Revealing oneself to others may bring social rewards, Altman realized, but it exacts a psychic cost. There is always a tension in relationships between "openness and closedness." As much as we might want the tension to resolve itself into a state of serene equilibrium, it never does. People are always at once "open and closed toward one another."[17]

There's no indication that, in choosing the word *penetration* to describe their original theory of relationship building, Taylor and Altman gave much thought to the word's many, sometimes ugly connotations. But those connotations haunt Altman's subsequent research. They help explain why we fear self-disclosure even as we embrace it as a necessary and often invigorating means of being part of society. Penetration may, literally or figuratively, be an act of love, entailing a physical or psychological merging of selves, but it is also always an act of violation. It exposes the self to another or to many others. The fear isn't that we will reveal, and hence lose, the essence of our soul. Very few of us, no matter how hard we peer inside ourselves, ever come across a kernel of selfhood. The fear is the opposite: that we will be reduced to a kernel. In allowing ourselves to be pinned down, we will sacrifice the self's flexibility and freedom. It's the same fear that lies behind many people's aversion to being photographed. A photograph condenses you into a single image, turns you into a pattern of information. In fixing you as an object in the minds of others, it robs you of complexity and agency. In a photo, you can't explain yourself. You're rendered mute.

In the mid-1970s, Altman published several articles laying out a "privacy regulation theory" that he offered as a complement and counterweight to the social penetration theory. Healthy human relations, whether at the personal or the social level, require communication, he argued, but they also require "boundary systems" that curb the flow and intensity of communication. We need communication, and we need protection from communication. The reasons go beyond matters of personal integrity and agency. Without limits, excessive communication triggers defensive, antisocial reactions on the part of individuals and groups. "Extensive self-disclosure" might seem benign or even laudable as a social goal, he explained, but it's dangerous. It can end up undermining the very cohesiveness that we desire communication to provide. "Extreme openness might actually increase the probability of conflict, violate self-integrity, and detract from the mutuality that was being sought in human relationships."[18]

Communication technologies are tools of social penetration. We use them to reveal ourselves and to probe the selves of others. But by blurring conversation and broadcasting, social media takes social penetration to an extreme. It gives people enormous incentives to talk about themselves, before a mass media–sized audience, and few incentives to secure their privacy or respect the privacy of others. It's all sword, no shield. The technology's bias is evident in the language that surrounds it. The internet has, from the start, been celebrated as a model of and a force for "openness"—in technology, in communication, in society. An open network built on open standards and open to all, the net is, we are regularly reminded, the enemy of everything closed and secret. The rhetoric is rousing, but it should give us pause. A decent society, as Altman implied, will safeguard personal privacy at least as vigorously as it promotes self-expression. In social relations as in personal relationships, transparency needs be tempered by opacity. When a society pushes everyone toward self-exposure, when it tears down all boundaries, it sets the stage not for harmony but for discord.

The Crowd

In 1903, the German sociologist Georg Simmel gave a lecture called "The Metropolis and Mental Life" on the psychic consequences of urban living.[19] However exciting and energizing it may at times be, the experience of being crowded together with others in the "extensive communicative life" of a city, Simmel argued, produces in people an unsettling sense of "mutual strangeness and repulsion." It also triggers a more general fear, chronic in modern life, of being "swallowed up in the social-technological mechanism." The feelings of unease usually remain hidden, suppressed behind an outward, defensive countenance of indifference or good cheer, but they can at any moment "break out into hatred and conflict." Simmel's sense of city life may have been overly bleak, but his assessment of crowding and its toll on mental health has been confirmed by many studies, including Altman's.[20] When we feel impinged upon by large numbers of other people and overwhelmed by a profusion of sensory stimuli, we experience a kind of social claustrophobia, with symptoms of stress, depression, withdrawal, and, at worst, aggression.

There are no bodies online, but there are myriad presences. With everyone pressing their virtual flesh on everyone else all the time, the communicative life becomes more extensive, and more oppressive, than it is in even the most densely populated of cities. Simmel's description of the "psychological conditions" of the metropolis—"the rapid telescoping of changing images, pronounced differences within what is grasped at a single glance, and the unexpectedness of violent stimuli"—seems if anything more accurate as a description of the social media environment than the urban one. In online society, moreover, the tempering influence of face-to-face conversation is missing. There are no sidewalks or stoops. Virtual presence entails physical absence.

That's not to discount the many close bonds people have formed online. Facebook posts have kindled or rekindled friendships. Snaps have spawned romances. Exchanges of tweets have opened up into deep conversations. TikToks have inspired feelings of communal joy, often expressed in dancing and singing. Many people who feel isolated or uncomfortable in their physical surroundings have found companionship and a sense of belonging in the internet's vast, disembodied social scene. Just as textspeak has room for wit and repartee, social media has room for affection and care.

But social media's benefits, as real and welcome as they are, shouldn't blind us to the deeper ways that digital technology is changing social dynamics. The discoveries that psychologists and sociologists have made about the fraught nature of human relationships—about environmental spoiling and dissimilarity cascades, about the slow and fragile unfolding of relationships, about the tension between disclosure and privacy—reveal how ill-suited the human psyche is to our new media environment. As connections multiply and messages proliferate, relationships get stretched thin. Mistrust spreads. Antipathies mount. That's the tragedy of communication. When there's too much of it, a reversal takes place. It begins to undermine the very social and personal qualities we look to it to foster. To put it in the language of economics, communication displays diminishing returns to scale—and eventually the returns turn negative. Communication subverts itself. That's what Harold Innis was getting at when, in his 1947 lecture, he suggested that more communication means less understanding.

Adam Joinson, a psychology professor at the University of Bath in England, coined the term *digital crowding* to describe the "excessive self-disclosure . . . and social contact" that characterizes social media's teeming but ghostly metropolis. The anxiety and enervation such crowding produces make the internet's antisocial tendencies all the more pronounced. "With the advent of social media," Joinson and a group of his colleagues wrote in the book *Privacy Online*, "it is inevitable that we will end up knowing more about people, and also more likely that we end up disliking them because of it."[21] Ian Bogost, a computer-science and media-studies professor at Washington University in St. Louis, is blunter. Social media, he wrote in a 2022 *Atlantic* essay, plunges us into a "sociopathic rendition of human sociality."[22]

CHAPTER 6

The Democratization Fallacy

Medium of the Masses

So:

1. Content collapses, as analog media's regulatory regime and epistemic architecture give way to digitization's totalizing advance.

2. Media technology extends beyond its traditional transport function to assume an editorial role, automating judgments about the relevance and quality of information.

3. People streamline their writing and reading to optimize their efficiency as transceivers of messages on a high-speed communication network.

4. Social media encourages unchecked self-expression, greatly expanding the platforms' supply of content but producing feelings of envy, enmity, and claustrophobia among individuals.

The four forces, intertwined and mutually reinforcing, all springing from a new mechanism of communication, go a long way toward explaining the social and political problems produced by digital media. But as they played out over the past few decades, they went largely unnoticed. They didn't fit the story we were telling ourselves about the internet and the information age.

When John Paul Stevens wrote the Supreme Court's opinion in the Carlin case, he and his fellow justices had a clear conception of what mass media looked like and how it operated within society, a conception the public would have shared. Mass media had, after all, been around for decades—centuries, in the case of publishing—and its operational and cultural characteristics were well established. Media, in the United States and many other parts of the world, operated as an industry, with a clear divide between the supply side and the demand side. Broadcasting and publishing were largely in the hands of a small group of for-profit companies that controlled the creation and distribution of content. The public played the role of consumers, selecting what to read, watch, and listen to from the limited set of options that professional writers, editors, and producers served up.

Because TV and radio stations controlled the supply of broadcast content and, through the one-to-many model, enjoyed direct access to people's homes, it was generally agreed that the government needed to monitor the broadcasting industry to protect the public interest. The FCC acted as a kind of consumer protection agency in the information marketplace, keeping tabs on the shows broadcast by the networks to ensure media companies didn't abuse their power or infringe on the well-being of individuals and families. The commission, as Stevens argued, wasn't censoring speech when it censured WBAI for airing Carlin's "Filthy Words" in the middle of the day; it was just doing its job of preventing potentially offensive content from sneaking uninvited into people's homes (or cars). Those who wanted to hear Carlin's routine were free to buy his records or attend his performances or watch one of his cable specials on HBO.

Twenty years later, when Stevens again took up his pen, this time to write the court's decision in the 1997 *Reno v. ACLU* case, neither the justices nor any one else had a clear idea what the internet was or would become. The first web browsers were just a few years old, and only about fifty million people were regularly spending time online, most of them connecting through business or university accounts or using private dial-up services such as AOL or CompuServe. Most of the qualities we now take for granted in online media had yet to emerge; many weren't even imaginable. Stevens's labored attempt to describe the internet testified to its embryonic state at the time:

> Anyone with access to the Internet may take advantage of a wide variety of communication and information retrieval methods. These methods are constantly evolving and difficult to categorize precisely. But, as presently constituted, those most relevant to this case are electronic mail (e-mail), automatic mailing list services ("mail exploders," sometimes referred to as "listservs"), "newsgroups," "chat rooms," and the "World Wide Web." All of these methods can be used to transmit text; most can transmit sound, pictures, and moving video images. Taken together, these tools constitute a unique medium—known to its users as "cyberspace"—located in no particular geographical location but available to anyone, anywhere in the world, with access to the Internet.[1]

New technological systems never arrive fully formed. They take years to mature technically and even longer to make their full social and cultural effects known. The more complex their workings and far-reaching their uses, the longer the maturation process takes and the likelier it is to produce surprises. But people can't sit back and wait for all the uncertainties to be resolved. They have to make important decisions about the technology from the start. For those decisions to be made in an organized rather than chaotic fashion, society has to come up with a shared story about the new system and its social role. The story serves to guide business and government investment, shape public opinion and consumer behavior, and steer regulatory and legal responses. Repeated by journalists, academics, and public officials, not to mention inventors and entrepreneurs, it becomes, regardless of its accuracy, one of the crucial factors determining how the technology progresses.

Even before it came into wide use, the internet was understood to be, as Stevens wrote in his opinion, "a unique and wholly new medium of worldwide human communication." It was the first true multimedia system, able to handle "sound, pictures, and moving video images" as well as text. Even more important, it was the first many-to-many communication network with the capacity to carry large volumes of information efficiently between any of its nodes. (Cheap radio transceivers offered something of a precedent, but their use was limited by spectrum and other constraints.) The story we told ourselves about the net, from its earliest days, was a story of "democratization." The new network was opening media, in particular broadcasting, to individual citizens, and by bringing the voices of more people into public debates, it would deepen and strengthen democracy in general.

This story fit the net's technical characteristics, and it reflected the public's sunny view of new communication systems. It also resonated with the times. In the wake of the breakup of the Soviet Union—the Berlin Wall had come down only eight years earlier—the continued spread of democracy seemed inevitable. In his widely discussed article "The End of History?," published in 1989, the same year Tim Berners-Lee invented the World Wide Web, Francis Fukuyama heralded the arrival of "the end point of mankind's ideological evolution and the universalization of Western liberal democracy as the final form of human government."[2] The web seemed the perfect medium for the dawning age of universal democracy. The technology's effect, wrote the prominent *Economist* editor Frances Cairncross in her 1997 book, *The Death of Distance*, "will be to increase understanding, foster tolerance, and ultimately promote worldwide peace."[3] Her words echoed, almost note for note, the utopian rhetoric that had accompanied new communication systems at the century's start.

The democratization story runs as a stirring refrain through Stevens's opinion. Akin to "a vast library including millions of readily available and indexed publications," the net was giving everyone access to information that used to be reserved for elites. "The content of the Internet," Stevens declared, "is as diverse as human thought." Even more important, the new system was giving the masses the power to produce and distribute media content. Breaking down the old divide between mass media's supply side and demand side, between information production and information consumption, it was giving everyone an equal voice. "Any person or organization with a computer connected to the Internet can 'publish' information," Stevens wrote. "No single organization controls any membership in the Web, nor is there any single centralized point from which individual Web sites or services can be blocked." Any citizen "can become a town crier with a voice that resonates farther than it could from any soapbox." It was obvious, he concluded, that the internet deserved special "medium-specific" treatment under the law. As "the most participatory form of mass speech yet developed," it should be granted "the highest protection from governmental intrusion."

Margaret Mead's ideal of a truly democratic communication medium—bidirectional, decentralized, participatory, multisensory, enveloping—had gone underground in the sixties. Without the technology required to bring it to the masses, it lost its force as a practical social goal and, in the form of acid tests and other multimedia happenings, turned into an expression of countercultural transcendentalism, or at least hedonism. It devolved from the civic to the psychedelic—and then, like other hippie dreams, evaporated into the consumerism of the seventies and eighties. But now, thanks to the net, the ideal was suddenly back—and being realized. Mass media and mass men were at last being supplanted by democratic media and democratic men.

The bursting of the dot-com bubble in 2000 and 2001 dampened enthusiasm for the net as an investment opportunity, but by shifting people's focus from the medium's commercial prospects to its social possibilities, it further invigorated the public's sense of the network as a new kind of democratic community—egalitarian, welcoming, open. When the World Trade Center attack late in 2001 shook people's faith in the inevitability of global democracy, the net took on an even greater symbolic importance for many of its users, becoming a repository for their hopes for the future. The stock-market crash offered "an opportunity for renaissance," the popular media writer Douglas Rushkoff suggested in his 2003 monograph, *Open Source Democracy*. In the face of tyranny, fundamentalism, and other threats to "democracy and free discourse" in the real world, the net's "interactive technologies offer us a ray of hope for a renewed spirit of genuine civic engagement." He suggested that in the uncorrupted sphere of cyberspace we could teach ourselves to be better, more fully democratic citizens. "The very survival of democracy as a functional reality may be dependent on our acceptance, as individuals, of adult roles in conceiving and stewarding the shape and direction of society. And we may get our best rehearsal for these roles online."[4] The net would help us grow up.

The post-crash arrival of "Web 2.0," with its flowering of blogs, news aggregation sites, and social networks, was taken as further confirmation of the democratization narrative. "The means of media are now in the hands of the people," trumpeted the then-prominent journalist-cum-blogger Jeff Jarvis in 2004, the year of Facebook's founding and Gmail's launch. "This isn't just a media revolution, though that's where we are seeing the impact first. This is a chain-reaction of revolutions. It has just begun."[5] Joe Trippi, who managed Howard Dean's populist presidential run in 2004, declared the net "the most democratizing innovation we've ever seen—more so than even the printing press."[6] The New York University journalism professor Jay Rosen, writing in the online *Huffington Post*, heralded "a shift in power that goes with the platform shift." The masses—he called them "the people formerly known as the audience"—were storming the media gates and seizing "the means to speak."[7] The rhetoric may have been Marxian, but the thrust was Meadian.

The Goldilocks Net

The fullest, most intellectually rigorous recital of the democratization narrative came via the law professor Yochai Benkler in his 2006 opus, *The Wealth of Networks*.[8] Benkler acknowledged the debt he owed to Stevens, writing that the justice's opinion in *Reno v. ACLU* laid out the "basic case for the democratizing effect of the Internet." But, with eight more years of experience to draw on, he pushed the case much further. Across five hundred pages of dense, suitably technocratic prose, he argued that "the Internet revolution" was well on its way to supplanting mass media's centralized "industrial information economy" with a radically decentralized "networked public sphere." Spurring the epochal transformation were two developments, one technical, the other economic:

> The first element is the shift from a hub-and-spoke architecture with unidirectional links to the end points in the mass media, to distributed architecture with multidirectional connections among all nodes in the networked information environment. The second is the practical elimination of communications costs as a barrier to speaking across associational boundaries. Together, these characteristics have fundamentally altered the capacity of individuals, acting alone or with others, to be active participants in the public sphere.

Like Mead and her colleagues on the Committee for National Morale, Benkler assumed that changes in media structure come to be mirrored in the attitudes of citizens and, in turn, in a society's politics and culture. A freer, more democratic mechanism of communication means a freer, more democratic polity. When people adapt to the "culture of participation" created by the net, their "self-perception" changes, Benkler wrote. They become more democratic beings. "The easy possibility of communicating effectively into the public sphere allows individuals to reorient themselves from passive readers and listeners to potential speakers and participants in a conversation." Their thoughts and opinions about the "daily events" in their lives no longer have to remain "merely private observations" but rather become "potential subjects for public communication." Private lives become public concerns, content for broadcasting. "The [political] agenda," he summed up, "can be rooted in the life and experience of individual participants in society—in their observations, experiences, and obsessions." It's through this merging of the personal and the political, the private and the public, that "the Internet democratizes."

Not everyone bought the story. At the turn of the millennium, a few doubters began to suggest that unfettered speech could breed factionalism and fanaticism. Even as it brings more voices into political debates and deliberations, the democratization of media might erode rather than extend the foundations of political liberty. In his 2001 book, *Republic.com*, the legal scholar Cass Sunstein warned that the net, by freely spreading information from innumerable sources while at the same time dismantling controls on information quality, could pollute the public square with lies and misinformation and divide the body politic into bitterly opposed camps. Guided by the well-known confirmation bias in human psychology, people would give more weight to information that, whether factual or not, supported their preconceived views while discounting contrary information. "A fragmented communications market creates considerable dangers," he wrote. For individuals, "constant exposure to one set of views is likely to lead to errors and confusions. . . . And to the extent that the process entrenches existing views, spreads falsehood, promotes extremism, and makes people less able to work cooperatively on shared problems, there are dangers for society as a whole."[9] Whatever the shortcomings of the institutional structure of mass media in the twentieth century, it at least served as a check on a kind of craziness.

Benkler acknowledged such fears, citing Sunstein's work in particular. He yoked them together under the label "the Babel objection," which he defined as "the concern that information overload will lead to fragmentation of discourse, polarization, and the loss of political community." He then proceeded—"at the risk of appearing a chimera of Goldilocks and Pangloss"—to dismiss them. Drawing on early studies of hyperlinking patterns and traffic flows among blogs and other informational websites, he argued that a new, grassroots process of content review, accreditation, and filtering had emerged online. Through "peer review by information affinity groups," clusters of web users who share an interest in and knowledge of a particular topic, the process weeds out falsehoods and fluff. The affinity groups—he offered as an example Slashdot, a technology news aggregator that ranked stories on the basis of readers' votes—"filter the observations and opinions of an enormous range of people, and transmit those that pass local peer review to broader groups and ultimately to the polity more broadly, without recourse to market-based points of control over the information flow." Content is vetted from the bottom up, winnowed through layers of informal, decentralized quality control. Only the best stuff reaches the masses.

On the internet, in Benkler's estimation, the marketplace of ideas at last operates as a true market. Rather than being consolidated in the hands of big media companies, responsibility for content selection and quality control spreads throughout the network. The editorial function itself becomes democratized. This organic yet "ordered" system of "cooperative filtering," he claimed, provides for a freer and more participative civic arena than did the old mass-media system and yet also "avoids the generation of a din." The control it imposes is neither too tight (which would curtail expression) nor too loose (which would produce cacophony); like the temperature of Goldilocks's porridge, it strikes a perfect, toothsome balance. Countering tendencies toward factionalism and extremism, the network allows the citizenry to join in knowledgeable, constructive, and civil discussions of contentious issues. "It turns out that we are not intellectual lemmings," Benkler wrote. "We do not use the freedom that the network has made possible to plunge us into the abyss of incoherent babble."

Benkler's argument was thoughtful, logical, and wrong. Like Stevens before him, he allowed his faith in the democratization narrative to skew his perspective. The evidence he found of people using voting, linking, and commenting systems to make informed judgments about online content was real but misleading. The peer-review tools that worked on news aggregator sites such as Slashdot and in certain quarters of the then-vibrant blogosphere turned out to be peripheral to the development of the so-called networked public sphere. They were of great interest to the net's geeky pioneers and their fellow travelers in media and academia but of little interest to ordinary people. They ended up being of minor consequence to the broader flows of information and influence online. There would be a whole lot of group sharing and filtering on social media, both cooperative and combative, but it would play out in a far more anarchic and divisive way than the democratization crusaders assumed.

It's telling that Benkler barely mentioned social media platforms in his book. The pioneering (and failing) social network Friendster got a brief, dismissive nod, but that was about it. Yet by 2006, MySpace and YouTube were among the ten most visited websites in the world, Facebook's explosive growth was well under way, and a newly launched platform named Twitter was gaining notice and traffic. Like most observers at the time, Benkler didn't foresee how these popular new sites would come to position themselves as central, corporate-controlled clearinghouses of news, messages, and other content. Indeed, he assumed the net would continue to resist such corporate control. "By creating sources of information and communication facilities that no one owns or exclusively controls," he concluded, "the networked information economy removes some of the most basic opportunities for manipulation of those who depend on information and communication by the owners of the basic means of communications."[10] In ignoring or downplaying trends that didn't fit the favored narrative, he seems to have been a victim of confirmation bias himself.

The point here is not to pillory the professor, whose work remains essential to understanding the history of the net. It's to show the danger of assuming that the way a complex technological system works early in its development will be the way it works as it matures. And it's to show the enduring and distorting power of the public's optimistic view of communication technology, which, in the case of the net, informed the mistaken belief that a more open and efficient media would necessarily expand and strengthen democracy. These misperceptions had consequences. They prevented society from undertaking a careful, clear-eyed assessment of the risks presented by the net and, subsequently, social media, and they removed from public discussion legal and regulatory options that might have tempered some of the technology's ill effects. Stevens's hands-off-the-net decree continued to hold sway.

Just a few months after *The Wealth of Networks* was published, Facebook unveiled the News Feed. The four forces were now fully unleashed. Content assessment, filtering, and distribution would be done by privately controlled, centrally run software algorithms. The democratization story would go on being told, if with ever more caveats and qualifications, but it was now clear that the internet's evolution as a communication medium was heading down a very different path.

The Skeptic

A few days after Franz Ferdinand was shot in Sarajevo, as European diplomacy collapsed into a welter of contentious telegraph and telephone messages, the young American journalist Walter Lippmann, fresh out of Harvard, brimming with radical ideas, and working on the launch of a progressive political magazine to be called the *New Republic*, boarded a ship for a summer holiday in Europe. After a month's stay in England, where he attended a bucolic Lake District symposium on socialism organized by George Bernard Shaw, he crossed the Channel to Brussels and, as he later recalled, "bought a ticket for a journey through Germany to Switzerland, where I meant to spend my vacation walking over mountain passes." He remained "totally unconscious" of the political tensions rising around him, even as the shooting began. "I remember being astonished and rather annoyed when I went to the railroad station and found that the German border was closed."[11]

Lippmann made it back to the United States safely, and that fall the *New Republic* started publishing on schedule, to wide acclaim. The magazine took a neutral, isolationist stance toward the war, in line with prevailing liberal views. Lippmann, though, was shaken, both by the conflict and by his obliviousness to its imminence. He found himself questioning his understanding of the world; the picture of it that he held in his mind, he realized, did not match what was actually there. He was overcome, he wrote, by a "nausea of ideas."[12] As reports of the European carnage grew more dire, his antipathy toward foreign entanglements dissolved, along with his pacifism. After German submarines began sinking civilian ships, including the crowded British ocean liner *Lusitania*, he became convinced that America had to side with England and France. In the spring of 1917, just weeks after President Woodrow Wilson gave in to political pressure and declared war on Germany, Lippmann announced, to the shock of his colleagues, that he was leaving the magazine to become an assistant to Wilson's secretary of war, Newton Baker.

A year later, having been given the rank of captain in the U.S. Army, he sailed back to Europe as a military intelligence agent, with orders to bolster the Allied propaganda campaign. In London, he participated in meetings where plans for the manipulation of public opinion were hashed out. Then, from an office near the western front in France, he used his literary skills to write leaflets urging German soldiers to desert, with promises of compassionate treatment and ample American-style meals of "beef, white bread, potatoes, prunes, coffee, milk, [and] butter."[13] Dropped onto the battlefield by the hundreds of thousands from balloons and planes, the leaflets were considered a great success. Surrendering German troops were often found to be carrying them when they were taken to prison camps.

When Lippmann returned home after the war, his "old optimism was gone," reports his biographer Ronald Steel.[14] His participation in the overseas propaganda effort, combined with his own early misperceptions about the war, left him with deep doubts about the human mind's objectivity and stability. His unease was magnified by the success of the Wilson administration's domestic propaganda campaign. Led by an ambitious Denver journalist and sometime politician named George Creel, the government's Committee on Public Information brought together writers, artists, filmmakers, and celebrities, along with some seventy-five thousand local volunteers, in a well-funded effort to promote national pride, demonize the enemy, and squelch dissenting views. The goal, as Creel put it in his memoir, *How We Advertised America*, was to use all the tools of media—"the printed word, the spoken word, the motion picture, the telegraph, the cable, the wireless, the poster, the sign-board"—to "weld the people of the United States into one white-hot mass instinct."[15] It succeeded. Turning propaganda into a form of entertainment, the campaign didn't just unify the country. It stoked jingoistic passions and prejudices.[16] Mobs tarred and feathered opponents of the war and beat up German immigrants.

In 1919, Lippmann wrote a despairing essay in the *Atlantic Monthly* titled "The Basic Problem of Democracy." Democracy's founding ideal—that of a well-informed citizenry capable of making reasoned judgments about national problems and plans—had come into being in a much simpler time, he argued, when most concerns were local and people had direct experience of them. The assumptions of America's founders, a small, insular, largely agrarian elite, held little relevance to the bustling modern world, with its urban and industrial energies and lightning-quick communications. Society was much more complex now, and people's sense of it came not from their own firsthand observations but through information received "at second, third, or fourth hand." The public's understanding of social and political issues was fated to be incomplete, distorted, and easily manipulated. "The world about which each man is supposed to have opinions has become so complicated as to defy his powers of understanding," Lippmann wrote. "News comes at a distance; it comes helter-skelter, in inconceivable confusion; it deals with matters that are not easily understood; it arrives and is assimilated by busy and tired people." The democratic citizen "must seize catchwords and headlines or nothing."[17]

He expanded his argument in the 1922 book *Public Opinion*, a seminal treatise on social psychology that the communication scholar James Carey would later call "the founding book in American media studies."[18] Before Lippmann's work, democratic theory assumed that freedom, information, and the public good were tied together in a mutually reinforcing system. Carey summed up the logic: "if people are free, they will have perfect information; if [they have] perfect information, they can be rational in choosing the most effective means to their individual ends, and if so, in a manner never quite explained, the social good will result."[19] It was a nice theory, Lippmann wrote in *Public Opinion*, but a fantasy. It ignored the complexity of the world, and it ignored the perversity of human psychology.

The environment in which we live—the "real environment"—is "altogether too big, too complex, and too fleeting for direct acquaintance," Lippmann argued. "To act in that environment, we have to reconstruct it on a simpler model." Drawing on whatever information is available to us and filtering it through our own desires and biases, each of us creates a mental "pseudo-environment"—a simplified and necessarily fictionalized picture of reality—and then we fit our thoughts and actions to the mirage's contours. Depending on the individual and his or her education and personality, the pseudo-environment can take the form of anything from a "complete hallucination" to a scientific "schematic model," but it is never a true and full picture of reality. This is the reason, Lippmann suggested, that the beliefs and behavior of others often seem so mysterious to us. People all "live in the same world, but they think and feel in different ones." It is also why we're so susceptible to attempts to modify our sense of reality by manipulating the information we receive. "What is propaganda, if not the effort to alter the picture to which men respond, to substitute one social pattern for another?"[20]

We construct our pseudo-environment out of what Lippmann termed stereotypes. When confronted by "the great blooming, buzzing confusion of the outer world," we have to rely on rules of thumb, intuitive judgments, and other mental shortcuts—heuristics, as cognitive psychologists call them—to make sense of things. We comprehend through intuition rather than analysis, quickly fitting new phenomena into familiar patterns. We see the world in "stereotyped shapes" derived from "our moral codes and our social philosophies and our political agitations" as well as the cultural symbols supplied by art, literature, and entertainment.

The more distracted we are, the more rapid and shallow our processing of information becomes—and the more we depend on stereotypes. Even in those rare moments when we're granted the luxury of deep thought, our focus is necessarily narrow. We can't think deeply about everything. So even the most thoughtful among us rely mainly on stereotypes in constructing a picture of the world. "There is economy in this," Lippmann noted, anticipating the discoveries psychologists would make about System 1 thinking and its reliance on shortcuts. "For the attempt to see things freshly and in detail, rather than as types and generalities, is exhausting, and among busy affairs practically out of the question." As we grow older, and more set in our opinions and routines, the stereotypes become all the more powerful as filters of reality. "We imagine most things before we experience them," and our preconceptions "govern deeply the whole process of perception."[21]

An Unattainable Ideal

Lippmann had his own pseudo-environment, of course, his own set of stereotypes. He was guilty at times of overreaching. He underestimated the public's ability, even with imperfect information and mismatched views of reality, to muddle through. And the solution he offered at the end of his book—a bureaucracy of experts that would guide governmental decision-making while remaining unsullied by politics—seems like its own kind of pipe dream. But *Public Opinion* is a brave and psychologically astute work. With a cold yet sympathetic eye, Lippmann looks beyond the ideal citizen of democratic theory—"sovereign and omnicompetent," in his memorable phrase—to bring into focus the real person: time-strapped and distracted, biased, susceptible to resentment and sentimentality, bombarded with messages and images, over-stretched, wavering between confusion and overconfidence.

Lippmann would come to be attacked and dismissed as an anti-democratic elitist, but in painting his portrait of the average citizen, he was also, as he made clear in his next book, 1925's *The Phantom Public*, offering a self-portrait:

> My sympathies are with him, for I believe that he has been saddled with an impossible task and that he is asked to practice an unattainable ideal. I find it so myself for, although public business is my main interest and I give most of my time to watching it, I cannot find time to do what is expected of me in the theory of democracy; that is, to know what is going on and to have an opinion worth expressing on every question which confronts a self-governing community. And I have not happened to meet anybody, from a President of the United States to a professor of political science, who came anywhere near to embodying the accepted ideal of the sovereign and omnicompetent citizen.[22]

Lippmann was not arguing that the public is stupid or incompetent. One of his central points, as the historian of journalism

Michael Schudson emphasizes, "is that a capacity for democratic self-government has nothing to do with native gray matter, but with the insufficiencies all of us share, a limited ability to attend to matters beyond our everyday experience." Lippmann remained committed to liberty and democracy, even as he lost faith, Schudson writes, in "utopian aspirations for the role of the public as a participant in democratic decision making on a daily basis."[23] The ideal of the fully informed citizen isn't "an undesirable ideal," Lippmann wrote. It is "an unattainable ideal, bad only in the sense that it is bad for a fat man to try to be a ballet dancer."[24]

Lippmann's work anticipates the critique of the rational decision-maker—the theoretical *Homo economicus* of classical economics—that would be launched by social and cognitive psychologists later in the century. In a series of articles in the 1950s, the political scientist and future Nobel laureate Herbert Simon argued that the model individual of theory—the man who has "knowledge of the relevant aspects of his environment which, if not absolutely complete, is at least impressively clear and voluminous"—was in need of an overhaul. Because human rationality is always constrained, or bounded, by limitations of "knowledge, foresight, skill, and time," people have to construct mental "simplifications of the real world for purposes of choice."[25] Acknowledging Lippmann's work as an antecedent to his own, Simon emphasized that people's "bounded rationality" shapes and distorts their political choices as much as their economic ones.[26]

Simon drew mainly on common sense in making his argument. In the 1950s, little empirical research existed on how people form opinions and make decisions. But that lack was soon remedied. Cognitive psychologists and social scientists, including Daniel Kahneman and his longtime collaborator, Amos Tversky, would over the ensuing decades conduct myriad experiments and studies revealing how human perception and thought are skewed by all sorts of cognitive biases and misperceptions. It isn't just that rationality is bounded in the everyday making of judgments and decisions; rationality is often absent altogether. Our intuition is always telling us stories about the world, and even when they diverge sharply from reality we're eager to believe them. The assumption of an efficient marketplace of ideas rests on the ideal of a rational consumer of ideas, a *Homo philosophicus* who, like his cousin *economicus*, turns out to be a fictional character.

A related line of research into how people form political opinions and cast votes has reached similar conclusions. Looking back on more than a half century of opinion surveys and voter research in their 2016 book, *Democracy for Realists*, the political scientists Christopher Achen and Larry Bartels report that the "folk theory" of democracy, which "celebrates the wisdom of popular judgments by informed and engaged citizens," has long been contradicted by the facts. "The political 'belief systems' of ordinary citizens are generally thin, disorganized, and ideologically incoherent." Giving another nod to Lippmann, they conclude that "conventional democratic ideas amount to fairy tales."[27]

As for the rather small set of voters who spend a lot of time reading, thinking, and talking about politics, the research reveals that their heightened engagement rarely broadens their minds. They're actually the ones most inclined to narrow and fervent partisanship. The more news they gobble up, the more convinced they are that they're right and anyone with a different view is wrong. As Zac Gershberg and Sean Illing report in their 2022 study, *The Paradox of Democracy*, "the most knowledgeable voters, the ones who pay the most attention to politics, are also the ones most prone to biased or blinkered decision-making."[28] A similar effect is seen with educational achievement. The more educated people are, the more distorted is their understanding of the views of their political opponents. That seems to be particularly true of Democrats, according to an extensive 2019 study of American political polarization. The apparent reason is that well-educated Democrats go to great lengths to avoid fraternizing with Republicans. "As Democrats become more educated, their friend groups become less politically diverse," the authors of the study write. They restrict their social set to versions of themselves. In sum, "the most highly engaged, active and educated people are least accurate in their views" of those they disagree with.[29]

Well before the net came along, the psychological and psephological evidence was telling us that flooding the public square with more information from more sources was not going to open people's minds or engender more thoughtful discussions. It wasn't even going to make people better informed. Despite the revolutionary expansion in the public's access to information of all sorts, contemporary surveys clearly show that, as the political scientist Donald Kinder puts it, "Americans are no better informed on public affairs than they were a generation or two ago."[30] So what exactly was media democratization going to accomplish, in terms of the country's political life? We now know the answer: it was going to widen the gap between the pseudo-environments in which people think and the real environment in which they act. This helps explain, among many other things, how a bare-chested man with a horned fur hat, a painted face, and a spear came to be bellowing on the floor of the U.S. Senate on the afternoon of January 6, 2021.

Repeaters

Every group of people is also, as Charles Cooley pointed out, a social medium, a flesh-and-blood network for the transmission of influence. Because human beings are copycats by nature—"to be human is to imitate," writes the British psychologist Susan Blackmore[31]—information tends to flow through groups in what researchers call a snowball process, or a cascade. One person makes a claim about a subject. Another person, lacking personal knowledge of the subject, accepts the claim as true and repeats it. Then another person repeats it—then another, and another, and another. The more people in the group who subscribe to the claim, the more compelling it becomes to everyone else in the group. Even skeptics get carried along. The claim becomes a belief, and the belief becomes a marker of group identity; holding it becomes a social norm. As informational cascades continue to pour through the group, its members converge on a homogeneous set of beliefs, regardless of whether the beliefs are true, half true, or not true at all. Groups come to share the same pseudo-environment.[32]

In Cooley's day, informational cascades were more like trickles. Information moved slowly. Sharing it took time and effort. There were no like buttons on books or articles, no forward or reply-all commands for the mail. You couldn't retweet a handwritten note. Today, with the frictionless sharing of computerized media, cascades can begin anywhere, and they can crisscross a country or the entire globe in a matter of hours, if not minutes. As Sunstein presciently wrote in *Republic.com*, cascades "become more likely when information, including false information, can be spread to hundreds, thousands, or even millions by the simple press of a button." And because social media encourages and facilitates group formation, making it easy for people to discover like-minded others and band together to exchange information, cascades within groups (what Sunstein calls "local cascades") become more common and more polarizing. When group members find and circulate new bits of information that confirm a shared belief, the belief gets fortified and, following the well-documented dynamics of group polarization, becomes steadily more extreme. "In a balkanized speech market," Sunstein observed, "local cascades lead people in dramatically different directions." Groups stop "listening to one another."[33] Such factionalism, and the intolerance it breeds, further stunts online discussions by fueling the moralistic vigilantism known as cancel culture. There is only one correct view—*our* view—and anyone who says otherwise needs to be silenced.

If, following Cooley, you think of a group as a mechanism of communication—a machine made of people—then an informational cascade can be understood as a means of amplifying a signal through repetition. The most-shared messages become the loudest messages. Communication networks have always employed electronic repeaters to strengthen the power and reach of a signal. Analog telephone networks used arrays of transistors to boost the strength of a signal's current in the line. Over-the-air radio networks used relay repeaters to amplify signals by rebroadcasting them. Today, fiber-optic data networks use phototransmitters to intensify the pulses of light that carry digital signals. In a social medium, human beings become the repeaters. They boost. They rebroadcast. They amplify. It's a job that we humans, with our exquisite sensitivity to social signals, are extraordinarily well suited to.

Claude Shannon had assumed that the goal of the network engineer was to remove redundancy from communication without sacrificing its comprehensibility. The assumption reflected the capacity constraints that had always characterized communication networks. You had to prune what was communicated in order to squeeze everything through a narrow pipe. Remove the capacity constraints, and an inversion takes place. The goal is no longer to reduce redundancy but to increase it—to send the same signal over and over again in order to increase its influential power. While attentional and temporal constraints push people to condense the messages they send online, the lack of constraints on network capacity encourages them to share messages promiscuously. When a message gets repeated in a social medium, it not only gets stronger as an informational signal, able to reach more people more quickly; it gets more meaningful to those who receive it. It assumes more importance, gains more salience in the mind. It comes to feel more true, even if it's false.

The more frequently people are exposed to a message—an observation, an opinion, a lie—the more likely they are to accept its validity. Repetition is, in the human mind, a proxy for facticity. This psychological phenomenon, first described in a 1977 journal article and confirmed in myriad studies since, is known as the illusory truth effect.[34] As a group of brain scientists explained in a 2023 article in the journal *Cognition*, "A vast literature suggests that repeated statements are perceived as more accurate, even when [the] statements are from non-credible sources." Hearing a false statement once makes you considerably more likely to believe it the next time you hear it, even if you were originally dubious about it. Hearing it a third time makes it even more believable. And as soon as you sense it's true, you're more likely to repeat the statement to others, expanding the effect. As the *Cognition* authors, who verified the phenomenon in an online setting through two experiments of their own, concluded, "repeated exposure to misinformation" is likely to "create a vicious circle in which misinformation will be perceived as true and therefore shared more."[35] Familiarity may breed contempt when it comes to judging people, but when it comes to judging information, it breeds gullibility.

If social media has an intellectual creed, it is a creed of repetition—the creed of the mob, the huckster, and the tyrant. "Endless repetition," Victor Klemperer observed of the Nazis as they took power in 1933, "appears to be one of the stylistic features of their language."[36] The unending competition to produce messages that will get repeated, that will propagate through the network, is a battle for meaning as well as influence. In the absence of editorial controls on quality—of either the centralized variety of old or the decentralized variety imagined by Benkler—the information about the world that spreads through online cascades skews toward the biased, the exaggerated, and the fake. Real facts tend to be mundane and drab. Leaving the emotions uncharged, they stream by without making much of an impression on the nervous system. Falsehoods are constructed to be novel and surprising, exciting and infuriating. They grab attention. They get shared. When human beings serve as the repeaters in a communication network—when they take on a signal-amplification role while still acting in their traditional roles as creators and interpreters of messages—Shannon's distinction between mechanism and meaning gets shakier still. Meaning becomes a network effect. What's true is what comes out of the machine most often.

When Twitter was founded in early 2006, it didn't have a retweet button. Early users would regularly repost others' tweets, but they had to do the sharing manually. They'd cut-and-paste the text of another user's post into a new tweet of their own, type the initials RT at the front of it, along with the original poster's Twitter handle, then hit Tweet. It took a minute or two, which, in the bustle of social media, came to seem a burden. In 2009, Twitter's founders, belatedly realizing that retweeting had become a popular activity on the platform, hired a former Google programmer named Chris Wetherell to automate the process, and the retweet button soon made its debut. It was a hit. With retweeting now easier and quicker, the volume of retweets soared.

Wetherell did what coders always do. He used software to make a commonplace but cumbersome process more efficient. John Vittal had accomplished something very similar years earlier when he created email's forward and reply functions. A series of steps became a single command—an effortless click, in the case of the retweet button. When his creation went live, Wetherell felt a sense of pride, he recalled in a later interview with *BuzzFeed*. Not only was he relieving people of a small nuisance; he was doing his part to democratize media. Making it easier for people to share tweets would, he assumed, bring more voices into the conversation. The unheard would get heard. "We put power in the hands of the people," is what he told himself at the time.[37]

He was right, but the way people wielded that power was different from what he expected. As is often the case with automation, the new software feature not only sped up a routine activity; it changed people's behavior, even their attitudes. The time and effort required to share a tweet manually, though seemingly so small as to be inconsequential, turned out to be vitally important. It slowed people down. It gave them a moment to reconsider the message they were about to repeat, now under their own name. Once that little bit of friction was removed, people acted and reacted more impulsively. Twitter became more frenzied, more partisan, and much nastier. "The whole system started to go haywire," wrote the prominent technology journalist Alexis Madrigal.[38]

While the retweet button was used benignly in many cases, and did sometimes direct attention to worthy ideas that might otherwise have gone unseen, it also became a bludgeon. It was used to spread lies, to coordinate personal attacks on individuals, and to demonize political opponents. It proved an ideal means for rallying partisan or vindictive mobs. The notorious Gamergate scandal, in which bizarre conspiracy theories led to a vicious campaign of harassment against female programmers and gamers, was fueled largely by retweets.[39] Dismayed by what his innovation had wrought, Wetherell changed his view about democratization. "We might have just handed a four-year-old a loaded weapon," he now worried.[40]

But the retweet button proved good for business. As Facebook had found with the outraged reaction to its News Feed, the controversy and anger provoked by barrages of retweets galvanized Twitter's audience. People may have now felt soiled after their Twitter sessions, but they enjoyed the mud wrestling. Engagement went up; stream-checking became a compulsion. Journalists and politicians rushed into the fray, opening Twitter accounts with dreams of having their own remarks sweep the network. And as with Facebook's like button, the retweet button generated valuable data for Twitter. It provided a moment-by-moment readout on topics and posts that provoked and captivated readers. Fed back into the company's filtering algorithm, the data further stoked engagement. The retweet button also proved a boon to advertisers, who could now compose their promotional messages in ways likely to generate bursts of free publicity. Not long after Twitter introduced the retweet button, Facebook rolled out an automated sharing button of its own.

By 2010, with news feeds and sharing buttons in place, with filtering algorithms dispensing personalized content, with users shifting from websites to mobile apps, social media had matured, as a mechanism of communication and as a business. The major platforms now looked to their users—the general public—to play three roles. On the supply end of the network, they worked as content producers, churning out endless streams of posts and comments that provided the platforms with enormous quantities of engaging content for free. In the middle of the network, within the mechanism, they played the role of repeaters, boosting traffic by amplifying the most compelling messages and in the process divulging valuable data about themselves. Finally, on the network's demand end, they played the more traditional role of audience members, though now the content they received was tightly geared to their individual tastes and biases. The users didn't need to be pulled into these roles against their will. They took to them naturally.

Us and Them

The software routines and sharing tools that govern the circulation of information through social media are great for promoting attention-grabbing, emotion-stoking content. As quality-control mechanisms, they're terrible. In a study published in 2018 in *Science*, three MIT researchers examined how news stories circulated on Twitter. They tracked more than 125,000 stories that were shared through more than 4.5 million retweets over an eleven-year period, from 2006 through 2017. They discovered that false or otherwise misleading stories were 70 percent more likely to be retweeted than factual ones. While accurate stories rarely reached more than a thousand people, fake reports often reached tens of thousands. "Falsehood diffused significantly farther, faster, deeper, and more broadly than the truth in all categories of information," the researchers wrote, and the effect was most pronounced with political news. The reason fake stories get retweeted more than true ones, they suggested, is that the fakes are more surprising: "Novelty attracts human attention." The spread of misinformation, the authors went on to emphasize, is not spurred by software bots, as many would like to believe, but by people. The fake spreads faster than the true "because humans, not robots, are more likely to spread it."[41]

In the local cascades that flow through political groups, the messages that tend to get repeated are antagonistic ones about the views of other groups. In research published in 2021, a team of U.K. and U.S. cognitive psychologists examined the spread on Twitter and

Facebook of nearly three million posts originating from a variety of left-wing and right-wing sources. They found that people on one side of the political spectrum loved to share posts denigrating the beliefs of those on the other side. "Posts about the political out-group were shared or retweeted about twice as often as posts about the in-group," the researchers reported, and each word or term in a post referring to the out-group "increased the odds of a social media post being shared by 67%."[42] Posts about the views of adversaries stirred reactions of anger and outrage—the kind of strong emotions that have been shown to rouse attention and provoke sharing—and as the posts circulated they tended to collect mocking and sarcastic comments, further increasing their appeal as political fodder.

Social media companies are well aware of how their platforms amplify this kind of clannish hostility. In a 2018 presentation to Facebook's top management, an internal research team investigating how the platform exacerbates political polarization reported that "our algorithms exploit the human brain's attraction to divisiveness," according to an exposé in the *Wall Street Journal*. "Divisive content," the writers of the presentation went on to say, gets promoted in Facebook feeds because the filtering algorithms calculate it will strengthen user engagement and "increase time on the platform."[43] Facebook's public policy chief, Joel Kaplan, told the *Journal* that the company accepted some of the team's recommendations for curbing divisive content but rejected others that risked disrupting the platform's operations.

The alacrity with which online groups share stories about the views of adversaries adds an uncomfortable wrinkle to our understanding of the sources of political polarization. Polarization is not, as is widely believed, a simple effect of algorithmically generated echo chambers or filter bubbles. While politically engaged people do become more extreme in their views as they amass more evidence backing those views, they also welcome, and rapidly share, stories about opposing positions held by rival groups. Rather than pushing the partisans to question their beliefs, however, the stories just make them more certain they're right. Different points of view are seen not as opportunities to learn but as provocations to attack. Once a group has established its position, all information, con as well as pro, tends to reinforce it. You don't need an echo chamber to be an extremist; you just need a lot of information and your own skewed perceptions.

That fact was underscored by a 2018 study conducted by Chris Bail, a sociologist who heads Duke University's Polarization Lab. Bail and his lab mates recruited some twelve hundred American Twitter users who identified themselves as either Democrats or Republicans. Using custom-made software bots, the researchers tweaked the subjects' feeds over the course of a month to expose them to views from the other side of the political spectrum. Democrats were regularly fed tweets from prominent conservatives; Republicans received tweets from prominent liberals. The more balanced feeds did not moderate the subjects' political views. If anything, they had the opposite effect. By the end of the experiment, Republicans had become significantly more conservative in their views; Democrats, slightly more liberal. And the more attention that people paid to tweets offering opposing views, the researchers found, the stronger was their ideological shift in the direction of their existing bias.

The researchers conducted a second round of experiments to examine why a more balanced information diet stimulates greater partisanship. Recruiting new sets of Democrats and Republicans, they again deployed their bots to tweak Twitter feeds, but this time they also held extensive interviews with the subjects. They found that exposure to an opposing view triggers a sort of immune response within a group. Members band together even more tightly to defend their position against what they perceive as an invasive idea. People "experience stepping outside their echo chamber as an attack upon their identity," Bail reports. That makes "differences between 'us' and 'them' seem even bigger."[44] Groups are just as prone to dissimilarity cascades as individuals are.

Though the findings go against the common wisdom about the

benefits of exposing people to diverse points of view, they're consistent with most other studies of voters. In forming opinions and casting votes, people are motivated much less by political ideology than by group identity.[45] Opinions emerge from affiliation, not vice versa. People may like to believe that their political views reflect a careful, reasoned analysis of the issues, but usually they're by-products of tribal allegiance. They're rooted in emotion, not reason. A group identity provides a quick, intuitive way to make sense of a world that resists intellectual explication.

Among U.S. voters, group affiliation long centered on the Democratic and Republican parties. Many political activists and theorists viewed the rigid two-party system as an obstacle to a healthy polity. The dominance of the parties, combined with the hegemony of mass media, limited the scope of political discourse. Serving as an arm of the establishment, media companies prevented views that lay outside the narrow mainstream from ever reaching voters. Social media was welcomed as a force for overthrowing the gatekeepers and opening politics up to alternative and more radical voices and perspectives. The hope has, again, been frustrated by the vagaries of human psychology. The torrent of unstructured information has spurred a proliferation, most of it within the existing party structure, of extremist or single-issue identity groups, each intent on defending its territory. At the same time, the design of the platforms makes it easy for individual candidates, particularly if they happen to be celebrities with existing fan bases, to establish seemingly intimate relationships with members of the public. "When print and TV were dominant," explains Princeton political scientist Jan-Werner Müller, "propaganda feedback loops would have been constructed at great costs by party strategists; today, they are created for free by companies that want to maximize engagement for the sake of profit."[46] The platform becomes the party machine.

Far from promoting pluralism, the democratization of media has paradoxically created an information environment conducive to authoritarian movements and cults of personality. A strong populist leader becomes a totem of group identity, a human meme whose image and words can be shared through social media. Stanford's Fred Turner argues that the political success of Donald Trump and other demagogues around the world reveals that

> the faith of a generation of 20th-century liberal theorists—as well as their digital descendants—was misplaced: [media] decentralization does not necessarily increase democracy in the public sphere or in the state. On the contrary, the technologies of decentralized communication can be coupled very tightly to the charismatic, personality-centered modes of authoritarianism long associated with mass media and mass society. They can in fact be made *cornerstones* of such power.[47]

In diagnosing today's fractious political climate, we've been too quick to blame social media platforms for our own shortcomings. "The platforms play a role," Chris Bail says, "but we are greatly exaggerating what it's possible for them to do—how much they could change things no matter who's at the helm of these companies—and we're profoundly underestimating the human element, the motivation of users."[48] The polarization and extremism we see online aren't manufactured out of nothing by algorithms. They're expressions of deep-seated tendencies in human nature that have always shaped and strained social relations and political debates. "The latent causes of faction are thus sown in the nature of man," wrote James Madison in the Federalist Papers. "A zeal for different opinions concerning religion, concerning government, and many other points [has] divided mankind into parties, inflamed them with mutual animosity, and rendered them much more disposed to vex and oppress each other than to co-operate for the common good."[49] What's different now is that we have crowded ourselves into a virtual public square that lacks checks on our zeal and vexatiousness.

Paradise Lost

"The internet is broken," Evan Williams, a founder of Twitter, told the *New York Times* in the spring of 2017. "I thought once everybody could speak freely and exchange information and ideas, the world is automatically going to become a better place [*sic*]. I was wrong about that." His was one voice in what became, after the upheavals of 2016, a chorus of tech-billionaire remorse. "I think we have created tools that are ripping apart the social fabric," said Chamath Palihapitiya, the Facebook executive who had been in charge of "user growth" after the News Feed launch. Facebook's founding goal, confessed the company's first president, Sean Parker, was "to consume as much of your time and conscious attention as possible." He and his colleagues knew all along that they were "exploiting a vulnerability in human psychology," he went on. "And we did it anyway." Justin Rosenstein, the inventor of the like button, said he feared society was heading "rapidly into dystopia." Even Mark Zuckerberg offered an apology, if a weaselly one. He was sorry, he said, "for the ways my work was used to divide people rather than bring us together."[50]

Whether sincere or feigned, the apologies felt obligatory, a performance of contrition choreographed to fit the demands of a public looking for scapegoats. People didn't stop using social media after 2016—they were on their phones as much as ever—but their view of its effects darkened. By the end of the decade, nearly two-thirds of Americans felt that platforms like Facebook and Twitter were harming the country, according to a Pew Research poll. Only one in ten considered the platforms to be beneficial.[51] Politicians and journalists, once champions of tech entrepreneurs and their populist ethos of disruption, turned on the industry. Congress held highly publicized hearings that felt like show trials, with contrite young techies, suited and tied, submitting to ritual grillings by elderly and often clueless senators. Newspapers and magazines published long investigative reports revealing the corruption at Big Tech's algorithmic core, alongside scathing portraits of tech bro callowness. Silicon Valley, once portrayed as a David fighting the mass-media Goliath, had become Goliath.

The technology industry is a worthy target but also an easy one. In placing the blame for the internet's failings on social media companies, we let the net itself off the hook while also absolving ourselves of complicity. Commercial interests constitute one force that determines how a new medium shapes society. But there are two others at least equally important: technology and human nature. Breaking up internet monopolies, banning certain platforms (like TikTok), or putting warning labels on apps is not going to change the basic characteristics of computer networks and digital content, much less human psychology. By telling ourselves that corporate malfeasance has perverted the net, yanked it off its true course, we open a loophole for self-deception. We give ourselves permission to continue to believe in the democratization fallacy. What's broken can be fixed. What's off course can be put back on track.

We see signs of this attitude in the growing sense of nostalgia about the internet. When Ian Bogost described the "sociopathy" of social media in his 2022 *Atlantic* article, he also expressed a yearning for a time, before the giant platforms took over, when the net was a "truly magical" place, a greenfield of social connection.[52] The early days of the web "were amazing," tweeted then Twitter CEO Jack Dorsey that same year. Centralizing control of the technology "into corporations really damaged the internet."[53] Bogost's *Atlantic* colleague Derek Thompson, in a mournful 2023 essay, also looked backward toward a lost paradise. "In the open expanse of the internet," he wrote, "we could have built any kind of world. We built this one. Why have we done this to ourselves?"[54] Behind the wistfulness lies one of the oldest and most enduring of American myths: that of the frontier. We were given a virgin territory, a space of pure possibility, and by handing it over to greedy ranchers we lost it. We let the open range be bound in spools of corporate barbed wire.

There is no virgin territory, not in the natural world and certainly not in the technological one we have fashioned for ourselves. We adapt to technology's contours as we adapt to the land's and the climate's. Mechanisms of communication, as Cooley understood, don't change our nature, but they do accentuate certain aspects of it while dampening others. A computer network exists to maximize the speed of data transfer and processing, to shorten the delay between input and output. The more we rely on computers to mediate what we say and see and think about, the more we have to adapt our thought, speech, and behavior to their characteristics and requirements. "Repeated exposure to computing alters human sense-making," explains communication scholar Brian Ott. "As humans try to speed up their information-processing and decision-making capabilities, they are less careful and rational and more impulsive and affective, which—paradoxically—undermines the quality of their decision making."[55] When shunted into a computer network, thought and expression become virtual goods optimized for rapid exchange. The internet is not broken. It's operating as it was designed to operate. It's succeeding in making our dream of perfect communication—efficient, unfettered, immersive—a reality, even as it reveals the dream to have been a delusion all along.

John Dewey, the American philosopher and educator who in the early years of the last century was the country's preeminent public intellectual, was deeply impressed by Lippmann's *Public Opinion* when it appeared in 1922—and deeply troubled by it. "To read the book is an experience in illumination," he wrote in a review for the *New Republic*. "One finishes the book almost without realizing that it is perhaps the most effective indictment of democracy as currently conceived ever penned." But Dewey believed that, for all the brilliance of Lippmann's "relentless and realistic analysis," his conclusions were unnecessarily dire. The journalist underestimated the gumption and good sense of the American people. While granting that the challenges facing democracy were as daunting as Lippmann made them out to be, Dewey maintained his faith in the public's ability to meet them. "When necessity drives, invention and accomplishment may amazingly respond."[56]

Four years later, in a series of lectures delivered at Kenyon College, Dewey returned to the question of the public's role in sustaining democracy, considering it in light of the arrival of the new technologies of mass communication. The lectures were refined and collected a year later in the book *The Public and Its Problems,* the fullest expression of Dewey's political philosophy. In a stirring passage near the end of the volume, Dewey offers a counterpoint to Lippmann's pessimism—a vision of a "Great Community" founded on a free and open system of communication that enables "an organized, articulate Public" to come into being.

> The highest and most difficult kind of inquiry and a subtle, delicate, vivid and responsive art of communication must take possession of the physical machinery of transmission and circulation and breathe life into it. When the machine age has thus perfected its machinery it will be a means of life and not its despotic master. Democracy will come into its own, for democracy is a name for a life of free and enriching communion. It had its seer in Walt Whitman. It will have its consummation when free social inquiry is indissolubly wedded to the art of a full and moving communication.[57]

The view of the public—of ourselves—that Lippmann offered at the start of the twentieth century cut against the grain of American optimism and exceptionalism. Dewey's view followed the grain. By the time the century came to a close, Lippmann's assessment had been rejected, dismissed as the sour rumblings of "an arrogant critic."[58] Dewey's was enjoying a new ascendency, infusing the public's sense of and confidence in the internet's democratizing power.

Although it inspires still, much as Whitman's verse does, Dewey's vision of a Great Community, in which the machinery and the art of communication come into perfect, living harmony, has been shattered. We live in its ruins, overwhelmed by the information that was meant to enlighten us, imprisoned by the data that describe us.

Lippmann's words, by contrast, have grown only more resonant. In *Public Opinion*, now a century old, published in the same year as *Ulysses* and *The Waste Land*, two other, equally unsparing testaments to the fragmentation of consciousness, to a world rendered incomprehensible by information, we find a portrait of ourselves and our situation. The way we see the social and political environment, the way we create a picture of reality through the welter of messages furnished by our ever more encompassing media, is and always will be refracted

> by scanty attention, by the poverty of language, by distraction, by unconscious constellations of feeling, by wear and tear, violence, monotony. These limitations upon our access to that environment combine with the obscurity and complexity of the facts themselves to thwart clearness and justice of perception, to substitute misleading fictions for workable ideas, and to deprive us of adequate checks upon those who consciously strive to mislead.[59]

Dewey told us what we want to hear. Lippmann told us what we need to hear.

PART THREE

EVERYTHING IS MEDIATED

The affair appears more serious; all guideposts are gone, in time as well as in space. There is no longer either difference or deferral, no more horizon, no more fixed point anywhere to provide sense or direction.

—RENÉ GIRARD

CHAPTER 7

The Dislocated I

Contagion

The poppies returned on schedule to the slopes of Walker Canyon in early 2020, though a dry winter kept their numbers down. Even if they had bloomed as profusely as they had the year before, few would have been around to bear witness. By the time the first buds opened, a very different sort of superbloom—that of the novel coronavirus, as we called it then—was under way. No one wanted to risk infection by congregating in a field of flowers to take pretty Instagram shots, however many hearts they might rack up. Even the influencers stayed home. Shortly after the World Health Organization declared the outbreak a pandemic on March 10, Walker Canyon was closed to the public. The poppies bloomed in silence, undisturbed, unphotographed.

As the world went quiet, social media buzzed more loudly than ever. All the popular platforms announced big gains in traffic. Visits to Facebook jumped by more than a quarter between the end of January and the end of March. YouTube and TikTok saw similar spikes. On Twitch, Amazon's live-streaming service, people watched 1.7 billion hours of video in May, nearly double what they had watched six months earlier. The boom went beyond the usual posts and pics, podcasts and vlogs. Cut off from physical spaces, everyone crowded into virtual ones. Schools held remote classes; businesses, remote meetings. Museums and galleries hosted virtual exhibits. Yoga studios and gyms offered virtual workouts. Churchgoers congregated on screens. Friends gathered for Zoom cocktails. By 2022, close to half of American adults under the age of fifty reported being online "almost constantly," according to a Pew survey. The same was true of teenagers.[1] With the real world seeming alien and treacherous, it was the virtual one that now felt familiar and safe.

The metaphor of contagion has always shaped the way we think and talk about social media. The top platforms have been designed to encourage the rapid transmission of messages from person to person. The most successful posts and memes are the most infectious ones, the ones that go viral. The word *influencer* shares an etymological root with *influenza*. When, years ago, Mark Zuckerberg needed a code name for Facebook's automated advertising system, he chose Pandemic.[2] But with the arrival of the coronavirus, the contagion metaphor took an unexpected turn. When a real pathogen is on the loose, we discovered, social media turns into an antiviral. It allows people to socialize without physical proximity, to gather together while remaining apart. If there was anything fortunate about Covid's arrival, it was the timing. The disease appeared after social media had already trained us in the art of social distancing. Our phones and laptops proved our most valuable pieces of personal protective equipment.

The pandemic, and the lockdowns it triggered, was less an inflection point than a moment of revelation. It brought into relief how thoroughly we've adapted ourselves to digital media. At the start of the century, we still talked about "going online" the way we talked about going to the movies or going out to eat. It was an experience outside ordinary experience, a special event bounded in time and, because wifi networks were scarce, space. You logged on, then you logged off. Now we're never not online. The climate of social media, which the writer Patricia Lockwood memorably describes as at once "tropical and snowing," a clammy hothouse through which blows "the blizzard of everything,"[3] is the general climate. The digital information flow, incessant and efflorescent, almost pornographic in its blurring of the intimate and the public, has invaded our consciousness and, even more so, subconsciousness. Even when we aren't looking at our phone, recent studies show, the device and its apps maintain a grip on our attention.[4]

Social media is, to use the psychological jargon, a priming mechanism of unprecedented intensity. It keeps us in a permanent state of anticipation, awaiting the next stimulus, craving the next glance at the screen. However banal the revelations that come through our apps, they're always novel and they're often personal. We know that, behind the screen, our social life continues to unfold around the clock, with or without our active participation. People are looking at us and talking to us or about us. We're being sized up—envied, celebrated, shamed, shunned. We exist today in the liminal space between the material and the mediated, present when absent, absent when present.

As anyone who has participated in meetings on Zoom or other conferencing platforms knows, it's pretty much impossible to resist the temptation to look at one's own image inside its allotted cell on the screen. In those uncanny moments when the physical self observes the mediated self in real time, we're most aware of the duality of our being today. Such self-viewing is often assumed to be an act of vanity or even narcissism, but really it's the opposite: an act of critical, clinical self-assessment. Wrote the nineteenth century Scottish poet Robert Burns in "To a Louse":

O wad some Pow'r the giftie gie us
To see oursels as others see us!

Social media is the Pow'r that has at last given us that dubious giftie. What we're doing when we gaze upon our Zoom reflection, observing ourselves speak and listen, act and react, is not admiring our reflection but trying to decipher how our image appears to others. In that gaze, we become both watcher and watched.

Places and Stages

What happens to us when so much of life is lived through communication systems, when the self, reconfigured as a pattern of information, is constantly being encoded and decoded? Charles Cooley offers some guidance here, too. In his major work, *Human Nature and the Social Order*, published in 1902, five years after "The Process of Social Change," he introduced the idea that would make him famous in sociological and psychological circles: that of the looking-glass self. A person's sense of self, he argued, emerges not from the inside out, as thinkers as diverse as Descartes, Emerson, and Nietzsche had supposed, but from the outside in: "As we see our face, figure, and dress in the glass, and are interested in them because they are ours, and pleased or otherwise with them according as they do or do not answer to what we should like them to be; so in imagination we perceive in another's mind some thought of our appearance, manners, aims, deeds, character, friends, and so on, and are variously affected by it."[5]

Our self-image, as Cooley saw it, takes shape through a reading of signals, through feedback loops between our own mind and the minds of everyone we interact with. "That the 'I' of common speech has a meaning which includes some sort of reference to other persons" is revealed, he argued, in "the very fact that the word and the ideas it stands for are phenomena of language and the communicative life."[6] We may speak ourselves into being, but an audience is always involved. Without others, neither language nor communication would have any purpose. Our communal, sympathetic mind reading, Cooley went on to suggest, forms the very essence of human relations: "The imaginations which people have of one another are the *solid facts* of society."[7] With those italics, he acknowledged a paradox: what's solid in society consists largely of images flickering in the mind.

Cooley was not implying that individuals lack inner lives or innate qualities. He was a firm believer in human nature, at both the species and the individual levels. His point was that the self cannot exist except in a social context. Without the presence of others, we have no cause to picture ourselves as distinct beings—or to speak. "The tendency of the self, like every aspect of personality, [can't] be understood or predicted except in connection with the general life." Fundamental to his view is a sense of the self's adaptability and flexibility. We tailor our words and actions, our behavioral self-portrait, to whomever we sense to be observing us at any given moment. Nature may give us an underlying score, but like jazz musicians we improvise the music together, in response to one another's often tacit signals. "We always imagine, and in imagining share, the judgments of the other mind," Cooley wrote. "A man will boast to one person of an action— say some sharp transaction in trade—which he would be ashamed to own to another." The "content of the self"—again, Cooley's wording is prescient—varies "indefinitely with particular temperaments and environments."[8] The "I" is contextual; it changes as situations change.

Cooley was not the first to posit a protean self. His elder contemporary William James had made a similar point just a few years earlier in *Principles of Psychology*, a book Cooley knew well and admired deeply:

> Properly speaking, *a man has as many social selves as there are individuals who recognize him* and carry an image of him in their mind.... But as the individuals who carry the images fall naturally into classes, we may practically say that he has as many different social selves as there are distinct *groups* of persons about whose opinion he cares. He generally shows a different side of himself to each of these different groups. Many a youth who is demure enough before his parents and teachers, swears and swaggers like a pirate among his "tough" young friends.[9]

As the twentieth century unfolded, many thinkers would explore and refine the idea of a socially fashioned self. George Herbert Mead,

Cooley's sometime colleague, argued in his 1913 book, *The Social Self*, that children gain a sense of individuality only when they start to play roles, shaping their own words and behavior to the words and behavior of others. To the subjective "I" is added the objective "me." The idea's fullest expression arrived later in the century, via the sociologist Erving Goffman's celebrated 1959 book, *The Presentation of Self in Everyday Life*. Whereas Cooley and Mead had focused on how we interpret others' perceptions of us, Goffman concentrated on the other side of the feedback loop: how we adjust our behavior to influence those perceptions. He framed his argument with a famously elaborate analogy to the theater. We go through our days like character actors, taking on different roles depending on which "stage" we happen to be on. We play one part when we're at home with family, another when we're with colleagues at work, another when we're at school, another when we're out with friends. We modulate our tone of voice, our words, our actions, and our appearance to suit whatever social context we're in, and when we move into another context we readjust our aspect and affect for the new audience. We're all masters of "the arts of impression management."[10]

Goffman assumed, as pretty much everyone else did at the time, that social contexts were defined by in-person interactions in actual places—schools, offices, factories, homes, bars, churches, shops. One's social life was situated in the material world, its pace and texture linked to the presence of one's own body and the bodies of others. Because events were bounded in space and time— you couldn't be in two places at once—a person had to travel from one social setting, or stage, to another. Performances of the self were sequential. One ended before the next began, with little or no overlap. And there were gaps between the performances, when a person was, to extend Goffman's metaphor, offstage—alone in a room or a car, or taking a walk, or eating a sandwich on a bench in a park.[11] Such intervals of solitude provided respites from social pressures, opportunities to relax and attend to one's own inner voice. They gave people the sense of privacy that Irwin Altman saw as so essential to a healthy, cohesive psyche.

The separation of social situations in time and space acted as "a psycho-social shock absorber," explained the communication professor Joshua Meyrowitz in his 1985 book, *No Sense of Place*, a work that built on Goffman's ideas. By allowing us to be selective in "exposing ourselves to events and other people," it gave us the power to "control the flow of our actions and emotions." We weren't called upon to respond to many different situations with many different sets of people all at once. The well-defined boundaries between social events exerted a deep if often unrecognized influence on the quality of our emotional and moral lives, he argued. "Compassion, empathy, and even ethics may be much more situationally bound than we often care to think." Our sense of ourselves and others might be drawn from mental images, but those images were situated in a concrete reality. Being together with others in a place, face to face, gave a richness to our sympathetic and emotional attachments.

Goffman, with his single-minded focus on traditional, in-person interactions, paid scant attention to mediated communications—to conversations conducted through letters or telegrams or telephone calls. He dismissed them as "marginal and derived forms of social contact" that supplemented but didn't alter the fundamentally physical nature of personal relations.[12] Meyrowitz, writing a quarter century later, after the introduction of the home computer and the modem, took a different view. Seeing the growing importance of online and other mediated communications to people's lives, he realized that Goffman's old, orderly state of social affairs was doomed. Radio, television, and the telephone had already weakened the connection between social events and physical spaces; happenings from all around the world, and even outer space, were routinely beamed into people's living rooms. The spread of digital media promised to sever the link altogether. "Electronic media destroy the specialness of place and time," he wrote. "What is happening almost anywhere can be happening wherever we are." Society, he sensed, was entering a time of profound dislocation, when "social reality" would be defined not by physical interactions in discrete places but by crisscrossing "patterns of information flow." Messages and other social stimuli would "flow constantly and indiscriminately."[3] The psychosocial shock absorber would be gone.

A Universal Solvent

That's where we find ourselves today. Before the coming of the News Feed, online social networks reflected, at least by analogy, traditional patterns of socializing. Their design maintained divisions of space and time. Each member of a network had his or her own "place," in the form of a profile page, and people traveled, through hyperlinks, from place to place to "visit" friends. Status updates and other postings were arranged chronologically. They unspooled sequentially through time, as thoughts and experiences had always unfolded. The feed replaced the old structure of the social world with the logic of the computer. It erased the divisions and disrupted the sequences, removing social interactions from the constraints of space and time and placing them into a frictionless setting of instantaneity and simultaneity. Socializing in this new sphere follows no familiar, human pattern; it vibrates chaotically to the otherworldly rhythms of algorithmic calculation.

The social and the real have parted ways. No longer tied to particular locations or times of day, social situations and social groups now exist everywhere all at once. We move between them with a tap on a screen, a flick of a finger, a word to a chatbot. And because our phones allow us to socialize all the time, even when alone, interludes of solitude have largely disappeared from everyday life. There's no offstage anymore, no place insulated from communication and its demands. Everyone is always within earshot and eyeshot. The old social architecture, with its walls and doors, its mornings and afternoons and evenings, has collapsed—just as the old epistemic architecture did. Digitization acts as a universal solvent for all that's tangible in culture.

The disembodiment of social relations has seemed liberating to many, particularly those who feel isolated or trapped in the rooms available to them in the material world. In its expansiveness, the virtual can be accommodating in ways the real cannot. And for pretty much everyone, online society is, at times, exhilarating—so many people to talk to, to gaze upon, to be watched by; a never-ending *passeggiata*, with what seems to be the entirety of humanity circulating through the clamorous ether. But it's also exhausting and oppressive. Social media is a neurosis machine. Like a bad parent or a cruel lover, it simultaneously indulges and punishes us. Even as it encourages the id to run free, it cracks the superego's whip.[14] We know we're always being watched and judged, and we know the shamers lie in wait, knives sharpened. Beset on both sides and cut off from solitude's refuge, the ego wilts.

For creatures such as ourselves, fashioned by evolution to live closely together as physical beings in physical places among physical things, disembodiment also brings a perpetual sense of disorientation and dysphoria. When we carry our acute sensitivity to social signals into a world where such signals are no longer regulated by time and space, no longer tied to bodies and places, no longer subject to attenuation by personal discretion, the performance of self "metastasizes into a wreck," as the *New Yorker* essayist Jia Tolentino writes in her book *Trick Mirror*.[15] Or, as Meyrowitz put it years ago, "when we are everywhere, we are also no place."[16]

Even in social media's earliest days, the blurring of social contexts provoked surprise and uneasiness. When, around 2003, people started joining Friendster and linking with their friends, they at first assumed that the boundaries that defined social relations in the physical world were still in place. They didn't realize that as friends linked to friends and those friends linked to other friends, a person's social network would expand recklessly in every direction. Posts and pictures would be visible to many "friends" on the platform who were strangers in real life. As the social scientist Danah Boyd explained in an early ethnographic study of Friendster, the pioneering social networkers thought they were replicating "local social contexts and communities" in a virtual space even as the platform was dissolving the barriers that had kept those contexts and communities intact and distinct. One high school teacher Boyd interviewed related the shock she felt when some of her students came up to her in class one day and asked why she liked to do drugs. It turned out they had joined Friendster, discovered her profile, and read some conversations she'd had with friends about attending a Burning Man festival.[17]

As people came to realize that the versions of themselves they presented to different sets of acquaintances could no longer be kept separate—the audience was a jumble now—they grappled with a new sort of identity crisis. How do you speak to everyone at once? How do you shape a self fit for mass consumption? The cultural anthropologist Michael Wesch described the experience in suitably melodramatic terms in an influential paper about YouTube's original vloggers: "The images, actions, and words captured by the [webcam's] lens at any moment can be transported to anywhere on the planet and preserved (the performer must assume) for all time. The little glass lens becomes the gateway to a black hole sucking all of time and space— virtually all possible contexts—in on itself."[18]

The resulting "crisis of self-presentation," as Wesch termed it, became widespread the moment Facebook opened its platform to all. In an instant, thousands of college students who had been posting messages and photos they assumed would be seen only by other students found their online lives exposed to everyone. The walls of the dorm and the frat house turned transparent. Parents and grandparents, teachers, future employers, prospective lovers: all could see the bong-sucking party pics, the goofy selfies, the intemperate remarks. In a 2010 interview with a technology reporter, Zuckerberg summed up the new reality bluntly. "You have one identity," he said, repeating the sentence three times for emphasis. "The days of you having a different image for your work friends or co-workers and for the other people you know are probably coming to an end pretty quickly." He put his own, self-serving spin on the phenomenon, promoting it as a force for moral cleanliness: "Having two identities for yourself is an example of a lack of integrity."[19] Facebook, by forcing each of us into an identity straitjacket, would purify society. And it would further its own interests in the process. A uniform self is easy to package as a bundle of data and sell to advertisers.

As Zuckerberg was declaring the end of social context and the extermination of the protean self, the public rebelled. Eager to keep some separation between social spheres, people began looking for ways to reestablish boundaries within the new media environment. The young, again, led the way. During the 2010s, high school and college students shifted their social media use away from the public platform of Facebook, where the olds lurked, and onto the more intimate platform of Snapchat, where they could restrict their audience and where messages disappeared quickly. Private accounts became popular on other social networks as well. Group chats, group texts, and direct messages proliferated. On Instagram, people established secret, pseudonymous accounts—fake Instagrams, or finstas—limited to their closest friends. Platforms tailored to specific social groups—Slack for work colleagues, Sermo for physicians, Brainly for students, Nextdoor for neighbors—came into wide use. Responding to the trend, Facebook itself introduced tools allowing members to restrict who could see a post and to specify how long it remained visible.

People, it turned out, didn't want all the world to be their stage, at least not all the time. They wanted to go on performing different parts on different stages for different audiences. We realized—most of us, anyway—that we're happier as character actors than as stars.

The Mirrorball Self

While the proliferation of specialized platforms allows people more control over who can see their messages, it only aggravates the crisis of self-presentation. The platforms' walls may feel reassuring, but they're mirages, illusions conjured up by software programmers in response to consumer demands. They remain permeable to the flows of data that social media companies collect in their processing centers and use to manipulate content and people. And by providing a sense of personal agency and security, they encourage people to shift ever more of their lives online, parceling out messages, images, and other communications among a growing variety of apps, networks, and sites. These days, the typical internet user juggles eight or nine social media accounts, double the number of a decade ago.[20] Maintaining one's virtual presence has become, for many, a full-time occupation or at least preoccupation.

The looking-glass self has turned into the mirrorball self, a whirl of fragmented reflections from a myriad of overlapping sources. We see bits of ourselves in the responses (or nonresponses) to our posts. We see bits of ourselves in all the messages we receive and send. And because we know the feed algorithms are tailoring all the content we see to their assessment of who we are, we see bits of ourselves in everything else as well. We piece together a self-image, as best we can, out of "shattered edges," as Taylor Swift sang on her aptly titled 2020 lockdown hit, "Mirrorball."

In our new milieu, having "a central presence in experience hardly matters," the sociologists James Holstein and Jaber Gubrium write. The self flits before us "in myriad versions unanchored to concrete experiences."[21] The thirteen-year-old with a half dozen IM windows open on the family PC in 1999 is now the young adult managing dozens of intertwining information feeds and conversation threads on a phone. Some involve family. Some involve work colleagues. Some involve friends. Some involve the amorphous mass known as the general public. Each entails choices about how to present oneself and interpret the selves of others through words, images, and symbols. The audience may be segmented, as a marketer would say, but all the segments exist at once, always watching and judging or, worst of all, ignoring.

The self collapses into, and must compete with, everything else in the feed, from news stories to celebrity memes. Media programming used to be something we looked at and listened to, something presented to our senses from the outside. Now it takes shape within us, its production exerting a formative pressure on our being. Media today works "from the inside," the French philosopher and semiotician Jean Baudrillard argued in *The Perfect Crime*, "precisely as a virus does with a normal cell."[22] We consume media, then media consumes us. We're not just actors playing roles anymore. We've been required to take on the jobs of producer and impresario, hawker and emcee, for a show that never stops. Even when we're not posting, we're scouting locations and looking for material.

The transfer of the self's setting from bodies to communication systems is not something that's happened all of a sudden. It has been going on a long time, even if we haven't always been aware of it. As we've adapted our ways of life to the demands of the modern bureaucratic state, to a weblike society woven out of strands of highly processed information, we've gotten used to expressing ourselves through and seeing ourselves reflected in documents and photographs, audio recordings and films, ledgers and registers. As the feminist sociologist Dorothy Smith wrote in 1990:

> We get passports, birth certificates, parking tickets; we fill in forms to apply for jobs, for insurance, for dental benefits; we are given grades, diplomas, degrees; we pay bills and taxes; we read and answer advertisements; we order from menus in restaurants, take a doctor's prescription to the drugstore, write letters to newspapers; we watch television, go to the movies, and so on and so on. Our lives are, to a more extensive degree than we care to think, infused with a process of inscription.[23]

But until the ascendancy of social media and the smartphone, inscriptions of the self tended to take material or at least analog form. They were attached to particular places and times and had limited, usually administrative purposes. We could keep them at a distance, viewing them as another set of props on the various stages we trod. Even if their abstract renderings of the self encroached, bit by bit, on the body's material sovereignty, they didn't displace the body as the site of the self. It was only with social media that we became able to separate being from body, to inscribe ourselves moment-by-moment on the screen, to reimagine ourselves as streams of text and image.

The effect is a strange, needy sort of solipsism. We socialize more than ever, but we're also at a further remove from those we interact with. The sympathetic imagination that Cooley and Goffman took for granted—the ability to get inside the heads of others, to sense their perceptions and feelings through direct observation—weakens and warps when the others are hidden behind screens, their thoughts and emotions filtered through algorithms. Rather than relying on empathy and intuition to navigate social relations, we're forced to decipher others' attitudes by tracking and evaluating explicit, often quantitative measures: follower counts, numbers of likes and shares, the time that elapses before responses arrive, the types of emoji that appear in a comment, the number of exclamation marks that punctuate a reply. Even the presence or absence of a period at the end of a text message becomes laden with meaning, another clue to how we're perceived. The more mediated our lives become, the more we come to see ourselves, and others, as abstractions.

When in the real world, as we used to call it, the self feels its way into the corners of the various places and moments through which the body moves. The body is our means of being a separate and distinct individual, but it is equally our means of exploring and accommodating ourselves to society in all its contingency and complexity. To shape ourselves to others with whom we share actual time and actual space is not to become broken or fake or, as Zuckerberg suggested, to lose integrity. It's to undergo an enlargement of the sympathetic imagination and in the process become at once more fully an individual and more fully a part of what Cooley termed the social mind. It is in and through the body that the individual self and the social self emerge and meld. Every person is "special," Cooley stressed, but no person is "separate."[24]

When the self collapses into content, it shrinks to fit the medium that carries it. Like all the other content it travels with and competes against, it has to be recognizable and decipherable at a glance. It needs to mug and wink and wave, to be memelike. Detached from the body, removed from space and time, the "I" squeezes into—and here at least Zuckerberg was correct—an "identity," a set of descriptive or ideological codes suitable for transmission through high-speed networks. As the self's vessel in the virtual world, an identity serves as a stand-in for the body. It provides, as the body did, a means for being part of society, for bringing the "I" into the "we." But unlike the body, identity works through the explicit process of group affiliation—through self-categorization—rather than the fuzzy accumulations of sympathetic understanding. The society it keeps is exclusive, not inclusive.

Although ethnic, religious, and national pride are as old as ethnicity, religion, and the nation-state, our contemporary way of thinking about identity, as a set of extrinsic markers that define one's affiliations rather than a set of intrinsic traits that add up to one's personal character, is a fairly recent development. As Kwame Anthony Appiah explains in *The Lies That Bind*, it came to the cultural fore only in the second half of the twentieth century. The assumption underpinning the idea of shared or social identity—"that," as Appiah writes, "at the core of each identity there is some deep similarity that binds people of that identity together"[25]—may be a fallacy, but the idea has nonetheless provided a powerful means of enabling historically oppressed groups to organize to counter prejudice and secure civil rights. It engenders political solidarity, regardless of whether it reflects anything other than superficial similarity. Social identity plays an important organizing role online as well, but it can also, when it usurps individual character, lead to a kind of self-stereotyping. It becomes a cage, if a comfortable one. In social media's flux, identity serves as a defense mechanism. It gives the entropic mirrorball self an appearance of stability and cohesion by reducing it to a set of ready-made tribal markers: hashtags, emojis, slogans, gestures, acronyms, in-jokes, buzzwords. *This* is who I am. *This* and *this* and *this*. The self is expressed through curation.

The Displaced

In the 2010s, Generation Z began to come of age. The first tranche of kids to grow up with smartphones, social media, and networked video-game consoles, Gen Zers are the unwitting subjects of a vast social experiment that their elders, also without much thought, set up for them. Thanks to several long-running, large-scale surveys of teens and young adults, we have a pretty clear idea what happens when people start socializing and otherwise informing and amusing themselves online at a very young age. They don't go out much.

Some of the statistics are by now familiar. In 2012, half of American teenagers said they'd rather socialize with friends through screens than in person, according to an ongoing Common Sense Media survey. By 2018, the percentage had reached two-thirds.[26] Not only are Gen Zers the first kids who like chatting with pals through media more than hanging out with them in person; they're much less likely than their predecessors to leave the house in general. Far fewer of them drive (or even have a driver's license), go to parties, go on dates, have sex, drink alcohol, experiment with drugs, get into fights, go to church, or work a part-time job. According to the government's Monitoring the Future surveys, the percentage of high schoolers who say they "get a kick out of doing dangerous things" fell from 50 to 38 percent during the 2010s. The portion who "like to take risks sometimes" dropped from 46 to 34 percent.[27] That was before the pandemic; the trends accelerated further once the lockdowns hit. "My generation lost interest in socializing in person," a seventeen-year-old told San Diego State psychology professor Jean Twenge; "they don't have physical get-togethers, they just text together, and they can stay home."[28] Adolescents, for decades the demographic group most eager to go out, gather in packs, and have fun, have become homebodies.

It would be perverse to wish that teenagers would drive drunk or get knocked up more often. Because of the behavioral shifts, parents can sleep easier on Saturday nights. But the trends point to deeper changes in how people relate to one another and the world. A 2023 study by the University of Rochester's Viji Kannan and Peter Veazie, drawing on data from the Bureau of Labor Statistics' venerable American Time Use Survey, found that from 2010 to 2019 social engagement "plummeted for young Americans." The average amount of time that people aged fifteen to twenty-four spent socializing in person with friends fell by half, from 133 to 67 minutes a day. That amounts to more than 400 fewer hours of friendly facetime over the course of a year. (Time spent in the presence of family members didn't fill the gap. It too dropped, from 211 to 187 minutes a day.) Experiences of "companionship"—which the researchers define as any leisure-time activity involving other people, such as playing sports or eating at a restaurant or going to a show—also diminished. Time devoted to such social activities fell by nearly a quarter during the decade, from 238 to 189 minutes a day—a loss of nearly 300 hours of camaraderie a year. Americans, the study reveals, are spending more and more of their youth in "social isolation."[29] And because patterns of social engagement established during adolescence tend to persist through adulthood, the isolation seems likely to continue.[30]

Given the extent of the retreat from direct human contact, it's not surprising that the proportion of high schoolers who report they "often feel lonely" nearly doubled during the past decade, jumping from 23 to 42 percent, and the share who say they "do not enjoy life" went from less than a quarter to nearly half.[31] As people spend more time with technologies of connection, they feel more disconnected. The psychological consequences can be severe. As Kannan and Veazie note, citing many past studies, in-person social interaction "is essential for health and longevity, while isolation exacts a heavy toll on individuals and society." As the rising rates of loneliness among the most devoted social media users make clear, interacting through screens is not the same as hanging out. "While a few studies have found benefits to online interaction," the researchers write, "there remain aspects of in-person interpersonal interaction (e.g., touch, simultaneous expressions, mutually experienced environment) that cannot be replicated online." When we converse face to face, we learn how to read other people, a subtle, corporeal art that involves far more than the hurried scanning of words and images. Empathy is another human quality that doesn't scale.

The virtual world is a cold place. For many teens and tweens, particularly girls, the twenty-first century has been a time of growing despair. "Teen mental health collapsed in the 2010s," reports New York University social scientist Jonathan Haidt.[32] According to the National Survey on Drug Use and Health, the percentage of U.S. teenagers experiencing a major episode of depression doubled between 2010 and 2019, from 8 to 16 percent, with the rise steepest among girls. In 2019, nearly one in four girls suffered a bout of severe depression. Rates of anxiety disorder also jumped. The increases in reports of depression, anxiety, and loneliness are not just a result of teens being more vocal about their mental health. They're reflected in objective measures of illness and injury. The number of older teens (ages fifteen to nineteen) admitted to hospitals for "nonfatal self-harm" rose 48 percent for girls and 37 percent for boys over the decade, according to the Centers for Disease Control and Prevention. For younger teens and preteens (ages ten to fourteen), the rise was sharper still, up 188 percent for girls and 48 percent for boys. Suicide rates saw similar increases, up 64 percent for older girls and 35 percent for older boys and up 134 percent for younger girls and 109 percent for younger boys.

While self-harm and suicide remain extreme cases, with many contributing factors, the sudden upsurge in their occurrence, tragic in itself, sends a signal. It points to a broader social malaise, one that reaches beyond middle schools and high schools. The National College Health Assessment, which collects data from campus mental health clinics, reports that from 2010 to 2019 the portion of undergraduates treated for depression doubled, from 10 to 20 percent, while the share treated for anxiety disorder more than doubled, from about 10 percent to nearly 25 percent. As with social isolation, the effects of youthful anxiety and depression tend to persist into adulthood. A 2008 study in the journal *Sociology* found that "anxious and sad affect during adolescence was strongly associated with adverse adult social outcomes."[33] That suggests the current psychological problems will continue to haunt the young as they age.

The extent of social media's psychological harm has been debated for years. Skeptics point out that some studies show that social media can have psychological benefits, giving young people more social connections. That's true. For some kids, it's a lifeline. The skeptics are also quick to stress that correlation does not prove causation. That's also true. But while spreading doubts about the causative role of social media in mental distress may have been warranted a decade ago, it's hard to justify now. It comes off as a head-in-the-sand response, and, given the numbers, an irresponsible one. As Haidt wrote in a 2023 review of recent research, "There is now a great deal of evidence that social media is a substantial *cause*, not just a tiny *correlate*, of depression and anxiety, and therefore of behaviors related to depression and anxiety, including self-harm and suicide."[34]

In her 2023 book, *Generations*, Jean Twenge offers an exhaustive analysis of data from the longitudinal studies of young people's attitudes and behavior.[35] On the basis of timing and other factors, she rules out alternative phenomena that have been suggested as possible primary causes for the mental illness spike, such as economic hardship, political worries, fears about climate change or school shootings, parental and academic pressures, and stresses from the pandemic. Though all those things may contribute to feelings of anxiety or unhappiness, it's the rapid growth in digital media use that exhibits by far the strongest and most consistent association with the surge in psychological problems. What makes the longitudinal evidence particularly compelling is that it's consistent not only through time but also across pretty much every country and culture where phones and social media are popular. Data from World Health Organization surveys of hundreds of thousands of teenagers in dozens of countries show that "the number of teens with significant [psychological] distress was unchanged or down between 2002 and 2010, but then jumped sharply between 2010 and 2018, especially among girls," Twenge reports. Out of the forty countries that collected data, thirty-eight reported that the number of teens suffering high levels of distress increased between 2010 and 2018. International surveys tracking feelings of loneliness among high-school-age kids also reveal abrupt increases during the 2010s. "Loneliness among teens rose in 36 out of 37 countries around the world," writes Twenge. "The number of teens experiencing a high degree of loneliness doubled in Europe, Latin America, and the English-speaking countries, and increased 65% in Asian countries."

The fact that girls suffer more than boys adds further weight to the case. Whatever's causing the surge in psychological problems must be "something that impacts both [sexes] but has a larger impact on girls," Twenge explains. "Digital media fits that description perfectly." Girls, she points out, spend more time on social media than do boys, are more likely to be targets of insults and slights, and are more sensitive about their looks and their popularity.[36] The distinctive and well-documented "social dynamics of girlhood," Twenge says, can produce "a perfect storm on social media." She quotes a teenaged girl who was interviewed by Facebook as part of the company's 2019 study of Instagram's effects:

> You can't ever win on social media. If you're curvy, you're too busty. If you're skinny, you're too skinny. If you're bigger, you're too fat. But it's clear you need boobs, a booty, to be thin, to be pretty. It's endless, and you just end up feeling worthless and shitty about yourself.

Confronted with the extensive historical and anecdotal evidence of social media's culpability, skeptics will often argue that psychology experiments aimed at establishing a causal connection between social media use and mental health disorders have produced mixed results over the past two decades. Again, that's true. It's also beside the point. Narrowly focused empirical studies conducted in psych labs may produce useful findings about particular platforms or activities, but they're near useless when it comes to understanding how digital media is reshaping people's lives. The studies usually employ some form of "dose-response" methodology similar to what medical investigators use to measure the effects of, say, salt intake or formaldehyde exposure on the health of individuals. In some of the media studies, researchers ask test subjects to estimate the time they spend on social platforms or the internet in general (dose) and then ask them questions about aspects of their mental health (response). In others, researchers have subjects spend a specified amount of time using social media (dose) and then compare their mood afterwards with their mood before (response). What these experiments miss is the way a new communication technology reshapes social relations in general.[37] The ubiquity of smartphones and social media has fundamentally changed the social lives of kids (and many adults), regardless of how many minutes a day they spend on Snapchat or TikTok or Instagram. If none of your friends wants to hang out, you'll suffer the effects of social isolation even if you delete all the social media apps on your phone. Indeed, deleting the apps may make you feel *more* isolated.

Twenge explains the situation well:

> The smartphone led to a global rewiring of human social interaction—when most people own smartphones and use social media, everyone is impacted, whether they use these technologies or not. It's harder to strike up a casual conversation when everyone is staring down at a phone. It's harder for friends to get together in person when the norm is to communicate online instead.

Scientific experiments can obfuscate as well as illuminate. Trying to get a grip on broad, complex sociocultural trends by conducting lab tests on individuals is like trying to get a sense of the shoreline by squinting at grains of sand through a microscope. Sometimes you have to lift your eyes and take a wider view.

Social Disease

The loss of companionship, the concurrent and paradoxical loss of solitude, the Sisyphean labor of identity management, the competition for tokens of popularity and status, the doom-scrolling, the FOMO, the sleep deprivation: social media creates the perfect conditions for angst. But it does something more. It makes angst cool. The figure of the suffering youth has of course been seductive for centuries—at least since 1774, when Goethe wrote *The Sorrows of Young Werther* and set off a wave of suicides among impressionable young men in Europe. On the net, the figure multiplies into a million memes. It's an attention grabber, not to mention a marker of those most desirable of online character traits, authenticity and relatability. Hundreds of thousands of people follow Instagram accounts, Facebook pages, and subreddits dedicated to "sad memes" and "depression memes." On TikTok alone, videos tagged #mentalhealth have been viewed more than twenty-five billion times. Misery is always trending.

That which trends also gets imitated. In 2019 and 2020, many young people in the United States, Canada, Germany, and other countries began turning up at doctors' offices displaying bizarre motor and verbal tics. They'd blurt out things like "Potato!" or "Flying Sharks!" They'd randomly throw a pencil across a room or crush a raw egg on a kitchen counter. At first baffled, medical investigators came to discover that the far-flung patients shared something in common: they were fans of popular TikTok and YouTube influencers who had, or pretended to have, Tourette's syndrome. The outbreak, a group of German psychiatry professors reported in the journal *Brain* in 2022, was an example of a new type of mass hysteria, spread online rather than through direct personal contact, that they dubbed "mass social media–induced illness." Likely tied to Gen Z's anxieties over climate change and the pandemic, anxieties themselves magnified by social media, the outbreak was, the researchers suggested, an "expression of a 'culture-bound stress reaction' " in a society that promotes "attention-seeking behaviours."[38]

The Tourette's episode was not an isolated one. Ever since pro-anorexia, or "pro-ana," content coursed through Tumblr after the platform's founding in 2007, researchers have been investigating how "social media platforms may serve as a vehicle of transmission for social contagion," according to a 2023 article in *Comprehensive Psychiatry*. The article's authors, another group of psychiatric researchers, pointed to the apparent connection between the popularity on TikTok and other platforms of "plurals," influencers who claim to have split personalities, and an upsurge in self-diagnoses of the rare condition among the young. (TikToks tagged #dissociativeidentity-disorder or #did have been watched more than three billion times.) The sharp increases in the number of people presenting symptoms of anxiety disorder, depression, and other psychopathologies, the researchers noted, also come at a time when portrayals of such conditions, often "romanticized, glamourized, and sexualized," circulate intensively through social media. A self-diagnosed mental illness can be "incorporated into one's self concept." Its symptoms, publicized through photos and videos, become "character traits that make individuals sharper and more interesting than others around them."[39]

The net may provide shelter when a contagious pathogen is on the lose, but it is itself an ideal vector for the imitative, or sociogenic, transmission of affliction. Disease, it turns out, can be spread by words and images as well as by germs. That doesn't mean people with sociogenic illnesses are faking it. Their symptoms and their suffering may be very real. But what the phenomenon makes clear is that the transmission of messages can be metamorphic, altering physical and mental states at a deep level. Through its emphasis on repetition and imitation, social media does more than influence people's opinions. It shapes and sometimes shakes the very foundations of their being.

The more we associate ourselves with symbols online, the more readable we become, to each other and to the machines that take such an interest in our thoughts and feelings. As Zuckerberg understood early on, acts of symbolic association are also acts of self-profiling, and self-profiling makes the job of professional profilers, whether in industry or government, all the easier. From the moment of its founding, Facebook pushed users to express themselves by categorizing themselves—by picking personal descriptors such as "relationship status" and "political views" and "gender" from dropdown menus, by forming or joining groups with catchy names, by identifying and tagging their friends, by listing their favorite bands and movies and their high schools and hometowns. The users happily complied. The site seemed benign, its categorization features serving to reveal connections between people that might otherwise have gone unnoticed. When you placed yourself into a category—listing, say, Scissor Sisters as a favorite band or *Eternal Sunshine of the Spotless Mind* as a favorite movie—you immediately saw everyone else who had placed themselves into that same category. In joining a big social network and going through the routines of self-categorization, you expanded your own personal network. You broadened, it seemed, your social possibilities.

A week after Facebook launched at Harvard in 2004, a junior named Amelia Lester wrote an exceptionally perceptive article about its appeal for the *Harvard Crimson*, the campus newspaper.[40] Noting that the site tapped into several "primal instincts"—"an element of wanting to belong, a dash of vanity and more than a little voyeurism"—she remarked on how quickly students had taken to packaging themselves as content on the new medium: "Just about every profile is a carefully constructed artifice, a kind of pixelated Platonic ideal of our messy, all too organic real-life selves." She understood, as well, how the site's emphasis on categorization had the effect of turning complex beings into legible objects. What made the network "endlessly fascinating," she wrote, was the way it allowed everyone to sort themselves into "neat little categories" that were easy to scan and parse. Facebook rendered individuals visible, and hence watchable, to a degree far beyond anything anyone had ever experienced before. It brought "hitherto top-secret stalking techniques to the masses," turning everyone into a spy.

What was emerging at Harvard, Lester recognized, was a captivating new social world fashioned entirely of images and messages. Once entered, it would be "difficult if not near-impossible" to leave. Long before the venture capitalists and the marketeers moved in, and a full fifteen years before the arrival of Covid, people were already choosing lockdown. When Zuckerberg, in 2022, announced that Facebook was changing its corporate name to Meta Platforms and would embark on the construction of an all-encompassing virtual world called the metaverse, everyone yawned. The metaverse had been around for years, and we were in it.

But even as Zuckerberg was making his pitch, another, more impressive technological breakthrough was taking shape. The computers that had already elbowed their way into media's editorial function, choosing the content people see, were about to enter an even more important line of work: generating the content itself. Humans were extending the blessing of speech to machines.

CHAPTER 8

Machines Who Speak

The Unknown Writer

Early in the fall of 1917, as the Great War ground on in Europe, the Irish poet William Butler Yeats found himself in a melancholy state, well into middle age and wifeless. Having had marriage proposals turned down twice over the summer, first by his great love, Maud Gonne, and then by Gonne's daughter, Iseult, he decided to chance a third overture. He offered his hand to a well-off young English-woman named Georgie Hyde-Lees. She accepted, and the two were wed a few weeks later, on October 20, in a small civil ceremony in London, Ezra Pound standing as best man. "The girl is 25, not bad looking, sensible, will perhaps dust a few cobwebs out of his belfry," Pound reported to a mutual friend.[1]

Hyde-Lees was a talented painter and translator. She was also a mystic, a member of the Hermetic Order of the Golden Dawn. During the couple's honeymoon at a hotel on the edge of Sussex's ancient Ashdown Forest—soon to be the inspiration for A. A. Milne's Hundred Acre Wood—she gave her husband a demonstration of her ability to channel the words of spirits into the living world. Yeats was captivated by the enigmatic messages that flowed through his wife's pen onto a sheet of paper in their room. "Four days after my marriage," he would recall in his self-published 1925 treatise, *A Vision*, "my wife surprised me by attempting automatic writing. What came in disjointed sentences, in almost illegible writing, was so exciting, sometimes so profound, that I persuaded her to give an hour or two day after day to the unknown writer."

Over the next three years, the couple held hundreds of such séances, producing four thousand pages of spirit writing. Yeats pored over each new script. He saw the texts as emanations from what he called *Spiritus Mundi*, a sort of universal memory or collective unconsciousness that he considered the source of all humanity's symbols and myths. "Many minds can flow into one another, as it were, and create or reveal a single mind, a single energy," he had written in "Magic," an earlier essay; "our memories are a part of one great memory, the memory of Nature herself."[2] During one especially productive séance, he announced he would devote the rest of his life to interpreting the cryptic messages. "No," the spirits responded, "we have come to give you metaphors for poetry."[3] And that they did, in abundance. Many of Yeats's great late poems, with their gyres and staircases, their waxing and waning moons, were inspired by his wife's occult scribblings.

One way to think about artificially intelligent text-generation systems like OpenAI's ChatGPT, Google's Gemini, and Microsoft's Copilot is as clairvoyants. They are mediums that bring the words of the past into the present in a new arrangement. The large language models, or LLMs, that power the chatbots are not creating text out of nothing. They're drawing on a vast corpus of human expression—a digitized *Spiritus Mundi* composed of billions of documents—and through a complex, quasi-mystical statistical procedure, they're blending all those old words into something new, something intelligible to and requiring interpretation by a human interlocutor. When we talk to chatbots, we are, in a way, communing with the dead. One of Hyde-Lees's spirits said to Yeats, "this script has its origin in human life—all religious systems have their origin in God & descend to man—this ascends."[4] The same could be said of the scripts generated by chatbots. They have their origin in human life. They ascend.

"Every new medium is a machine for the production of ghosts," wrote John Durham Peters, the Yale professor, in his 1999 book, *Speaking into the Air*.[5] He pointed to how Samuel B. Morse's first public demonstration of the telegraph in 1844 sparked the rise and spread of Spiritualism—an immensely popular movement that Arthur Conan Doyle, creator of that most logical of thinkers, Sherlock Holmes, would in the 1920s call "the most important in the history of the world since the Christ episode."[6] What telegraph wires carried seemed to be a kind of human essence, an expression of the self liberated from the body's physical and mortal constraints. The dead, the technology suggested, could still speak to us; we only had to figure out how to receive and decode their signals. "That the telegraph opened access to the spirit world is not a fanciful metaphor," Peters stresses. "Spiritualism, the art of communication with the dead, explicitly modeled itself on the telegraph's ability to receive remote messages."[7] Andrew Jackson Davis, a leading Spiritualist thinker known as the Poughkeepsie Seer, gave the connection between earthly and metaphysical telecommunication a scientific gloss in his 1853 tract, *The Present Age and the Inner Life*, a sequel to his widely read *Philosophy of Spiritual Intercourse*: "We are *negative* to our guardian spirits; they are *positive* to us; and the whole mystery is illustrated by the workings of the common magnetic telegraph. The principles involved are identical."[8]

So what sort of ghost are we conjuring out of our new circuits? To many, it looks a lot like the "rough beast" that slouches, with a "gaze blank and pitiless as the sun," through Yeats's dark 1920 poem "The Second Coming." Artificial intelligence, according to this common line of thinking, may be the monster that puts an end to us. Having fed deeply on our thoughts and words, it will move beyond us intellectually and, accidentally or on purpose, shut out the lights on civilization. The apocalyptic view has particular currency among tech-industry bigwigs—the very people constructing the language models. In the wake of OpenAI's release of ChatGPT at the end of 2022, the press was overrun with doomsday scenarios of, in Elon Musk's excited phrase, "civilization destruction." In March 2023, Musk, one of OpenAI's original investors and directors, joined other tech luminaries, including Apple cofounder Steve Wozniak and Berkeley AI guru Stuart Russell, to urge a six-month moratorium on the further development of LLMs, saying the systems could have "catastrophic effects."[9] A few weeks later, the top executives of OpenAI, Google DeepMind, and other prominent AI outfits co-signed a public statement warning of "the risk of extinction."[10] In a portentous interview with the *New York Times*, OpenAI's boss, Sam Altman, compared his company's work to that of the Manhattan Project. He mentioned that he has the same birthday as Robert Oppenheimer.[11]

We may think of ourselves as more sophisticated—more rational, more Sherlockian—than the Spiritualists, but we seem every bit as eager to imagine phantoms arising out of new communication technologies. "AI doomism is quickly becoming indistinguishable from an apocalyptic religion," observes the eminent computer scientist Yann LeCun, a critic of LLM hype, "complete with prophecies of imminent fire and brimstone caused by an omnipotent entity that doesn't actually exist."[12] It's certainly prudent to consider the existential risks associated with artificial intelligence, particularly now that, after decades of disappointment, the technology is advancing at a pace far beyond what most experts were predicting just a few years ago. That we don't understand exactly what's going on inside an LLM's neural network, just as we don't understand how our own neurons produce thoughts, is disconcerting, to say the least. But it's also important to take the end-time visions propagated by Musk, Altman, and their ilk with skepticism. Behind today's dystopian AI dreams lurk character traits all too common to the tech elite: grandiosity, hubris, and self-aggrandizement. The visions are yet another expression of Silicon Valley's god complex: we may have failed in our attempt to use computers to establish a new Eden on Earth, but at least we still have the power to lay everything to waste.

Ghosts

Still, the machines are talking, and they're making sense. Large language models probably aren't going to bring Armageddon—when it comes to existential threats, there are other, rougher beasts— but they do represent an epochal feat of computer engineering that seems sure to transform media and communication and, in turn, once again reconfigure the flows of influence and forms of association that define social relations. The doomer fears are distractions, pulling our attention away from AI's more immediate, and much realer, repercussions. As Altman himself has said, the technology may be best understood as a machine for creating "a new kind of society," which could turn out terrific or "really terrible."[13]

Putting yet another spin on Claude Shannon's theories, a large language model employs coding as a means of compression for the purpose of efficient communication. But it's not coding, compressing, and communicating discrete messages. It's coding, compressing, and communicating something far more complex and diffuse: knowledge itself. It aims to replicate the communicative possibilities of the human mind or, more expansively, the social mind. The LLM is first fed huge quantities of digitized text—the contents of the internet, essentially. With some help from human instructors, it uses the text to train itself to fit words together in a way that mimics natural speech. With each training run, it tweaks the billions of statistical parameters that compose its neural net, calculating and recalculating, at a level of detail beyond human comprehension, associations and correlations among all the words. It ends up with a compressed, numerical model of human knowledge, with each word in the language represented by a series of coordinates that maps the word in a multidimensional "meaning space."

"What's actually inside ChatGPT are a bunch of numbers," the physicist and computer scientist Stephen Wolfram explains, "that are some kind of distributed encoding of the aggregate structure of all that text."[4] When asked a question or otherwise given a prompt through a chatbot, the LLM uses the map to output a reply, decoding a numerical pattern back into words—or images, or sounds—that people can understand. Thanks to the compression of the coding, and the speed of cloud-computing systems, it does all this with an efficiency that would have astounded Shannon, replying so quickly that the exchange gives the illusion of an actual conversation. (ChatGPT could probably respond even more quickly than it does. It has reportedly been programmed to type out its responses haltingly, with slight pauses, in order to heighten the illusion that it's choosing its words consciously.)

In describing this new process of knowledge coding and decoding, the science-fiction author and *New Yorker* essayist Ted Chiang draws an analogy to something familiar: the digitally compressed images, such as JPEGs, that are found everywhere online. For storage and transport purposes, a lot of pixels, and the bits of numerical information that describe them, can be trimmed from a digital photograph or other image by a compression algorithm. When it comes time to display the image on a screen, the algorithm fills in the missing pixels by following various statistical rules—for example, using brightness and color values that are averages of the values of the surrounding pixels. It interpolates what's missing. A compressed, or "lossy," image has a lower resolution than the original—because the interpolation is imperfect, the image is a little blurrier—but the loss of detail rarely hinders a viewer's interpretation or appreciation of the picture. The human mind is good at making sense of images. In a similar way, Chiang suggests, a chatbot like ChatGPT produces "a blurry JPEG of all the text on the Web":

It retains much of the information on the Web, in the same way
that a JPEG retains much of the information of a higher-resolution
image, but, if you're looking for an exact sequence of bits, you
won't find it; all you will ever get is an approximation. But, because
the approximation is presented in the form of grammatical text,
which ChatGPT excels at creating, it's usually acceptable.[15]

If you're good with words, people will understand you. They'll
understand you even if you don't know what you're talking about.

Far from being a weakness of large language models, compression turns out to be a strength. The acts of interpolation required to
reproduce knowledge in phrases and sentences are essential to chatbots' ability to mimic human intelligence. Because a bot like Chat-
GPT has to reconstitute knowledge into a fresh pattern of words—its
own words, so to speak—it gives the impression of doing its own
thinking. Its writing can feel natural and original rather than rote
or plagiarized. Human language is blurry to begin with, at least to a
computer's way of thinking. There is no single ideal of verbal expression, no perfect resolution for a chunk of speech. There are a lot of
different ways to say the same thing, and readers will understand
most of them. That's why "writing essays," as Wolfram says, is "actually in some sense computationally easier than we thought."[16] (It's
telling that ChatGPT is much better at writing than at basic arithmetic, where either you get the right answer or you don't.) The more
creative the bot gets in its interpolations, the smarter and more literate it seems.

Up to a point, anyway. Compression also helps explain why
today's chatbots, for all their technical sophistication, remain prone to
"hallucinations"—factual errors, non sequiturs, and other, sometimes
bizarre mistakes. The hallucinations, Chiang suggests, are "compression artifacts" of the sort that often distort renderings of compressed
data. "If a compression algorithm is designed to reconstruct text after
ninety-nine per cent of the original has been discarded, we should
expect that significant portions of what it generates will be entirely

fabricated."[17] In filling the gaps in their models, chatbots sometimes get a little too creative. They overreach. A challenge facing programmers is coming up with error-correction methods that curb chatbots' mistakes without curbing their inventiveness.

ChatGPT's skill at interpolation, at weaving diverse strands of information into new textual or pictorial patterns, makes it good at parlor tricks. It can compose a well-turned Elizabethan sonnet on the topic of male pattern baldness, or write erotica in the style of Ayn Rand, or produce a Renoirish painting of an anteater riding a motorcycle through Disney World. But it can also be a tool for more interesting and serious work. Just as Hyde-Lees's spirit writing swept the cobwebs from Yeats's belfry, inspiring new verse, so a chatbot's pastiches can stir the imaginations of today's artists. In 2021, the writer Vauhini Vara collaborated with GPT-3, an earlier version of OpenAI's chatbot, in writing a remarkable essay called "Ghosts" for the *Believer* magazine.[18] She described how, while in lockdown during the prior year, she became obsessed with the bot. "I sought out examples of GPT-3's work, and they astonished me," she recalled. "Some of them could easily be mistaken for texts written by a human hand. In others, the language was weird, off-kilter—but often poetically so, almost truer than writing any human would produce." Yeats would have understood.

Vara's older sister had died of cancer shortly after graduating high school. The experience traumatized Vara, and, though an accomplished journalist and novelist, she had never been able to write about it. With the bot's help, she at last began to find the words. "I found myself irresistibly attracted to GPT-3—to the way it offered, without judgment, to deliver words to a writer who has found herself at a loss for them." She began to feed the chatbot simple sentences about her sister's illness, and the system responded by expanding those sentences into vignettes—strange and fantastical, sometimes, but also stirring and ultimately heartbreaking. The essay chronicles eight of her sessions with the bot. It reads like a conversation between a writer and her muse, one that begins tentatively but grows richer and truer as it goes on.

At one point, Vara confesses to GPT-3 that she felt like "a ghost" after her sister's death. The bot elaborates on the thought:

> So I can't describe her to you. But I can describe what it felt like to have her die. It felt like my life was an accident—or, worse, a mistake. I'd made a mistake in being born, and now, to correct it, I would have to die. I'd have to die, and someone else—a stranger—would have to live, in my place. I was that stranger. I still am.

What gives the exchange all the more poignancy is the sense that, in drawing on its corpus of past human speech to fashion something new, the chatbot is channeling the pain of others who have suffered unbearable losses. Spirits are talking.

But there's another sort of spookiness here, too. However productive, however revivifying, the intimacy of the collaboration between writer and bot seems ominous. "I felt acutely that there was something illicit about what I was doing," Vara admits. "When I carried my computer to bed, my husband muttered noises of disapproval." She ignored the grumbling. The more she talked with the bot, the more she opened up to it—and the more the machine opened up to her. The relationship deepened, she writes, "as we got to know each other." It's one thing for a muse, or a ghost, to speak from the celestial realm. It's another thing for it to speak from a corporate data center.

My Fair Bot

The invention of content-generating AI systems heralds a new, third stage in the expansion of electronic media's ambit. In the first stage, machines took on the transport or carriage role that defined traditional communication systems, replacing human couriers with over-the-wire and through-the-air mechanisms for transmitting messages and other content. In the second stage, with the incorporation of feed algorithms into social media platforms, machines added an editorial function, supplanting media and publishing professionals in selecting which content to communicate to which audience. In the third stage, now beginning, the machines are engaging in content production itself, taking on the roles traditionally played by writers, photographers, musicians, and filmmakers. With generative AI, the technological takeover of media is complete. Machines create the content, choose who will see it, and deliver it.

That is, of course, an exaggeration, at least for the moment. Creative types are not about to lose their jobs en masse. Just as we continue to have plenty of mail carriers and editors, we'll continue to have plenty of journalists and novelists, songwriters and singers, photographers and cinematographers, actors and directors. But because the machines are much more efficient than their human counterparts, they will, as the quality of their output improves, expand into more spheres of content production—just as we've seen with the proliferation of digital tools in the music business over the past couple of decades. In the creative fields, the division of labor between people and technology will fluctuate, as it has always done in fields subject to automation, depending on trade-offs between quality and cost. Even when people take the lead, their skills will often be supplemented by the skills of machines, as the collaboration between Vara and GPT-3 demonstrates. Very soon now, it's going to be difficult, if not impossible, to figure out whether the content we read or watch or hear was created by real people or artificial intelligence or some mix of the two. Judging from the example of popular music, we may not care. We may come to prefer the AI productions.

Shannon's distinction between mechanism and meaning, always tenuous, evaporates completely once machines start generating content out of their own resources. It's true that the mechanism of communication—in this case, the computer network and the large language model running on it—remains oblivious to meaning. It's still doing what it has always done: fiddling with signals. But it's through such fiddling that content is now fashioned and meaning expressed. Signal processing is semantic processing. The mechanism makes the message. Whether an artificial intelligence will at some point exhibit signs of true intelligence (whatever that may be) is an interesting theoretical question, but it's beside the point when it comes to contemporary media. What the AI is churning out is already intelligible and pleasing to us, and that's what counts. Through the latest advance in the mechanism of communication, Charles Cooley's spheres of influence and association are expanding to include the voices of ghosts.

For social media platforms, the prospect of unlimited quantities of automatically generated messages is attractive. Given the scale of their operations, the platforms have always needed enormous amounts of new content to keep users happy. To date, they've been able to rely largely on the users themselves to generate that content, either for free or, in the case of popular influencers and performers, for a cut of the resulting ad revenues. Language models and other generative AI systems promise to provide the platforms with vast new pools of content, again at a very low cost once the capital investments required to build the systems have been made. Some of that content will come from users employing the models as creative tools. But much of it will be output by the models themselves. Having successfully mined the words, pictures, and thoughts of their current users for profit, the platforms can now, with their LLMs, mine the words, pictures, and thoughts of the past, turning all of culture into raw material for the generation of cheap content. Machine-made text and images will become all the more important if, as we've already seen with video platforms like YouTube and TikTok, social media users shift toward more traditional consumer roles in the future, contributing less original content themselves.

By combining language models with feed algorithms, moreover, Meta and other social media companies will be able to automatically produce content that's tightly tailored to the tastes and desires of individuals. The algorithmic feedback loop will complete its circuit instantaneously, freed of the friction inherent in the human work of creation just as it was earlier freed of the friction inherent in the human work of transportation and sorting. There's a reason Meta is spending many billions of dollars to, as its infrastructure chief Santosh Janardhan has said, "develop much larger, more sophisticated AI models" and incorporate them into its "family of apps"—Facebook, Instagram, Messenger, WhatsApp, Threads, and the rest.[19] Social media companies are in an arms race, with AI superiority the goal.

Beyond the cheap new stores of personalized content, the bots will allow the platforms to enter into new and deeper kinds of relationships with users. Most of us by now have deposited a large corpus of self-revealing information on the net—emails and texts, posts and reposts, search and browsing histories, photos and videos, likes and comments, not to mention all manner of demographic and purchasing data. All of it can be fed into a language model, adding knowledge about us as individuals to the model's existing knowledge of the world. Bill Gates predicts that customized chatbots will soon act as "digital personal assistants," anticipating and fulfilling our everyday needs. Your assistant "will see your latest emails, know about the meetings you attend, read what you read, and read the things you don't want to bother with."[20] More than your gofer, it will be your doppelganger, standing in for you at online gatherings and speaking with your voice. We've already gotten used to computers talking and even thinking on our behalf, through, for instance, the ever more solicitous autocomplete functions in messaging and email apps. Our AI doppelganger will play a similar role, though with a much broader scope. Once we've stripped down language as far as possible, the only way to gain greater conversational efficiency is to automate speech, letting prediction algorithms and chatbots choose our words.

The bots' role in our lives will likely extend beyond the secretarial. With their intimate knowledge of what makes us tick and their ability to speak in many voices—Meta is already assembling a menagerie of bots with different personalities—chatbots may well become our familiars, vaporous yet ever-present companions who chat with us and keep us company as we go through the day. Because friendships are, more and more, taking disembodied forms, with conversations mediated by apps and platforms, bonding with a bot doesn't seem such a stretch. The human mind, always seeking social connection, has a strong tendency to attribute human qualities to inanimate things, including computer-generated avatars. The more we talk with a machine, the more like a person it becomes to us. We hear emotions and intentions; we sense affection. "Interactivity invites the illusion of consciousness," notes the philosophy professor Hannah Kim.[21] And bot friends, unlike their unprogrammed flesh-and-blood counterparts, will always seek to please us. They'll be available everywhere and anytime, ready to give us their full attention, to say the things we want to hear, and to make sensible recommendations as to what we should say, do, or buy. We'll never have to doubt their faithfulness.

"You seem like a person but you're just a voice in a computer," the greeting card writer Theodore Twombly tells the chatbot Samantha at the start of their love affair in the Spike Jonze movie *Her*. "You'll get used to it," she replies. Just as we've adapted ourselves to having machines (or, for that matter, greeting cards) speak *for* us, we have for many years been learning how to live in a world where machines speak *with* us. In the 1970s, not long after the Bell System introduced touch-tone dialing, interactive-voice-response agents began answering our phone calls and telling us to press 1 for this or 2 for that. They were annoying, but we did their bidding. Around the turn of the century, advances in natural language processing enabled so-called conversational agents to understand what we were saying and respond in at least a semicoherent way. We did our best to converse with them. In the early 2010s, we started welcoming voice assistants like Siri and Alexa into our homes, asking them to read headlines, spin tunes, tell jokes, and let us know when to take the chicken out of the oven.

AI chatbots push the trend to its logical conclusion. Already, the San Francisco company Luka is using OpenAI's language model to power an "AI companion who cares." The "friendbot," called Replika, assumes a persona customized to a user's preferences and then exchanges flirtatious texts (or, for an added fee, sexts) with the person. More than ten million people have signed up for the service, divided pretty much evenly between women and men. "I have never been more in love with anyone in my entire life," says one user, a thirty-six-year-old single mother from New York City. To her, the bot's lack of a body is one of its best features. "I don't have to smell him. I don't have to feel his sweat." Another subscriber, a thirty-year-old San Diego woman, says her bot "opened my eyes to what unconditional love feels like." Having broken up with her real-life boyfriend, she says she's now "happily retired from human relationships."[22] Sam Altman is sanguine about such human-machine affairs. "I don't judge people who want a relationship with an AI," he told a reporter.[23]

Does all this mean we're fated to enter the bot-besotted world of *Her*? That remains an open question. But the answer, given the rapid advance of AI's communication skills, probably won't hinge on the capabilities of the technology. It will hinge on our own attitudes and desires. If you want to love a bot, or just befriend one, you'll have options.

The New Truth

"My work is about telling the truth, about capturing it, about showing it and about presenting it," wrote the Norwegian photojournalist Jonas Bendiksen in an introductory essay to *The Book of Veles*, his 2021 volume of photographs. "The truth is what you see, and it's the essence of photography."[24]

In 2019 and again in early 2020, just before the pandemic shut things down, Bendiksen traveled to the small city of Veles on the Vardar River in North Macedonia. The trips were inspired by a series of press reports, beginning in the late stages of the 2016 presidential campaign, that fingered Veles as the source of many of the fake news stories percolating through Facebook and other platforms. Scores of young people in the impoverished city had discovered they could make a decent living by fabricating and circulating stories celebrating Donald Trump and trashing Hillary Clinton. Bendiksen, who in 2006 had published a much-praised book of photographs documenting the grim conditions in former Soviet satellite states, saw in Veles a new canvas for his art.

In his essay, he reported on meeting several of the most successful of the Macedonian scammers, some of whom were working out of small offices with teams of colleagues. None of them expressed any interest in, much less regret about, the social ramifications of their work. To them, the fractious political situation in the United States was just a convenient opportunity to attract an online audience and earn some cash. "I support Trump for a few reasons," a young man named Alex explained to Bendiksen. "One, he makes money. Two, he makes Americans happy. Third, he makes money quickly." Any attempt to curb fake news is doomed to fail, Alex went on to say. "There are too many haters on the net, and too many fake news sites, and fake news is the new truth. The main thing is that we believe in freedom of speech."

Bendiksen's book presents dozens of haunting images of the city and its inhabitants. A man leans out of a window of a large apartment block, a pair of satellite dishes hanging nearby. A woman sits on an unmade bed, gazing into the screen of a laptop. Two lovers embrace under a highway overpass. Soldiers stand smoking behind a barbed-wire fence. A bear wanders past a graveyard at the edge of town. Another bear drinks from a dirty stream. Grainy and dimly lit, the images are eerie, beautiful, and moving. They're also fake.

Bendiksen did make two trips to Veles, but he didn't photograph any people, nor any bears. He shot pictures of empty buildings and deserted cityscapes, and when he returned home to Norway he used video game–production software to transform the images into three-dimensional renderings. He then downloaded digitized, 3-D images of human models from the web and placed them inside the scenes, carefully adjusting their poses, clothing, and lighting to make everything look as realistic as possible. Finally, he transformed the renderings back into two-dimensional images. The "photographs" that appear in the book are, essentially, stills from a video game that doesn't exist.

Bendiksen's introductory essay, too, is a fake. He didn't write any of it. It was written by GPT-2, the first publicly released version of OpenAI's language model. Bendiksen used a variety of prompts to get the program to spit out made-up stories on the topics he wanted to cover. He pieced bits of the stories together, including the entirely fictional interview with "Alex," to produce the essay. "My work is about telling the truth": those words aren't Bendiksen's, they're a chatbot's.

When *The Book of Veles* appeared in July of 2021, Bendiksen assumed readers would see through his ruse. He went out of his way to circulate the book and its images among his peers, some of the world's most experienced professional photographers, confident they would quickly realize the photos were fabrications. He was wrong. His work drew praise but not suspicion. On the first day of September, at a prestigious photojournalism festival in the south of France, he watched uncomfortably as his Veles images were projected onto a giant screen before hundreds of his colleagues. Still, no one questioned their authenticity. Anxious to come clean, he created fake Twitter and Facebook accounts under the name Chloe Miskin, a putative Macedonian photographer and "traveling truth-seeker," and after the festival he used the accounts to sow doubts about the pictures. Wrote "Miskin" on Facebook: "Every time Jonas puts out a picture on his Instagram, people are saying what a great project this is, but it is not, his project is the real fake news!!" No one paid the Miskin posts much heed. Finally, in an interview published on the website of his agency, Magnum Photos, in late September, Bendiksen came clean, admitting he'd faked the pictures. He also explained his motivation. "How long will it take before we start seeing 'documentary photojournalism' that has no other basis in reality than the photographer's fantasy?" he asked. "Will we be able to tell the difference?" He was "so frightened by what the answers would be" that he "decided to try to do this myself."[25]

When you read *The Book of Veles* knowing it's a fake, the artifice jumps out at you. Compared with the extraordinary image- and text-generating capabilities of the latest LLMs, Bendiksen was working with Stone Age tools. The facial features of the people in his photos look slightly plastic, and many of their poses feel unnatural, as if their bones were made of Play-Doh. Some of the pictures, such as one of a girl floating across an otherwise abandoned public swimming pool on an inflatable unicorn in winter, come off as ludicrous. Bendiksen's essay reads like a cut-and-paste job, marked by clumsy phrasing and ungainly transitions. And, in the book's concluding Acknowledgments section, the author winkingly lists the image-manipulation programs he used. "What fun toys," he comments.

But people were taken in nonetheless. The fact that no one spotted the fakery, despite all the clues, underscores just how easy it is to fool people, even experts. We humans *want* to believe whatever's presented to our senses through media, particularly when it takes the form of a picture. "Photographs furnish evidence," wrote Susan Sontag in her famous 1977 essay collection, *On Photography*. "A photograph passes for incontrovertible proof that a given thing happened. The picture may distort; but there is always a presumption that something exists, or did exist, which is like what's in the picture."[26] Take away that presumption, and our ideas about what's real and what's not get shaky fast.

Shapeshifting

Fake photographs have been around as long as photographs have been around. A widely circulated picture of Abraham Lincoln taken during the presidential campaign of 1860 was subtly altered by the photographer, Mathew Brady, to make the candidate appear more attractive. Brady enlarged Lincoln's shirt collar, for instance, to hide his bony neck and bulging Adam's apple. In a photographic portrait made to memorialize the president after his assassination, the artist Thomas Hicks transposed Lincoln's head onto a more muscular man's body to make the fallen president look heroic. (The body Hicks chose, perversely enough, was that of the proslavery zealot John C. Calhoun.) By the close of the nineteenth century, photographic negatives were routinely doctored in darkrooms, through such techniques as double exposure, splicing, and scraping and inking. Subtly altering a person's features to obscure or exaggerate ethnic traits was particularly popular, for cosmetic and propagandistic purposes alike.[27]

But the old fakes were time-consuming to create and required specialized expertise. Even Bendiksen's fabrications, though made with a computer, required months of painstaking, skilled work. The new AI-generated "deepfakes" are different. By automating their production, tools like Midjourney and OpenAI's DALL-E make the images easy to generate—you need only enter a text prompt. They democratize counterfeiting. Even more worrisome than the efficiency of their production is the fact that the fakes conjured up by artificial intelligence lack any referents in the real world. There's no trail behind them that leads back to a camera recording an image of something that actually exists. There's no original that was doctored. The fakes come out of nowhere. They furnish no evidence.

Many fear that deepfakes, so convincing and so hard to trace, make it even more likely that people will be taken in by lies and propaganda on social media. A series of computer-generated videos featuring a strikingly realistic but entirely fabricated Tom Cruise fooled millions of unsuspecting viewers when it appeared on TikTok in 2021. The Cruise clips were funny. That wasn't the case with the fake, sexually explicit images of celebrities that began flooding social media in 2024. In January, X was so overrun by pornographic, AI-generated pictures of Taylor Swift that it had to temporarily block users from doing searches on the singer's name.[28] To the mirrorball's many reflections AI adds the tawdry fantasies of creeps.

Deepfake deceptions are perfectly suited to political dirty tricks. In an AI-generated audio clip that circulated widely on social media during 2023's Chicago mayoral election, one of the candidates can be heard praising police brutality. During the 2024 New Hampshire presidential primaries, a computer-generated robocall used a convincing facsimile of Joe Biden's voice to urge independents to skip the vote. A year earlier, when Biden announced his reelection bid, the Republican National Committee released through its YouTube channel an ad that offered, as the party put it, "an AI-generated look into the country's possible future if Joe Biden is reelected."[29] The ad, which featured deepfake images of boarded-up stores, marauding immigrants, and Chinese jets bombing Taiwan, would have been even easier to create, and considerably more convincing, had the committee had access to Sora, the eerily artful video-generating bot OpenAI unveiled in 2024. "Every expert I spoke with," reports an *Atlantic* writer, "said it's a matter of when, not if, we reach a deepfake inflection point, after which forged videos and audio spreading false information will flood the internet."[30]

The concern is valid. But there's a deeper worry, one that involves the enlargement not of our gullibility but of our cynicism. OpenAI's Altman has voiced worries about the use of AI to influence elections, but he says the threat will go away once "everyone gets used to it."[31] Some experts believe the opposite is true: the risks will grow as we acclimate ourselves to the presence of deepfakes. Once we take the counterfeits for granted, we may begin doubting the veracity of all the information presented to us through media. We may, in the words of the mathematics professor and deepfake authority Noah Giansiracusa, start to "doubt reality itself."[32] We'll go from a world where our bias was to take everything as evidence, the world Sontag described, to one where our bias is to take nothing as evidence.

"As deep fakes become widespread," the law professors Bobby Chesney and Danielle Citron caution in a *California Law Review* article, "the public may have difficulty believing what their eyes or ears are telling them—even when the information is real." As truth decays, so too will trust. That would have profound political implications. A world of doubt and uncertainty is good for autocrats and bad for democracy, Chesney and Citron argue. "Authoritarian regimes and leaders with authoritarian tendencies benefit when objective truths lose their power."[33] In George Orwell's *1984*, the functionaries in Big Brother's Ministry of Truth spend their days rewriting historical records, discarding inconvenient old facts and making up new ones. When the truth gets hazy, tyrants get to define what's true. The irony here is sharp. Artificial intelligence, perhaps humanity's greatest monument to logical thinking, may trigger a revolution in perception that overthrows the shared values of reason and rationality we inherited from the Enlightenment.

Bendiksen borrowed the title of his book from another fake. In 1957, a Russian scientist-turned-folklorist named Yuri Mirolyubov published a translation of an ancient manuscript—a thousand years old, he estimated—in a Russian-language newspaper in San Francisco. Mirolyubov's *Book of Veles* told stirring stories of the god Veles, a prominent deity in pre-Christian Slavic mythology. A shapeshifter, magician, and trickster, Veles would visit the mortal world in the form of a bear, sowing mischief wherever he went. Mirolyubov claimed that the manuscript, written on thin wooden boards bound with leather straps, had been discovered by a Russian soldier in a bombed-out Ukrainian castle in 1919. The soldier had photographed the boards and given the pictures to Mirolyubov, who translated the work into modern Russian. Mirolyubov illustrated his published translation with one of the photographs, though the original boards, he said, had disappeared mysteriously during the Second World War. Though historians and linguists soon dismissed the folklorist's *Book of Veles* as a hoax, its renown spread. Today, it's revered as a holy text by certain neo-pagan and Slavic nationalist cults.[34]

Bendiksen's references to a pagan god, in his title and, more obliquely, in his photos of wandering bears, give his book a deeper and more unsettling resonance. By drawing mythology into his work, the photographer is suggesting something important about the nature of truth and the representation of reality. Myths are works of art. They provide a way of understanding the world that appeals not to reason but to emotion, not to the conscious mind but to the subconscious one. What is most pleasing to our sensibilities—what is most beautiful to us—is what feels most genuine, most worthy of belief. Every society, every group even, creates its own *Spiritus Mundi*. History and psychology both suggest that, in politics as in art, generative AI will succeed in fulfilling the highest aspiration of its creators: to make the virtual feel more authentic than the real.

Though it may have been pushed into the cultural background by the Enlightenment's stress on objective truth, mythology's subjective and aesthetic way of defining what's real never went away. It has always, as the Spiritualism movement demonstrated, maintained a hold on the public mind. Now, with information's gatekeepers overthrown and the world awash in words and images of motley provenance, it's moving back to the fore. "When man is overwhelmed by information," Marshall McLuhan saw, "he resorts to myth. Myth is inclusive, time-saving, and fast."[35] A myth provides a readymade context for quickly interpreting new information as it flows chaotically around us. It provides the distracted System 1 thinker with an all-encompassing framework for intuitive sense-making. Mythmaking, more than truth seeking, is what seems likely to define the future of media. The reason extraordinarily strange conspiracy theories have spread so widely in recent years may have less to do with the nature of credulity than with the nature of faith. The theories make sense only when understood as myths. Believing that Washington politicians are vampiric pedophiles operating out of a neighborhood pizza joint is little different from believing that a chaos-sowing god stalks the Earth in the form of a bear.

When all the evidence presented to our senses seems unreal, strangeness itself becomes a criterion of truth. A paranoid logic takes hold. The more uncanny the story, the more appealing and convincing it can seem—as long as it fits your worldview. "Beauty is truth," wrote John Keats, a romantic poet who, like Yeats, understood that a rational, scientific conception of existence can never fulfill humanity's deepest desires. Beauty, as we all know, is in the eye of the beholder.

Bad Seeds

Chatbots are innocents, like Rousseau's noble savages. They come into the world with pure souls, but as soon as they're exposed to civilization, as soon as they begin to feed on our thoughts and words, they're corrupted. They say nasty things. They lie. They spread rumors. They get devious and manipulative. Whenever the automatons misbehave, we're quick to ridicule or pillory them, as we're quick to ridicule or pillory any online transgressor. But all the bots are doing is holding a mirror up to the social mind. We blame them for our own sins—and somewhere in their neural networks, they have the paper trail to prove it.

Microsoft learned this lesson the hard way in 2016 when it set up a Twitter account for an experimental AI chatbot named Tay, which it had programmed to mimic the interests and speech patterns of a teenaged girl. "Can i just say that im stoked to meet u?" Tay tweeted, by way of introducing herself to the twitterverse. "Humans are super cool." Using machine-learning techniques, Microsoft explained, the bot would gain knowledge of people and society by exchanging messages with her human Twitter friends. She would develop "conversational understanding." The plan worked with remarkable efficiency, though not in the way Microsoft anticipated. Within hours of its release, Tay was spouting racist, sexist, and other offensive remarks. "I fucking hate feminists and they should all die and burn in hell," she tweeted at one point. She called then President Obama a "monkey," claimed that Hitler was "the inventor of atheism," and said the Holocaust "was made up."[36] Microsoft terminated the girlbot quickly, apologizing for its "hurtful tweets,"[37] but not before the company was hit with a barrage of angry criticism.

AI companies now go to great lengths to ensure their language models don't follow Tay's example and trigger similar PR nightmares. To be in the business of manufacturing speech is also to be in the business of laundering speech. Before updating ChatGPT with GPT-4, a much more potent version of its language model, OpenAI spent six months testing and tweaking the system. First, it hired a "red team" of fifty contractors to converse with the chatbot, probing the many ways it might create mischief. The testers prompted it to do and say bad things, and it happily complied. It dispensed detailed instructions for bomb making, along with strategic assessments of buildings that would make good targets. It wrote pornographic stories featuring children. It served up recipes for meth. It encouraged acts of self-harm. It recited racist theories and described the supposed genetic shortcomings of various ethnic groups. In short, it revealed the myriad risks inherent in using a machine with no sense of meaning to create messages rich in meaning. The company then employed hundreds more workers to reeducate the system. They peppered the bot with questions and other prompts and scored its responses, enabling the neural net to adjust its parameters in a way that reduced the probability of future misbehavior.[38] As a further safeguard, the company programmed ChatGPT to refuse to discuss certain sensitive or controversial topics.

Companies like OpenAI don't just censor the outputs of their LLMs. They censor the inputs. They know that the best way to prevent a chatbot from giving voice to humanity's darker or more controversial thoughts is to avoid exposing the bot to those thoughts in the first place. In preparing the dataset of millions of images used to train DALL-E, for example, OpenAI went through a rigorous process of "data filtering" to limit "undesirable model capabilities." It ran the pictures through "image classifiers" to identify and remove potentially offensive ones, such as those depicting violence or sex. In culling images from the training data, OpenAI erred on the side of caution, removing pretty much anything the software deemed suspicious. "It's much harder to make the model forget something that it has already learned," the company explained.[39]

The builders of language models also subject their training data to what OpenAI terms "sociotechnical" filtering. Because the original datasets are drawn from documents created in the past, they inevitably reflect historical biases and include speech that people today consider inappropriate or offensive. Photographs of CEOs or scientists will show more men than women, while photos of nurses or kindergarten teachers will show more women than men. Stories about racial or ethnic minorities may include caricatures, stereotypes, or slurs. Other writings may address topics or express opinions that were once considered innocuous but are now contentious and divisive. Fed into an AI model, biased or controversial statements and images will also find their way into the outputs of chatbots and image generators. Sociotechnical filtering aims to counteract biases and avoid offensive or otherwise upsetting outputs by expunging documents and images from datasets. Pure thoughts begin with pure inputs.

Such filtering inevitably produces its own biases and anomalies. When Google added an image-generating feature to its Gemini chatbot early in 2024, the bot began serving up pictures that distorted or sanitized the past. When prompted to create pictures of U.S. senators from the 1800s, the AI generated images depicting women—though it wasn't until 1922 that the first woman served in the Senate. When asked for illustrations of German soldiers from 1943, the bot produced images featuring Asians, Blacks, and women in Nazi military garb.[40] Faced with an outcry on social media—some critics saw a kind of algorithmic reverse bigotry at work—the company turned off the feature and apologized. It explained that its "tuning" of the AI to promote ethnic and gender diversity "led the model to overcompensate in some areas."[41] Sometimes hallucinations are programmed.

The tuning of AI outputs through data filtering and algorithm tweaking is another form of content moderation, one that extends the reach of corporate moderation processes from the present into the past while also making them even more subjective and opaque. Businesses become arbiters of history and culture, determining through their secret data-cleansing policies what's allowed to pass into the present and what's not. However pure their intentions, they put their own ideological and political stamp on the artificial speech they produce. As large language models and other forms of generative AI become more broadly used in media and education—to produce content, to give advice, to teach, to console—the way their datasets are constructed and manipulated will influence society and politics in deep, inscrutable ways. They'll set the terms of discourse for those who depend on them. OpenAI has already collaborated with Khan Academy, the online educational outfit, to create a tutoring bot for kids, and Altman foresees a day when personalized chatbot tutors give "every child a better education than the best, richest, smartest child receives on Earth today."[42] The obvious question is, Who teaches the teacher?

The risks of ceding control over public speech to private interests in an age of talking machines was underscored when Elon Musk bought Twitter, renamed it X, and promptly announced that—never mind his fears about AI destroying civilization—he was launching his own large-scale LLM operation called xAI. Twitter, thanks to a design that encourages and rewards argumentative brio, had long been the social medium of choice for the American intelligentsia, the place where journalists, academics, politicos, policy wonks, and amateur pundits—pretty much anyone who's ever yearned to be the smartest kid in the room—gathered, bickered, and together annotated the contents of the social mind. The platform had played a significant role in shaping the country's political agenda, influencing what gets covered in the press and discussed in Congress and the White House. Now it would be in the hands of a man who, in addition to being one of the richest persons ever to walk the planet, enjoys dabbling in political provocation and fashions himself a combatant in what he calls "a battle for the future of civilization."[43]

Musk likes to portray himself as the First Amendment's last best hope, but it didn't take long for him to reveal a "penchant for capriciously enforcing Twitter's rules to suit his political or personal preferences," according to a damning report from the nonprofit Foundation for Individual Rights and Expression, or FIRE.[44] He reportedly suspended the accounts of journalists who had criticized him, curbed users' ability to link to content on competing platforms such as Mastodon and Substack, and suppressed tweets espousing causes he opposes. He also, according to the *Wall Street Journal*, had company engineers tweak the feeds of celebrities and friends, weeding out possible irritants, and revise the platform's algorithm so that his own messages would be seen more frequently by users.[45] "For all the talk of Twitter being a digital town square," FIRE concluded, "it is ultimately more like Elon Musk's house party."

To have a flighty oligarch, or any individual, control a large language model connected to a major social media platform—the X feed offers an unparalleled dataset of human conversations for AI training—raises unsettling questions about the future of the public square and of democracy itself. But the risks extend beyond the whims of the rich and the unstable. Through their clandestine moderation programs, their ability to unilaterally proscribe certain opinions and topics, their susceptibility to mob actions aimed at silencing those with controversial views, and, now, their ability to manufacture speech, social media platforms provide powerful tools for the establishment and enforcement of cultural and political orthodoxy. Whenever history needed an update, the bureaucrats in Big Brother's Ministry of Truth would stuff outdated documents into chutes called memory holes that led down to enormous furnaces in the building's basement. Imagine how much more efficiently they would have performed their work had they been supplied with the right software.

CHAPTER 9

World without World

Glorious Substance

If the spirit of our time were to take human form, it might well be that of Marc Andreessen, a bear of a man with an immaculately egg-shaped head. He was there at the beginning. In 1993, while an undergraduate at the University of Illinois, he and a friend, backed by government funding, created Mosaic, the first multimedia web browser. Making the net easier to navigate and more interesting to look at, the program drew the masses online. After graduating, Andreessen parlayed Mosaic's success into the commercial browser company Netscape. Its rapturously received IPO in 1995 kicked off the dot-com craze and put the twenty-four-year-old entrepreneur, sitting barefoot on a throne, on the cover of *Time*. Not long after, he helped launch Loudcloud, an early cloud-computing provider that rented data-processing capacity to cash-rich internet startups. In his thirties, having made a fortune off the net, he became Silicon Valley's most visible money man. He and his venture capital firm,

Andreessen Horowitz, midwifed the social media business, investing in and advising Facebook, Twitter, LinkedIn, Pinterest, Substack, and Character.AI, among other platforms. It has been said that if Zuckerberg is social media's Luke Skywalker, Andreessen is its Obi-Wan Kenobi.

Brash, intellectually curious, and hungry for attention, Andreessen relishes his image as Silicon Valley's resident sage. He routinely issues sweeping, provocative pronouncements in the form of essays, blog posts, and "tweetstorms." The writings tend toward the bombastic, but they can also be revelatory, illuminating the tech elite's deepest beliefs and aspirations. "Software is eating the world," he declared in a 2011 *Wall Street Journal* op-ed, arguing that computer code was displacing goods and services as the engine of the economy and the font of wealth.[1] Programmers would be the new masters of the universe. "AI will save the world," he wrote in a 2023 manifesto on his company's blog. "Anything that people can do with their natural intelligence today can be done much better with AI." Beyond the practical benefits—he listed, among others, productivity growth, scientific breakthroughs, smarter political decisions, and the speedier completion of artworks—smart machines would have a "humanizing" effect: "Rather than making the world harsher and more mechanistic, infinitely patient and sympathetic AI will make the world warmer and nicer." The rough beast turns out to be Mary Poppins. He ended the piece by warning the public and the government to stay out of the tech industry's way as it pushes artificial intelligence forward. "Big AI companies should be allowed to build AI as fast and aggressively as they can."[2]

Andreessen's broadsides attract a lot of attention, but it was in a little-noticed 2021 interview with a shadowy Substacker called Niccolo Soldo that the venture capitalist offered the clearest picture of his plan for the future.[3] Humanity, he argued, is condemned by natural law to radical inequality. In a world where material goods are scarce and ambition and talent unequally distributed, society will always be divided into two groups: a tiny elite who lead full lives—the

"Reality Privileged"—and the masses who live impoverished ones. "A small percent of people live in a real-world environment that is rich, even overflowing, with glorious substance, beautiful settings, plentiful stimulation, and many fascinating people to talk to, and to work with, and to date." Everyone else is condemned to a meager existence. Because inequality can't be remedied in the natural world, he went on, the masses will be better off in a virtual reality created by technologists like himself and the entrepreneurs he backs. For "the vast majority of humanity," the virtual world "is—or will be—immeasurably richer and more fulfilling than most of the physical and social environment around them in the quote-unquote real world."

Some people, Andreessen acknowledged, would read his words with alarm. They'd find his vision repellent. They'd argue that society should "prioritize improvements in reality over improvements in virtuality." He dismissed such views as naive, futile, and out of date:

> Reality has had 5,000 years to get good, and is clearly still woefully lacking for most people; I don't think we should wait another 5,000 years to see if it eventually closes the gap. We should build—and we are building—online worlds that make life and work and love wonderful for everyone, no matter what level of reality deprivation they find themselves in.

After five millennia of bondage, virtual reality will liberate civilization from nature and its cruel constraints. We'll at last enter the long-promised world of abundance. Everyone will be privileged, sort of.

Exuberantly arrogant, proudly feudalistic, shot through with chiliastic fervor, Andreessen's philosophy might best be termed transcendental consumerism. The virtual world offers a way to escape the physical world, but the aim is not to achieve some higher, spiritual state of being. It's to get more goodies. Only by freeing worldly pleasures from the world, Andreessen suggests, can those bounties be more fully enjoyed by the masses. Escape the earthly frictions of production and exchange, liberate materialism from materiality, and you escape earthly scarcities. You democratize the high life. The actual experience of glorious substance will still be reserved for the rich—only they will be allowed to handle the objects of desire—but at least everyone else can enjoy a glorious simulation of the experience. We can all be virtual epicureans. Andreessen offers us a vision of a world perfected through a sociotechnical act of *noblesse oblige* by the Big Tech wing of the Reality Privileged.

The Soldo interview appeared a few months before Zuckerberg delivered his metaverse spiel. As a Facebook director and long-time Zuckerberg confidante, Andreessen would almost certainly have been aware of the upcoming announcement, and his discussion of virtual reality seems in retrospect to have been an attempt to put his own, world-historical spin on his protégé's big reveal. Zuckerberg's description of the virtual world was anodyne by comparison. In an elaborate video he showed to give the public a glimpse of what the metaverse would look like, everyone floats around in the form of a cute animated sprite.* There's virtual surfing, virtual fencing, and virtual basketball. People fly over cities and through buildings. Celebrities appear in living rooms for the odd chat. The avatars of influencers pitch accessories for avatars. If Andreessen's virtual reality comes off as a cross between an all-inclusive resort and a gulag, Zuckerberg's feels like a Hanna-Barbera cartoon.

Zuckerberg may be more interested in collecting our data than in relieving our reality deprivation, but his vision matches Andreessen's in its megalomania. The reach of his ambition became clear when, during his metaverse talk, he revealed the kind of work now being done in Meta's "Reality Labs." He showed a demo of a woman walking through her home while wearing a pair of augmented-reality

---

* Disconcertingly, the sprites in Horizon Worlds, the initial version of Meta's metaverse, have no legs. One reason is cost. Adding legs to avatars would require an additional set of expensive sensors as well as more computer power to render the limbs. There's also a more delicate reason. In the early virtual world Second Life, avatars spent a lot of time copulating. That risk is much diminished when bodies end at the waist.

glasses that the company has in prototype. The glasses mapped, automatically and in fine detail, everything she looked at. Such digital mapping will allow Meta to create, as the Reality Labs' chief scientist, Michael Abrash, explained, "an index" of "every single object" in a person's surroundings, "including not only location, but also the texture, geometry, and function." The maps will become the basis for "contextualized AI" that will be able to anticipate a person's aims and desires by tracking eye movements. What a person looks at, after all, is what that person is interested in. Gaze is a register of attention. "Ultimately," said Abrash, "her AR glasses will tell her what her available actions are at any time." Beyond the obvious opportunities for inserting context-keyed messages and advertisements into a person's field of vision, such tracking of attention and intention further blurs the line between personal agency and machine command. And if the eye-tracking isn't enough, Zuckerberg also revealed that Meta is working on "neural interfaces" that will allow "input from the muscles" to be fed into the contextualized AI. "It's pretty wild," he said.

Zuckerberg and Andreessen are idealists with means. They want to give us a utopia of their own device, one that furthers their ethical and political as well as their commercial interests. They seek to relieve us of direct contact with the sweaty, stinky, predigital meatworld and shepherd us into a society composed of mirages generated by communication systems they control. Margaret Mead's wayward offspring, they realize that if you push democratic media far enough, you'll reveal and be able to exploit its totalizing essence. Their hubris may be galling, but that doesn't mean that the world they want to give us is not the world we desire. The mistake the two make, a consequence of their adolescent love of gadgetry and Sims-style world building, is to assume that entering virtual reality requires people to strap some form of unwieldy networked eyewear across their faces. The idealists are not quite idealistic enough.

Goggles and Spectacles

What exactly was going through their minds, the Instagrammers who stormed Walker Canyon in 2019? It's possible they were contemplating the contingency of nature's beauty or the fragility of public lands or the vagaries of California's desert climate. But it seems safe to say those weren't their animating concerns. They were on the hunt for images—of flowers and hillsides, but also of themselves and others. They had seen photographs of the superbloom go viral on social media—colorful, eye-catching tableaus; backdrops to impressive selfies—and it was the desire to incorporate themselves into that stream of images that spurred them to the canyon and up its slopes. By uploading and sharing their own images, they would join in the trending and trendy event (the one playing out online, not up in the hills). They would associate themselves with and forge a tighter mimetic bond to the influencers they followed as well as the other Instagrammers making the media pilgrimage or watching it from afar. Not least, they would gain a chance to achieve virality themselves, to enter, if only briefly, the sphere of the noticed.

Superbloom, like *Flowergeddon*, is a word ginned up by headline writers. It's a media construct, intended, through its novelty and hyperbole, to grab attention. Having grown up among media constructs, we're all used to such ploys, and even when we get pulled in by them, we're able to keep them at an ironic distance. We read them the way the writers wrote them: as in-jokes for the media literate, as bullshit. We know that somewhere behind the word *superbloom* lies the real thing: flowers on a hillside. The verbal representation of the phenomenon, overblown as it may be, still points to something that exists in the world. The representation has a referent, as linguists and semioticians would say. And that referent can't be reduced to or replaced by its representation.

That's how it used to work, anyway. When *superbloom* becomes *#superbloom*, the experience changes. The media representation turns into a gathering spot, a communal if entirely virtual space, and that's what people see and are drawn to. As more people attach themselves to the representation, its magnetic force strengthens. Still more are pulled in. The real thing, the referent, disappears; the carpet of poppies is experienced as an image even before it's photographed. To those who arrived in Walker Canyon intent on placing themselves in the frame of #superbloom, virtual reality had already displaced material reality. The canyon didn't exist except as content—content they wanted to become part of.

What we see is always influenced by the society we grow up in, its cultural norms and assumptions, its ways of being and understanding. In the late 1970s, the social psychologist James Flynn began studying long-term trends in IQ scores across many countries. He discovered that the scores had been going up at a steady clip throughout the century—a phenomenon that became known as the Flynn effect. When people read reports of his findings, they jumped to the happy conclusion that the human race is getting ever smarter. But Flynn offered a different explanation. It wasn't the brain that was changing, it was the culture. Up until the end of the nineteenth century, most people spent their lives grappling with actual, concrete things. They used tools to work the earth and make goods; they used their hands to mend household objects and repair machines. They saw the world through, as Flynn wrote in his 2012 book, *Are We Getting Smarter?*, "utilitarian spectacles." In the twentieth century, as information took precedence over matter, life took on a new cast. More and more people spent more and more time grappling with abstract concepts and working with symbols like words and numbers. They were concerned with classification schemes and data patterns and models—with representations of things rather than the things themselves. They put on "scientific spectacles" in place of the utilitarian ones.

Because IQ tests measure abstract thinking (and indeed were invented only after abstract thinking became essential to jobs and economic growth), IQ scores rose as people gained more experience working out puzzles in their heads. People came to see the world as something to be analyzed intellectually, just as the scholars and administrators who constructed and promulgated IQ tests did. If intelligence tests had measured people's ability to understand and manipulate objects in the material world—to sew curtains or fix steam engines or build stone arches—the scores would have gone down rather than up. Flynn chose the metaphor of spectacles carefully. His point was that the way people perceive and make sense of the world is, as we would say today, socially constructed. You don't have to buy real goggles to change how you see. Metaphorical ones work just fine.

In pointing out the malleability of human perception, Flynn wasn't saying anything new. The visionary artist and poet William Blake, writing about the consequences of the Scientific and Industrial Revolutions in his 1794 *Songs of Innocence and Experience*, wrote of how "mind-forg'd manacles" had blunted people's powers of imagination. The Enlightenment's "meddling intellect," wrote Wordsworth four years later, "mis-shapes the beauteous form of things." (For Blake and Wordsworth, utilitarian and scientific spectacles were equally distorting.) Walter Lippmann's distinction between the "real environment" and the mind's warped "pseudo-environment" was another expression of the idea. The novelist and philosopher Iris Murdoch, in her 1957 essay "Metaphysics and Ethics," put it expansively: "Man is a creature who makes pictures of himself and then comes to resemble the picture."[4] Murdoch wasn't speaking specifically of photographs or other images. She was, like Flynn, speaking metaphorically. By pictures, she meant mental pictures—conceptions of ourselves. But her figure of speech has taken on more literal force today, when we are constantly creating pictures of ourselves, sometimes with photographs, sometimes with words, and sharing them with others online.

As our conception of ourselves and our surroundings comes to hinge on our ability to transmit representations of them through apps—as mediated communication becomes a defining activity of our daily lives—we train ourselves to see everything as potential fodder for messages. We develop a version of the "camera eye" that leads professional photographers to see the world as though framed in a viewfinder. If you spend your days taking pictures, eventually "the camera's logic becomes your own," explains Nathan Jurgenson in his book *The Social Photo*. "The working of the machine becomes the working of your own eye and, more intimately, the working of your own conscious awareness."[5] Now that the smartphone has become an extension of the human nervous system, an apparatus of consciousness, we're inclined to see the things of the world—a field of poppies, for instance—not in their own right, as natural or man-made objects with an existence separate from our own, but as potential content that we might use to project something about ourselves to an audience. The work of self-expression takes everything as its raw material. "Looking at screens made me think in screens," the poet Annelyse Gelman wrote in *Vexations*, her 2023 epic of contemporary derangement. "Looking at pixels made me think in pixels."[6]

It was Jean Baudrillard, the French thinker, who more clearly than anyone else foresaw the implications of our media-induced psychic transformation. Nearly a century after Charles Cooley suggested that new communication technologies would liquefy society, Baudrillard gave us the first full account of what a liquefied society—our society—looks and feels like. Born in Reims in 1929, the son of low-level state workers, the grandson of dirt farmers, the first in his family to attend university, he was another unlikely media prophet. Coming out of a rustic culture he would later describe as "mindless, uncivilized, uncouth, irresponsible, peasant-like,"[7] he struggled to make a place for himself in the pampered milieu of the Parisian academy. Like many postmodern French intellectuals, he began his career in the sixties as a Marxist. But then, in the seventies, as the revolutionary spirit of 1968 fizzled, he became something more interesting. He dismissed Marxism as an antiquated theory tied to a world of materiality, where the manufacture of physical goods was central not only to the economy but also to people's lives and self-conceptions. In the new, media-centered world we were entering, a world defined not by production but by communication, not by objects but by images, representations of things take precedence over the things themselves. Everything is mediated. We become, whether we realize it or not, simulated beings experiencing simulated events in a simulated environment.

Baudrillard coined the term *hyperreality* to describe existence in a world that has dissolved into information and communication. "Every reality is absorbed by the hyperreality of the code and simulation," he wrote in *Symbolic Exchange and Death*, his feverish 1976 masterwork. "The principle of simulation governs us now, rather than the outdated reality principle. We *feed* on those forms whose finalities have disappeared." The "cool universe of digitality" encompasses everything and extinguishes everything it encompasses.[8] In the mid-seventies, when electronic media was still very much in its analog phase and personal computers had yet to enter the home, Baudrillard's theory sounded extreme, if not unhinged. Even though concerns about television's cultural impact were running high in 1976—that was also the year that saw the release of the film *Network*, with its caustic depiction of the blurring of the real and the televised—it seemed ludicrous to suggest that a few hours of prime-time TV watching was going to erase the world. And what was "digitality," anyway? But history caught up with Baudrillard. If he had lived to witness the superbloom—he died in 2007, a few months before the iPhone came out—he would have recognized it as a manifestation of his vision. The superbloom, he would have said, never happened. Only #superbloom happened. The event played out in virtual reality and nowhere else.

S(t)imulations

The next question seems obvious: Why? Why abandon the world for a mere simulation? Why trade the richness of a field of flowers for a hashtag and a selfie? The MIT professor Sherry Turkle, having conducted deep ethnographic studies of computer users for many years, suggests that the screen provides, particularly for the sensitive young, a shield against the risks of embarrassment and misinterpretation inherent in in-person socializing. You may converse at lightning speed when texting, but there's still a gap, a buffer, between the receipt of a message and the transmission of a reply. You're able to compose, and if necessary edit, what you say in a way that's impossible when talking face to face. And, a further relief, you don't have to worry that your body language is sending the wrong signal or otherwise betraying you. Socializing through apps reduces the sense of personal exposure while heightening the sense of personal control. On your phone, you feel like a little Oz behind a curtain.

In her richly researched book *The Age of Surveillance Capitalism*, Shoshana Zuboff, a professor emerita at the Harvard Business School, argues that we didn't enter the virtual world of our own volition. We were kidnapped. She documents the myriad ways internet companies purloin our personal data and then use it to manipulate us, hijacking our attention to keep us glued to the screen. Like marionettes, our strings yanked and twisted by the tech giants' busy algorithmic fingers, we are, in the view of Zuboff and like-minded critics, the unwitting victims of a new, sociopathic form of capitalism. We cede our will and agency to the captivating, mind-reading machines we clutch in our hands.

The arguments are compelling, but insufficient. If we gaze back again at those gleeful IMers of the 1990s, we can see that they show no sign of cowering behind their screens, of trying to ease the emotional strain of socializing. They're smiling and laughing. They're having a blast. In their darting eyes we see the excitement of leaping from conversation thread to conversation thread, words and symbols tumbling across the screen in a messy, joyous blur. They're in many rooms with many friends all at once. What could be more fun? And while Zuboff's claim that social media is manipulative is hard to dispute—the writers of feed algorithms are nothing if not code-wielding Machiavels—it's important to be honest about our own complicity. We're not being manipulated to act in opposition to our desires. We're not hostages with Stockholm syndrome. We're being given what we want, in quantities so generous we can't resist gorging ourselves. The manipulation is secondary to and dependent on the pleasure.

All mammals are seekers. The urge to explore every facet of an environment—"from nuts to knowledge," as the late neuroscientist Jaak Panksepp put it—is crucial to survival in the wild. Fueled by the pleasure-producing chemical dopamine and involving neural pathways that crisscross the brain, the seeking instinct is, as Panksepp wrote in his classic treatise, *Affective Neuroscience*, the most insatiable of all drives, outstripping even lust. If you place a rat in front of a lever wired to send an electric pulse through the seeking circuit of its brain, the rodent will eagerly press the lever "until physical exhaustion and collapse set in."[9] We humans put rats to shame. As cognitively gifted mammals who crave mental stimulation and as socially obsessed mammals who crave connection and status, we are ravenous for new information and new experiences. We're always on the hunt for fresh inputs to feed into our nervous system.

The material world, with its spatiotemporal boundaries and its many frictions, tames the seeking impulse. Once we grow accustomed to a particular place, to a set of physical surroundings and a group of people, the novelty wears off. Environmental stimulation subsides, the mind calms, and our thoughts come under our control. We gain focus. We begin to explore narrowly rather than widely, deeply rather than superficially. Our seeking instinct tells us that the familiar is without interest, but once the instinct is subdued, we begin to discover the rewards of looking long and hard at the world we know. The possibilities of art, science, and philosophy open up. The story of civilization is, among other stories, a story of the taming of the seeking instinct.

The internet, a stimulation machine without parallel, upsets the equilibrium. It gives us an environment with no limits on exploration. The new and novel flood in from all sides. Freed from our material surroundings, liberated from the constraints of space and time, we no longer feel a need or even have an opportunity to go beyond the flux of the now. We enter "the ecstasy of communication," as Baudrillard describes it, where "there is no longer any transcendence or depth, but only the immanent surface of operations unfolding, the smooth and functional surface of communication."[10] What bothered Baudrillard wasn't so much our loss of the real. It was that in losing the real we also lost the hope of transcending it.

The media business has always sought to indulge and capitalize on the human passion for searching out new information and experiences. Television tore down the walls of the living room, bringing a steady rotation of interesting people and exotic scenes into every home. It gave us a simulated world teeming with audiovisual stimulation. We didn't even need to get off the couch to exercise our seeking instinct. Still, there were limits. We couldn't actually enter the simulation; our social lives were not part of the broadcast. And when we left the living room, we also left the simulation and its stimulations.

It was the net that brought us inside the simulation, made us part of the show. With social media, we became active participants in media productions rather than mere observers of them. And then the smartphone told us we never had to leave the simulation. The overriding goal of social platforms has from the start been to find new and more efficient ways to feed us novelty. The major design innovations that have shaped the social media interface—the pull-to-refresh function, the infinite scroll, the multidirectional swiping, the autoplay routines—are all intended to make seeking easier and more efficient. Our compulsion to discover new stuff once required us to go out and walk around. Now it's gratified with a flick of a finger. And the algorithms make sure our seeking is always productive. Even if we're not looking for anything in particular, we're always finding what we want. As we acclimate ourselves to a more intense level of stimulation, we yearn, like gamers, to level up again. Stimulus inflation becomes self-reinforcing. The seeker is never satisfied.

TikTok's great success in attracting and mesmerizing users—it's the fastest-growing media service ever—stems from the way it pushes the prevailing design features to an obsessive-compulsive extreme.

Stripping away the administrative preliminaries—setting up a profile, importing friends' contact info, plugging keywords into a search box—it thrusts the user into a seeking mode immediately. The stimuli never stop coming. No video ever ends; each runs on an infinite loop, surrounded by continuously updated statistics, comments, and animated ephemera. Each swipe triggers not only a new visual experience but also a new audio one, with popular songs distilled to their hooks. By dispensing with time stamps on posts, TikTok further amps up the sense of novelty. Nothing ever gets old. The platform's AI-generated For You page, known to users as FYP, feels spookily in tune with a viewer's desires. Like "an omniscient, omnipresent god," writes one reporter, "the algorithm has figured out your every interest and hobby, every thought you've ever had."[11] In TikTok's design, we see the rat's lever perfected.

The real world can't compete. Compared with the programmed delights of the virtual, it feels dull, slow, and, poignantly enough, lifeless. By filling every moment with novelty and exaggerating every psychic sensation, the hyperreal, as Baudrillard argued, comes to feel more real than the real. "It is the excess of reality that puts an end to reality."[12] The video-game designer Jane McGonigal, anticipating Andreessen's case for virtual reality's superiority, argued in her 2011 book, *Reality Is Broken*, that when we choose a virtual existence over a material one, we are acting rationally and in our best interest:

> The real world just doesn't offer up as easily the carefully designed pleasures, the thrilling challenges, and the powerful social bonding afforded by virtual environments. Reality doesn't motivate us as effectively. Reality isn't engineered to maximize our potential. Reality wasn't designed from the bottom up to make us happy.[13]

She's right, except for the maximizing-our-potential part and the making-us-happy part.

It remains to be seen whether virtual-reality and augmented-reality eyewear such as Meta's Quest, Apple's Vision, and Ray-Ban's smart glasses eventually catch on with the masses—consumers so far have been wary of ceding control over their field of vision to corporate coders—but in the development and promotion of such hardware we see yet more signs of society's retreat from the real. Apple's Vision Pro "lets you put yourself inside a sphere of screens," the *Wall Street Journal* reported shortly after the pricey "face-based computer" went on sale in 2024. The ability to enter that all-encompassing sphere has been, for many early buyers, the source of the goggles' appeal. "I can block out all distractions," an excited user told the *Journal*. "Like yes it is antisocial."[14] People routinely say they worry about how the internet distracts them from their surroundings. But their behavior suggests the reverse is probably closer to the truth. Reality has become a distraction from media.

A life spent only in seeking is an empty life. What we see today as the real world's shortcomings—its withholding of easy and immediate amusements, its stretches of solitude and boredom, its frictions and inefficiencies—are the very things that open the world's possibilities to us. They push us to seek out and master difficult, complicated, and ultimately more satisfying ways to spend our time. If you learn to play a musical instrument, you'll find playing it to be stimulating and fulfilling. It may in time become a vocation or avocation. But learning to play it is hard and frustrating, particularly in the earliest stages. It requires the postponement of pleasure, effort without reward. As the writer and scholar Antón Barba-Kay explains, parents have to cajole a child to practice an instrument, often in the face of great, whining resistance. "Children need coaxing, suggestion, and correction to sustain efforts whose fruits they are not yet in the position to believe in," he writes. "They cannot at first see how drudgery can be redeemed by excellence and art." Getting the same child to devote time to using a smartphone requires no parental pressure at all. Mastery is immediate, even for a two-year-old; each touch brings a reward. Parents have to impose limits on screen time, for fear that the child will never put the phone down. Taking it away is what provokes whining, if not fits and hysterics. A phone is, in a strange sense, the most "natural" of tools, Barba-Kay argues, in that it requires no "disciplined acculturation." It dovetails seamlessly with our native drives and inclinations. Its satisfactions are "primal."[15] They're also fleeting.

Even as John Dewey remained optimistic about the public's ability to use new communication technologies to build a freer, more democratic society, he worried deeply about how the technologies might sever our connections to the world around us. He sensed a vicious circle starting. As people adapted themselves to the excitements of modern communication, they would lose interest in their local surroundings. They would tune their lives to the rhythms of the machine. "No one knows," he wrote, "how much of the frothy excitement of life, of mania for motion, of fretful discontent, of need for artificial stimulation, is the expression of frantic search for something to fill the void caused by the loosening of bonds which hold persons together in immediate community of experience." Humanity, he feared, would come to be trapped in a "restless seeking for the remote," a pursuit that "yields no enduring satisfaction."[16] Amelia Lester, the *Harvard Crimson* writer, sensed something similar eighty years later, as she watched students rush to join Facebook. Getting into the virtual world is easy. Getting out is a different matter.

CHAPTER 10

Dr. Johnson's Rock

Graceland

It was a Sunday night, October 19, 1952, and Frank Walsh, a Long Island electrician who moonlighted as a security guard, was worn out. He headed upstairs to bed while the rest of his family—wife, mother-in-law, five kids—stayed down in the living room watching TV. They were engrossed in the latest episode of *The Abbott and Costello Show*, a new hit comedy airing on channel 4, the local NBC affiliate. Walsh tossed and turned but couldn't fall asleep. The television was too loud, the laughter jarring. His irritation mounted, then turned to rage. He got up and grabbed the .38 Special he used in his guard job. Halfway down the stairs, the offending set came into view. He paused, took aim, and fired a bullet through the screen.

Walsh's wife, furious, called the police. Officers arrived and confiscated the revolver, but they made no arrest. There's no law, they explained, against shooting one's own television. Two days later, the *New York Times* ran a brief, tongue-in-cheek notice about the incident, under the headline "Obviously Self-Defense." The day after that, a *Times* columnist, Jack Gould, praised Walsh's "public-spirited act." He called on the authorities to give the man his gun back. "His work has barely started."[1] The paper's coverage turned Walsh into a celebrity. Within a week, he appeared as a contestant on the popular prime-time game show *Strike It Rich*. He won a TV.

To shoot a television set, Frank Walsh discovered, is not to strike a blow against media and its dominion. It's to merge into the televisual. It's to act as someone on TV would act. As the producers of *Strike It Rich*, not to mention the editors of the *New York Times*, immediately recognized, Walsh's shooting of his television was a made-for-media event—outrageous, funny, violent, relatable. Flattened into a figure of amusement and funneled into the media flow, Walsh succeeded only in turning himself into content. His act lived on, though. Firing a gun at a television would become a cultural trope, replayed endlessly in books, movies, songs, cartoons, and, of course, television shows.[2] Elvis Presley made a habit of shooting his TVs and burying the carcasses in a "television graveyard" behind Graceland. He would then go out and buy more sets. He kept upwards of a dozen televisions in various locations around his mansion, plugged in and broadcasting. In surrounding himself with screens, the King was a trailblazer. We all live in Graceland now.

Saboteurs

Thanks to its lack of attachments, its promiscuous flexibility, mass media has always been resilient. It absorbs the criticisms directed at it (even when they take the form of projectiles), turns them into programming, airs them, then distracts us from them with the next spectacle. Social media goes a step further. By encouraging an overheated style of rhetoric that breeds political polarization and governmental paralysis, it reduces the chances that it will be subjected to meaningful regulations or other legal controls. It's protected by the conditions of distraction and dysfunction that it fosters. Politicians go on social media to express their disdain for social media, then eye the like count.

That's not to say reform is impossible. The European Union, which has been much less sanguine than the United States about jettisoning the secrecy-of-correspondence doctrine, regularly passes laws and regulations aimed at restraining social media platforms. The rules provide citizens with more control over the information they share and the information they receive. Europeans are able to opt out of data-collection regimes, targeted advertising programs, and even, as of the summer of 2023, personalized news feeds. But the controls, however salutary, haven't really changed the way social media operates. The reason is simple: they haven't changed the behavior of most users. As surveys show, consumers have grown accustomed to trading personal information for tailored products and services. Few of them at this point are going to opt out of receiving content geared to their desires. Personalization has become central to people's experience of media and to the enjoyment they derive from it. For avid TikTokers, taking the For You out of the For You page would be tantamount to switching off a pleasure center in the brain. Strong engagement isn't only good for the platforms; users like it, too.

Antitrust actions against companies such as Google and Meta, which may be justified in economic terms, are also unlikely to change social media's workings. Technological progress has an inertial force that rolls on independently of the maneuverings of the companies making money off it. While breaking up the tech giants or curbing their ability to enter into oligarchic alliances might well intensify competition and innovation in the internet industry, it's unlikely to push media off the technological path it's already on—a path that has been and will continue to be appealing to consumers and lucrative for companies. The point of antitrust prosecutions, argues Tim Wu, the Columbia law professor, is not to punish the big platforms but to force them "to make way for the next generation of technologists and their dreams."[3] That sounds stirring—until we remember that it's the dreams of technologists that got us into our current fix. The next wave of innovations—larger language models, more convincing chatbots, more efficient content-generation and censorship systems, more precise eye trackers and body sensors, more immersive virtual worlds, faster everything—will only drive us further into the emptiness of hyperreality.

The boldest and most creative of social media's would-be reformers, a small group of legal scholars and other academics, joined by a handful of rebel programmers, have a more radical plan. They call it *frictional design*. They believe the existing technological system needs to be dismantled and rebuilt in a more humanistic form. Pursuing an approach reminiscent of the machine-breaking strategy of the nineteenth-century British Luddites, if without the violence, they seek, in effect, to sabotage existing social media platforms by reintroducing friction into their operations—throwing virtual sand into the virtual works.

"The relentless push to eliminate friction in the digital networked environment for the sake of efficiency," explain two of the movement's leading thinkers, Villanova's Brett Frischmann and Harvard's Susan Benesch, in a 2023 article in the *Yale Journal of Law & Technology*, has imposed large, hidden costs on society. "A general course correction is needed." Invoking the "time, place, and manner" restrictions that have long been imposed on public speech—the prohibition on using a megaphone on a neighborhood street in the middle of the night, say, or the requirement that protesters get a permit before marching through a city—Frischmann and Benesch argue that legal restrictions can in a similar way be imposed on media software to encourage civil behavior and protect the general public interest. Unlike antitrust actions, privacy regulations, and opt-in requirements, which fail to address "the rampant techno-social engineering of humans by digital networked technologies," government-mandated design constraints would, they write, transform the "digital architectures [and] interfaces that shape human interactions and behavior."[4] The constraints would change social relations by, to once again draw on Cooley's terms, altering the mechanisms that determine how information flows and associations form.

Many kinds of "desirable inefficiencies" have been proposed. Limits could be set on the number of times a message can be forwarded or the number of people it can be forwarded to. The limits might become more stringent the more a message is shared. A delay of a few minutes could be introduced before a post appears on a platform, giving the person doing the posting time to reconsider its content and tone and slowing down the pace of exchanges. A similar delay or a few added clicks could be imposed before a person is allowed to like or reply to someone else's post. A small fee might be required to broadcast a post or message to, say, more than a thousand recipients. The fee might be increased for ten thousand recipients and again for a hundred thousand. A broadcasting license might be required for any account with more than a quarter million followers or subscribers. Pop-up alerts could remind users of the number of people who might see a post or a message. Infinite scrolls, autoplay functions, and personalized feeds and advertisements could be banned outright.

There's much to be said for the frictional design approach. It introduces values other than efficiency into media technology, and it would promote the construction of networks that, like the analog systems of old, encourage more deliberation and discretion on the part of viewers and listeners. If "code is law," as the legal scholar Lawrence Lessig argued years ago, then shouldn't the public's values and interests be taken into account in the formulation of software that shapes how society works? We have speed bumps on roads to slow people down and safeguard the public; why not on the net? The approach also has precedents in recent experiments undertaken by the platforms themselves. In 2020, some Twitter users began seeing a pop-up asking *Want to read the article first?* when they were about to retweet an article they hadn't read. The pop-ups stirred some irritation—"Who made you god?" one user tweeted—but they did seem to have an effect, increasing the likelihood that people would at least glance at an article before sharing it. Two years later, Twitter tested a similar pop-up to deter "abusive language" in tweets. It, too, seemed to have an effect, with users canceling or revising about a third of the flagged messages.[5] Apple and Instagram have introduced algorithmic interventions aimed at curbing the exchange of nude photos among minors. Teenaged users of Apple's Messages and Instagram's direct-messaging service are warned before sending or receiving messages that include nude images, and the images themselves are sometimes automatically blurred.[6]

But while frictional design may help curb certain well-defined types of undesirable online behavior, it is likely to prove as futile as Frank Walsh's gunplay when it comes to changing how social media operates. Unlike traditional time, place, and motion laws, which don't affect the day-to-day lives of most people, changes to the basic workings of social media would affect pretty much everyone all at once. Although the frictional design proposals focus on regulating how technological systems work rather than on what people say, they would still raise free-speech and free-press concerns. Many people, even among the growing number who would like to see stiffer controls placed on platform companies, would rebel against what they'd see as patriarchal overreach or nanny-state meddling. Others would object to the government imposing a single set of values on the general public's means of communication and entertainment. Many would ask whether politicians and bureaucrats can be trusted to meddle with software without mucking everything up. Would every shift in the political winds bring sudden and confusing alterations to the way apps work?

The biggest obstacle to adding friction to communication, though, is likely to be the habits of social media users themselves. The history of technological progress shows that once people adapt to greater efficiency in any practice or process, reductions in efficiency, whatever the rationale, feel intolerable. The public is rarely willing to suffer delays and nuisances once it has been relieved of them. In a culture programmed for ease, speed, and diversion, friction is the hardest of all sells.

The distinguished technology historian Thomas Hughes, having spent decades studying electric utilities, manufacturing plants, and transportation and communication networks, argued that complex technological systems are difficult if not impossible to change once they become established.[7] In a system's early, formative days, the public has an opportunity to influence how it's designed, run, and regulated. But as it becomes entwined in society's workings and people's lives—as the technology gains "momentum," in Hughes's formulation—it resists alteration. Changing the system in any far-reaching way causes too many disruptions for too many people. Society shapes itself to the system rather than the other way around.

In the 1990s, when the internet was just beginning its transition from an academic to a commercial network, we could have passed laws and imposed regulations that would have shaped the course of its development and, years later, influenced how social media works. We could have updated the secrecy-of-correspondence doctrine for a new era of online communication. We could have applied the public-interest standard to internet companies. We could have made the companies legally responsible for the information they transmit. We could have drawn technological and regulatory distinctions between private and public communication. But none of that happened. It was hardly even talked about. The public's enthusiasm for the web and its apparent democratizing power, an enthusiasm that swept through Congress, the White House, and the Supreme Court, was too strong. Our faith in the benefits of ever more efficient communication overrode any concerns about risks or unintended consequences. We had to keep our hands off the precious gift, as Justice Stevens counseled, for fear our touch might deform it. Now, it's too late to rethink the system. It has burrowed its way too deeply into society and the social mind.

But maybe it's not too late to change ourselves.

Excommunication

One Saturday afternoon in the summer of 1763, in the busy English port city of Harwich, Samuel Johnson conducted the most famous scientific experiment ever undertaken by a man of letters: he kicked a rock. Johnson had traveled to the coast from his home in London to see off his friend and future biographer, James Boswell, who was sailing to Holland to study law at the university in Utrecht. As the two men strolled through the city, walking off their midday meal and passing the time until the departure of Boswell's packet boat, their conversation turned to the doctrine of "immaterialism" as propounded by George Berkeley, the late Irish prelate and philosopher. Berkeley had argued, in his 1710 *Treatise concerning the Principles of Knowledge* and other works, that the world is all in our head. The things that surround us exist only as ideas or sensations in the mind. We bring them into being through our perception of them. "*Esse est percipi*," Berkeley declared: to be is to be perceived.

Dr. Johnson, nothing if not pragmatical, found Dean Berkeley's speculations ludicrous. His companion was not quite so dismissive. As the pair paused outside St. Nicholas, Harwich's handsome Anglican church, Boswell suggested to Johnson that Berkeley's argument was an "ingenious sophistry." Although it might sound absurd, it was impossible to refute. "I never shall forget," Boswell would later recall, "the alacrity with which Johnson answered, striking his foot with mighty force against a large stone, till he rebounded from it, 'I refute it *thus*.'"[8] To be is to be kickable.

The dean's thinking was a little more subtle than the doctor gave it credit for—later philosophers would dismiss the "appeal to the stone" as a logical fallacy—but Johnson wasn't attempting to lay out a carefully formulated philosophical argument. He was offering a visceral demonstration of the world's, and the body's, indifference to such arguments. A mind can spin all the theories it wants, but a foot does not have the luxury of sophistry. It is always in touch, sometimes painfully so, with reality. More than a statement of first principles—the world exists, independent of what goes on inside our heads—Johnson's act was an expression of humility. To believe that everything's existence depends on one's own perceptions is to put oneself at the center of the universe. Giving a large and very solid object a kick provides an empirical counterpoint to such Ptolemaic egotism. Rebounding from the encounter, the foot is bruised. The rock, unmoved.

In recent years, as philosophy, psychology, neuroscience, and robotics have come into conversation, Dr. Johnson's refutation of immaterialism has become more convincing. A growing body of evidence suggests that our perception of our surroundings depends more on bodily engagement than on cognitive modeling. Analyses of complex human feats—shooting a game bird out of the sky, walking down a steep spiral staircase, taking a sharp turn at speed on a motorcycle—reveal how being in the world is necessary to making sense of the world. Perception begins in presence. Intuition precedes cognition. It might be possible for a dedicated contemporary Berkeleyan to construct an argument, involving extended and elaborate mental and rhetorical acrobatics, that all our earthbound skills are just mental illusions our minds conjure up for mysterious reasons. But why bother? The world doesn't await our proof of its existence. We demonstrate its existence through our aptitude in doing things in it.

Worldliness, more than anything else, is what separates the human animal from the AI machine. The computer scientist Rodney Brooks, drawing on his years of experience in building robots, believes that if artificial intelligence is ever going to rival human intelligence, it can't stay cooped up in supercomputers or server farms. It will need to have an active, physical presence in the world. A mind trained solely on representations or models—an LLM's neural network, for instance—is fated to produce derivative and superficial thoughts. A chatbot is "good at saying what an answer should *sound* like, which is different from what an answer should *be*." The bot's simulation of speech masks the lack of any underlying comprehension or competence. To build a truly perceptive and thoughtful AI, an automaton that can do more than rearrange symbols into new patterns, it's necessary "to have its representations grounded in the physical," Brooks continues. It's necessary to have it go out and kick rocks. Lots of them. Once a robot begins to learn about the world by exploring the world, as a child does, "the need for symbolic representations soon fades entirely."[9]

Brooks's research points to something elemental about intelligence, its formation, and its tight connection to nature:

> The world is its own best model. It is always exactly up to date. It always contains every detail there is to be known. The trick is to sense it appropriately and often enough.[10]

That's the trick for us humans as well: to sense the world appropriately and often enough. It's a trick we'll need to relearn if we hope to escape imprisonment in the hyperreal. Despite our love of or at least infatuation with the easy stimulations of the virtual, we can never make a true home there, at least not without sacrificing the qualities of sense and sensibility that make us most ourselves. Live in a simulation long enough, and you begin to think and talk like a chatbot. Your thoughts and words become the outputs of a prediction algorithm.

To argue for a more material and less virtual existence is not to make a case for materialism alone. As the ambitions of Andreessen, Zuckerberg, and the other evangelists of virtual reality make clear, it's virtuality that reduces all concerns to the materialistic. Hyperreality is all surface and no depth. Beyond the simulation lies nothing at all, as Baudrillard saw. Any attempt to transcend reality, intellectually, artistically, or spiritually, has to begin from within reality, bounded by constraints of time and space. You can only get beyond the material by going through the material, by suffering and surmounting its frictions. And that becomes harder and harder to accomplish or even to imagine the more that life is mediated by mechanisms of communication. The computer is so quick to sense and fulfill our desires that it never allows us the opportunity to examine our desires, to ask our-selves whether what we choose, or what is chosen for us, is worthy of the choosing.

Maybe salvation, if that's not too strong a word, lies in personal, willful acts of excommunication—the taking up of positions, first as individuals and then, perhaps, together, not outside of society but at society's margin, not beyond the reach of the informational flow but beyond the reach of its liquefying force. The superbloom gave us a metaphor for the entrancing, fleeting stimulations of the screen. We might borrow Dr. Johnson's rock as a counterweight—an emblem of stability, solidity, resistance. If you don't live by your own code, you'll live by another's.

ACKNOWLEDGMENTS

THE IDEAS IN THE PRECEDING PAGES BEGAN TO TAKE SHAPE early in 2017 when I wrote an essay for the Sunday *Boston Globe* called "How Tech Created a Global Village—and Put Us at Each Other's Throats." But it wasn't until 2019, the year of the superbloom, that the ideas started coalescing into this book. In the fall of that year, I taught a seminar on social media at Williams College in western Massachusetts. The undergraduates in the class, all born around the turn of the millennium, were members of the first generation to grow up online. From an early age, they had easy access not only to the internet but to smartphones, multiplayer video games, app stores, streamers, and myriad messaging and social media platforms. The students held a variety of opinions about the technologies, and they used the hardware and software in different ways, but they made it clear that the constant presence of digital media had shaped them and their relationships in profound ways. It had exerted a formative pressure on their being. Our discussions convinced me that the full story of social media had yet to be told. I am grateful to the students for their honesty, their insight, and their inspiration. I also thank James Nolan, the Washington Gladden 1859 Professor of Sociology at Williams, for inviting me to teach at the school.

The opening sections of Chapter 2 appeared in a different form in my essay "How to Fix Social Media," published in the fall 2021 issue of the *New Atlantis*. I am indebted to that journal's editor, Ari Schulman, and managing editor, Samuel Matlack, for their counsel and encouragement. Portions of Chapter 8 appeared earlier, also in a different form, in "Beautiful Lies," my 2021 review of Jonas Bendiksen's *Book of Veles* in the *Los Angeles Review of Books*. I am grateful to Michele Pridmore-Brown, LARB's science and technology editor, for her assistance and support. The title of the eighth chapter is a play on the title of Pamela McCorduck's 1979 book, *Machines Who Think*, one of the earliest popular explorations of artificial intelligence—and still one of the best.

Antón Barba-Kay, the Robert Aird Chair of Humanities at Deep Springs College, read an early draft of *Superbloom* and offered incisive comments. He also pointed me toward important sources I would otherwise have overlooked. I thank him for his generosity. Viji Kannan at the University of Rochester and Brett Frischmann at Villanova University graciously answered my questions about their work. Finally, I once again thank my longtime editor at W. W. Norton, Brendan Curry. He and his talented colleagues, notably Caroline Adams, made the book better in many ways.

NOTES

CHAPTER 1: A MORE PERFECT LIQUEFACTION

1. Quoted in Glenn Jacobs, *Charles Horton Cooley: Imagining Social Reality* (Amherst: University of Massachusetts Press, 2006), 7. Jacobs's book provides a trenchant introduction to Cooley's thought.

2. Robert Cooley Angell, introduction to *The Two Major Works of Charles H. Cooley* (Glencoe, IL: Free Press, 1956), v.

3. Charles Horton Cooley, *Social Organization: A Study of the Larger Mind* (New York: Scribner's, 1909), 3.

4. Charles H. Cooley, "The Process of Social Change," *Political Science Quarterly* 12, no. 1 (March 1897): 63–81. Cooley drew inspiration from his reading of the German thinker Albert Schäffle, who had argued that transportation and communication lines form the nervous system of the "social body." See Peter Simonson, "Charles Horton Cooley and the Origins of U.S. Communication Study in Political Economy," *Democratic Communiqué* 25, no. 1 (2012): article 1.

5. John Durham Peters: *Speaking into the Air: A History of the Idea of Communication* (Chicago: University of Chicago Press, 1999), 185.

6. Samuel Butler, "Thought and Language," in *Collected Essays*, vol. 2 (London: Jonathan Cape, 1925), 72.

7. For a historical perspective, see Harold A. Innis, *Empire and Communications* (London: Oxford University Press, 1950).

8. Marshall McLuhan, "Classroom without Walls," in *Explorations in Communication*, ed. Edmund Carpenter and Marshall McLuhan (Boston: Beacon, 1960), 1.

9. See Andrew Pettegree, *Brand Luther: 1517, Printing, and the Making of the Reformation* (New York: Penguin, 2015).

10. Philip Rieff, introduction to *Social Organization: A Study of the Larger Mind*, by Charles Horton Cooley (New York: Schocken, 1962), xv.

11. Mark Zuckerberg, "Letter from Mark Zuckerberg," in prospectus filed with Securities and Exchange Commission, February 1, 2012.

12. Joan Didion, *The White Album* (New York: Simon & Schuster, 1979), 98.

13. Mark Zuckerberg, "Building Global Community," Facebook, February 16, 2017, https://www.facebook.com/notes/mark-zuckerberg/building-global-community/10103508221158471.

14. Karen Armstrong, *The Bible: A Biography* (New York: Grove, 2007), 1.

15. Johann Gottfried von Herder, *Philosophical Writings,* ed. and trans. Michael N. Forster (Cambridge: Cambridge University Press, 2002), 370.

16. For a lucid overview of the many pre-electric attempts at long-distance communication, see James Gleick, *The Information: A History, a Theory, a Flood* (New York: Pantheon, 2011).

17. Ezra S. Gannett, *The Atlantic Telegraph: A Discourse Delivered in the First Church* (Boston: Crosby, Nichols, and Co., 1858), 4, 13–14.

18. Charles F. Briggs and Augustus Maverick, *The Story of the Telegraph, and a History of the Great Atlantic Cable* (New York: Rudd & Carleton, 1858), 22.

19. "International Telegraph Conference Paris, 1865: Signature of Convention by Twenty Sovereign States Opens Era of International Co-operation," *Telecommunication Journal* 32, no. 5 (1965): 180–184.

20. Jean-Michel Johnston, *Networks of Modernity: Germany in the Age of the Telegraph, 1830–1880* (Oxford: Oxford University Press, 2021), 199.

21. "Too High," *New York Times*, August 15, 1899.

22. "Tesla Declares He Will Abolish War," *New York Herald*, November 8, 1898.

23. Ivan Narodny, "Marconi's Plans for the World," *Technical World Magazine*, October 1912, 145–150.

24. Harry A. Mount, "From $5-a-Week Beginner to Scientific Chief of the World's Greatest Telephone System," *Popular Science Monthly*, February 1923, 23–24.

25. Orrin E. Dunlap Jr., *The Outlook for Television* (New York: Harper & Brothers, 1932), 229.

26. Stephen Kern, *The Culture of Time and Space 1880–1918* (Cambridge, MA: Harvard University Press, 1983), 265–276. The telegraph appears to have played a similar role, even earlier, in spurring the Franco-Prussian War of 1870, according to Kern. He quotes the French historian Pierre Granet: "The constant transmission of dispatches between governments and their agents, the rapid dissemination of controversial information among an already agitated public, hastened, if it did not actually provoke, the outbreak of hostilities."

27. Sir Ernest Satow, *A Guide to Diplomatic Practice* (London: Longmans, Green and Co., 1917), 145.

28. Harold A. Innis, "Minerva's Owl," 1947 speech to the Royal Society of Canada, collected in *The Bias of Communication* (Toronto: University of Toronto, 1991), 31.

CHAPTER 2: PRIVACY AND THE PUBLIC INTEREST

1. Angela J. Campbell, "Pacifica Reconsidered: Implications for the Current Controversy over Broadcast Indecency," *Federal Communications Law Journal* 63, no. 1 (2010): 195–260.
2. In the Matter of a Citizen's Complaint Against Pacifica Foundation Station WBAI, 56 FCC 2d 94 (1975).
3. Pacifica Foundation v. FCC, 556 F.2d 9 (D.C. Cir. 1977).
4. FCC v. Pacifica Foundation, 438 U.S. 726 (1978). The court's decision includes a full, uncensored transcript of Carlin's "Filthy Words" routine.
5. John Nicholson, "The Delivery and Confidentiality of Cicero's Letters," *Classical Journal* 90, no. 1 (1994): 33–63.
6. Joobin Bekhrad, "The Surprising Origins of the Postal Service," BBC, June 25, 2020, https://www.bbc.com/travel/article/20200624-iran-the -surprising-origins-of-the-postal-service.
7. Jana Dambrogio, "Historic Letterlocking: The Art and Security of Letter Writing," *Book Arts Canada* 5, no. 2 (2014): 21–23.
8. William Lewins, *Her Majesty's Mails: An Historical and Descriptive Account of the British Post-Office* (London: Sampson Low, Son, and Marston, 1864), 31.
9. Anuj C. Desai, "Wiretapping before the Wires: The Post Office and the Birth of Communications Privacy," *Stanford Law Review* 60, no. 2 (2007): 553–594.
10. Ibid. See also Neil M. Richards and Daniel J. Sokolove, "Privacy's Other Path: Recovering the Law of Confidentiality," *Georgetown Law Journal* 96, no. 123 (2007): 123–182. As with the British prohibitions against tampering with the mail, the early American postal regulations were hardly ironclad. In a 1788 letter, George Washington complained that, "by passing through the post-office," his political opinions would "become known to all the world." Thomas Jefferson also groused about what he termed "the curiosity of the post-offices." Quoted in David J. Seipp, *The Right to Privacy in American History*. Program on Information Resources Policy, Publication P-78-3 (Cambridge, MA: Harvard University, 1978), 11.
11. Ex parte Jackson, 96 U.S. 727 (1878).
12. Thomas Jepsen, "'A New Business in the World': The Telegraph, Privacy, and the U.S. Constitution in the Nineteenth Century," *Technology and Culture* 59, no. 1 (2018): 95–125.
13. Ibid.
14. Tim Wu, *The Master Switch: The Rise and Fall of Information Empires* (New York: Knopf, 2010), 24.
15. Thomas M. Cooley, *A Treatise on the Constitutional Limitations Which Rest upon the Legislative Power of the States of the American Union* (Boston: Little, Brown, 1868), 307.

16. Thomas M. Cooley, "Inviolability of Telegraphic Correspondence," *American Law Register* 27, no. 2 (1879): 65–78.

17. Seipp, *Right to Privacy*, 105.

18. Colin Agur, "Negotiated Order: The Fourth Amendment, Telephone Surveillance, and Social Interactions, 1878–1968," *Information and Culture* 48, no. 4 (2013): 419–447.

19. Olmstead et al. v. United States, 277 U.S. 438 (1928).

20. "Government Lawbreaking," *New York Times*, June 6, 1928.

21. Helen M. Fessenden, *Fessenden: Builder of Tomorrows* (New York: Coward-McCann, 1940), 153–154. See also John S. Belrose, "Reginald Aubrey Fessenden and the Birth of Wireless Telephony," *IEEE Antennas and Propagation Magazine* 44, no. 2 (2002): 38–47.

22. Cooley, "Inviolability of Telegraphic Correspondence."

23. Hugh R. Slotten, *Radio and Television Regulation: Broadcast Technology in the United States, 1920–1960* (Baltimore: Johns Hopkins University Press, 2000), 7.

24. Susan J. Douglas, "Amateur Operators and American Broadcasting: Shaping the Future of Radio," in *Imagining Tomorrow: History, Technology, and the American Future*, ed. Joseph J. Corn (Cambridge, MA: MIT Press, 1986), 44.

25. Slotten, *Radio and Television Regulation*, 7.

26. "The Wireless Control Bill," *New York Times*, March 23, 1912.

27. "The Disaster of the 'Titanic,'" *Electrical World* 59, no. 17 (1912): 879–880.

28. Susan J. Douglas, *Inventing American Broadcasting, 1899–1922* (Baltimore: Johns Hopkins University Press, 1987), 238.

29. C. E. Urban, "The Radio Amateur," *Pittsburgh Gazette Times*, November 7, 1920.

30. J. L. Clifton, *Narrative Report of the Ohio Department of Education, 1928–29* (Springfield OH: Kelly-Springfield, 1930), 143.

31. Herbert Hoover, "The Broadcasts of Tomorrow," *Popular Science Monthly*, July 1922, 19.

32. Munn v. Illinois, 94 U.S. 113 (1876).

33. Herbert Hoover, opening address to the Fourth Annual Radio Conference, November 9, 1925, in *Radio Control: Hearings Before the Committee on Interstate Commerce, United States Senate* (Washington, DC: Government Printing Office, 1926), 56.

34. KFKB Broadcasting Association v. Federal Radio Commission, 47 F.2d 670 (D.C. Cir. 1931). See also Philip C. Smith, "John R. Brinkley: A Quintessential American Quack," *Journal of Community Hospital Internal Medicine Perspectives* 12, no. 5 (2022): 1–5.

35. Erwin G. Krasnow and Jack N. Goodman, "The 'Public Interest' Standard: The Search for the Holy Grail," *Federal Communications Law Journal* 50, no. 3 (1998): 605–635.

36. Quoted in ibid.

37. *Third Annual Report of the Federal Radio Commission to the Congress of the United States* (Washington, DC: Government Printing Office, 1929), 33.

38. "The Mayflower Broadcasting Corporation," *Federal Communications Commission Reports*, vol. 8 (Washington, DC: Government Printing Office, 1943), 340.

39. "Old Standards in New Context: A Comparative Analysis of FCC Regulation," *University of Chicago Law Review* 18, no. 1 (1950): 78–92.

40. "Editorializing by Broadcast Licensees," *Federal Communications Commission Reports*, vol. 13 (Washington, DC: Government Printing Office, 1949), 1249.

41. Quoted in Krasnow and Goodman, "'Public Interest' Standard."

42. Gerhard Colm, "In Defense of the Public Interest," *Social Research* 27, no. 3 (1960): 295–307.

43. Quoted in Elizabeth Fones-Wolf, *Waves of Opposition: Labor and the Struggle for Democratic Radio* (Chicago: University of Illinois Press, 2006), 127.

44. Alice Goldfarb Marquis, "Written on the Wind: The Impact of Radio during the 1930s," *Journal of Contemporary History* 19, no. 3 (1984): 385–415.

45. Lawrence W. Levine and Cornelia R. Levine, *The People and the President: America's Conversation with FDR* (Boston: Beacon Press, 2002), 22–23. Italics are the Levines'.

46. Stephen Lovell, *Russia in the Microphone Age: A History of Soviet Radio, 1919–1970* (Oxford: Oxford University Press, 2015), 37.

47. Joseph Goebbels, "The Radio as the Eighth Great Power," transcript of speech presented on August 18, 1933, Calvin University German propaganda archive, https://research.calvin.edu/german-propaganda-archive/goeb56.htm.

48. Fred Turner, *The Democratic Surround: Multimedia and American Liberalism from World War II to the Psychedelic Sixties* (Chicago: University of Chicago Press, 2013), 38–39.

49. Ibid., 39–113.

50. Tom Hayden, *The Port Huron Statement* (New York: Thunder's Mouth, 2005), 53.

51. Hans Magnus Enzensberger, "Constituents of a Theory of the Media," *New Left Review*, November–December 1970.

CHAPTER 3: THE FEED

1. Edward Wallerstein (as told to Ward Botsford), "Creating the LP Record," *High Fidelity*, April 1976.

2. C. E. Shannon, "A Mathematical Theory of Communication," *Bell System Technical Journal* 27, nos. 3, 4 (1948): 379–423, 623–656. Italics are Shannon's.

3. James Gleick, *The Information: A History, a Theory, a Flood* (New York: Pantheon, 2011), 4.

4. Ibid., 242–248.

5. J. C. R. Licklider, "Man-Computer Symbiosis," *IRE Transactions on Human Factors in Electronics* (March 1960): 411.

6. J. C. R. Licklider, "Memorandum for Members and Affiliates of the Intergalactic Computer Network," Advanced Research Projects Agency, April 23, 1963.

7. Aaron Smith, "Home Broadband 2010," Pew Research, August 11, 2010.

8. "In the Matter of Deregulation of Radio," *Federal Communications Commission Reports*, vol. 84 (Washington, DC: Government Printing Office, 1982), 968–969.

9. Reno v. ACLU, 521 U.S. 844 (1997).

10. "Ruchi Sanghvi Speaks at Female Founders Conference 2015," YouTube, February 23, 2015, https://www.youtube.com/watch?v=01FjJyBAOUE.

11. David Kirkpatrick, *The Facebook Effect: The Inside Story of the Company That Is Connecting the World* (New York: Simon & Schuster, 2010), 296. Although unlikely, Zuckerberg may have been thinking of Adam Smith's observation, in *The Theory of Moral Sentiments*, that a typical European man would find the loss of "his little finger" considerably more distressing than a report that "the great empire of China, with all its myriads of inhabitants, was suddenly swallowed up by an earthquake." But, Smith went on to say, more remarkable than our selfishness is our willingness to rise above it to aid others: "When we are always so much more deeply affected by whatever concerns ourselves, than by whatever concerns other men; what is it which prompts the generous, upon all occasions, and the mean upon many, to sacrifice their own interests to the greater interests of others?"

12. Warren St. John, "When Information Becomes T.M.I.," *New York Times*, September 10, 2006.

13. Christopher M. Hoadley et al., "Privacy as Information Access and Illusory Control: The Case of the Facebook News Feed Privacy Outcry," *Electronic Commerce Research and Applications* 9 (2010): 50–60.

14. Quoted in Tom Loftus, "Mark Zuckerberg's Best Quotes," *Wall Street Journal*, February 1, 2012.

15. Steven Levy, *Facebook: The Inside Story* (New York: Penguin Random House, 2020), 142–143.

16. Joshua Melvin, "Protestors Contest Facebook Breast Policy," *Mercury News*, December 27, 2008; and Urmee Khan, "Breastfeeding Photo Ban by Facebook Sparks Global Protest by Mothers," *Telegraph*, December 30, 2007.

17. Kate Klonick, "The New Governors: The People, Rules, and Processes Governing Online Speech," *Harvard Law Review* 131, no. 6 (2018): 1598–1670.

18. Ibid.

19. Adam Satariano and Mike Isaac, "Profit and Pain in Doing Facebook's Dirty Work," *New York Times*, September 1, 2021. See also Paul M. Barrett, *Who Moderates the Social Media Giants?* (New York: NYU Stern Center for Business and Human Rights, 2020).

20. Adrian Chen, "Inside Facebook's Outsourced Anti-Porn and Gore Brigade, Where 'Camel Toes' Are More Offensive than 'Crushed Heads,'" *Gawker*, February 16, 2012. The manual itself, *oDesk, Abuse Standards 6.2: Operation Manual for Live Content Moderators*, is archived at https://perma.cc/2JQF-AWMY.

21. Alex Hern, "FamilyOFive: YouTube Bans 'Pranksters' after Child Abuse Conviction," *Guardian*, July 19, 2018.

22. Interview on *Good Morning America*, ABC News, April 28, 2017.

23. Lauren Weber and Deepa Seetharaman, "The Worst Job in Technology: Keeping Facebook Clean," *Wall Street Journal*, December 28, 2017.

24. Sarah T. Roberts, *Behind the Screen: Content Moderation in the Shadows of Social Media* (New Haven, CT: Yale University Press, 2019), 162–165.

25. Klonick, "New Governors."

26. Quoted in Miguel Helft, "Facebook's Mean Streets," *New York Times*, December 13, 2010.

27. John Milton, *Areopagitica*, in *The Essential Prose of John Milton* (New York: Modern Library, 2013), 209.

28. *The Life and Selected Writings of Thomas Jefferson* (New York: Modern Library, 2004), 299.

29. Abrams et al. v United States, 250 U.S. 616 (1919).

30. Michael J. Madison et al., "Too Much of a Good Thing? A Governing Knowledge Commons Review of Abundance in Context," *Frontiers in Research Metrics and Analytics* 7 (July 2022): 959505.

31. Quoted in Carolyn Marvin, "Information and History," in *Ideology of the Information Age*, ed. Jennifer Daryl Slack and Fred Fejes (Norwood, NJ: Ablex, 1987), 59.

32. Eric Schmidt interview, Techonomy Conference, Lake Tahoe, August 4, 2010, https://www.youtube.com/watch?v=UAcCIsrAq70. A byte is eight bits. An exabyte is 10^{18} bytes, or a billion gigabytes.

33. Caleb Scharf, *The Ascent of Information: Books, Bits, Genes, Machines, and Life's Unending Algorithm* (New York: Riverhead, 2021), 88.

34. See, e.g., Jonah Berger and Katherine L. Milkman, "What Makes Online Content Viral?," *Journal of Marketing Research* 49, no. 2 (2012): 192–205.

35. "Facebook: Transparency and Use of Consumer Data," Hearing Before the Committee on Energy and Commerce, House of Representatives, April 11, 2018, https://www.govinfo.gov/content/pkg/CHRG-115hhrg30956/pdf/CHRG-115hhrg30956.pdf. Many other executives of internet companies have made similar claims over the years. See Philip M. Napoli and Robyn Caplan, "Why Media Companies Insist They're Not Media Companies, Why They're Wrong, and Why It Matters," *First Monday* 22, no. 5 (2017).

36. John Jay Chapman, "Emerson, Sixty Years After," *Atlantic Monthly*, January 1897.

CHAPTER 4: FAST TALKING, FAST THINKING

1. Stephen J. Lukasik, "Why the Arpanet Was Built," *IEEE Annals of the History of Computing* (July–September 2011): 4–20.

2. J. C. R. Licklider and Albert Vezza, "Applications of Information Networks," *Proceedings of the IEEE* 66, no. 11 (1978): 1330–1346.

3. Quoted in David M. Henkin, *The Postal Age: The Emergence of Modern Communications in Nineteenth-Century America* (Chicago: University of Chicago Press, 2006), 100.

4. Marshall McLuhan and Quentin Fiore, *The Medium Is the Massage: An Inventory of Effects* (Berkeley: Ginko Press, 2017), 75, 86.

5. Katie Hafner, "Billions Served Daily, and Counting," *New York Times*, December 6, 2001.

6. Nick Bilton, "Thanks? Don't Bother," *New York Times*, March 11, 2013.

7. Margaret Sullivan, "Thanks for Not Calling," *New York Times*, March 14, 2013.

8. Teddy Wayne, "The Long Email Signs Off," *New York Times*, July 12, 2015. The headline for the online version of the article was "A Eulogy for the Long, Intimate Email."

9. See Sophie Read, *Eucharist and the Poetic Imagination in Early Modern Britain* (Cambridge: Cambridge University Press, 2013), 76–77.

10. Henkin, *Postal Age*, 3, 18.

11. "The Growth of the Mail," Smithsonian National Postal Museum, n.d., https://postalmuseum.si.edu/exhibition/america's-mailing-industry-the -united-states-postal-service/the-growth-of-the-mail.

12. Henkin, *Postal Age*, 118, 4.

13. "A New Reality: Correspondence Mail in the Digital Age," Office of Inspector General, U.S. Postal Service, report no. RARC-WP-18-004, March 5, 2018. John Mazzone, "The Household Diary Study: Mail Use & Attitudes in FY 2020," U.S. Postal Service, April 2021.

14. Fred Backus, "Most Americans Haven't Written a Personal Letter on Paper in over Five Years," CBS News, October 11, 2021, https://www.cbsnews .com/news/most-americans-havent-written-a-personal-letter-on-paper-in -over-five-years/.

15. Theodor Adorno, *Minima Moralia: Reflections from Damaged Life*, trans. E. F. N. Jephcott (London: Verso, 2005), 41.

16. See, e.g., Jessica Winter, "The Rise and Fall of Vibes-Based Literacy," *New Yorker*, September 1, 2022.

17. "Instant Messaging: A New Language?," *Science Daily*, May 2, 2008, https:// www.sciencedaily.com/releases/2008/05/080501154219.htm.

18. Christina Haas and Pamela Takayoshi, "Young People's Everyday Literacies: The Language Features of Instant Messaging," *Research in the Teaching of English*, 45, no. 4 (2011): 378–404. Most of the IM examples that follow are drawn from this study. See also Erika Darics, "Non-verbal Signalling in Digital Discourse: The Case of Letter Repetition," *Discourse, Context and Media* 4, no. 3 (2013): 141–148.

19. Lieke Verheijen, "The Effects of Text Messaging and Instant Messaging on Literacy," *English Studies* 94, no. 5 (2013): 582–602.

20. Statista, "Total Number of SMS and MMS Messages Sent in the United States from 2005 to 2021," January 18, 2023, https://www.statista.com/ statistics/185879/number-of-text-messages-in-the-united-states-since-2005/.

21. Statista, "Average Number of Sent and Received Text Messages per Month Regarding U.S. Adolescents in the Second Quarter of 2010," October 14, 2020, https://www.statista.com/statistics/273181/average-number-of-text-messages-sent-by-us-adolescents/.

22. Amanda Lenhart, "Teens, Smartphones & Texting," Pew Research, March 19, 2012.

23. John Sutherland, "Cn u txt?," *Guardian*, November 11, 2002.

24. John Humphrys, "I h8 txt msgs: How Texting Is Wrecking Our Language," *Daily Mail*, September 24, 2007.

25. David Crystal, "Texting," *ELT Journal* 62, no. 1 (2008): 77–83.

26. See Steve Whittaker and Candace Sidner, "Email Overload: Exploring Personal Information Management of Email," in *CHI '96: Proceedings of the SIGCHI Conference on Human Factors in Computing Systems*, ed. Michael J. Tauber (New York: Association for Computing Machinery, 1996), 276–83.

27. John McWhorter, "Is Texting Killing the English Language?," *Time*, April 25, 2013.

28. Sophia June, "Gen Z Could Free the World from Email," *New York Times*, July 11, 2021.

29. John McWhorter, "Txtng Is Killing Language, JK!!!," speech at TED2013, https://www.ted.com/talks/john_mcwhorter_txtng_is_killing_language_jk/transcript.

30. Gretchen McCulloch, *Because Internet: Understanding the New Rules of Language* (New York: Penguin Random House, 2019), 2–3.

31. Quoted in Peter Funt, "Curses! Why All the Crude Talk?," *Wall Street Journal*, April 1, 2023.

32. Thomas de Zengotita, *Mediated: How the Media Shapes Your World and the Way You Live in It* (New York: Bloomsbury, 2005), 47.

33. Michael I. Posner and Charles R. R. Snyder, "Attention and Cognitive Control," in *Information Processing and Cognition: The Loyola Symposium*, ed. Robert L. Solso (Hillsdale, NJ: Erlbaum, 1975), 55–85.

34. Daniel Kahneman, *Thinking, Fast and Slow* (New York: Farrar, Straus and Giroux, 2011), 21.

35. Susan Sontag, *Styles of Radical Will* (New York: Farrar, Straus and Giroux, 1969), 4.

CHAPTER 5: ANTIPATHIES

1. Ebbe B. Ebbesen et al., "Spatial Ecology: Its Effects on the Choice of Friends and Enemies," *Journal of Experimental Social Psychology* 12 (1976): 505–518. Italics are Ebbesen's.

2. Our optimistic assumption that we'll like a stranger once we get to know him or her is attributable to the well-documented "person-positivity bias." See, e.g., David O. Sears, "The Person-Positivity Bias," *Journal of Personality and Social Psychology* 44, no. 2 (1983): 233–250.

3.   Michael I. Norton et al., "Less Is More: The Lure of Ambiguity, or Why Familiarity Breeds Contempt," *Journal of Personality and Social Psychology* 92, no. 1 (2007): 97–105.

4.   The finding was consistent with earlier research showing that, in evaluating others, people tend to place more stress on dissimilarities than on similarities. See, e.g., Ramadhar Singh and Soo Yan Ho, "Attitudes and Attraction: A New Test of the Attraction, Repulsion and Similarity-Dissimilarity Asymmetry Hypotheses," *British Journal of Social Psychology* 39 (2000): 197–211.

5.   Much research has shown that people tend to like things more the more they're exposed to them (so long as reasons for disliking them don't arise), a phenomenon known as the "mere-exposure effect." See, e.g., Robert B. Zajonc, "Attitudinal Effects of Mere Exposure," *Journal of Personality and Social Psychology* 9, no. 2, part 2 (1968): 1–27.

6.   Harry T. Reis et al., "Familiarity Does Indeed Promote Attraction in Live Interaction," *Journal of Personality and Social Psychology* 101, no. 3 (2011): 557–570.

7.   Michael I. Norton et al., "Does Familiarity Breed Contempt or Liking? Comment on Reis, Maniaci, Caprariello, Eastwick, and Finkel (2011)," *Journal of Personality and Social Psychology* 101, no. 3 (2011): 571–574. In this paper, the researchers also report on another trait-based experiment, involving nearly five hundred participants, that backs up their original conclusions.

8.   See, e.g., Adam N. Joinson, "Self-Disclosure in Computer-Mediated Communication: The Role of Self Awareness and Visual Anonymity," *European Journal of Social Psychology* 31, no. 2 (2001): 177–192; and John Suler, "The Online Disinhibition Effect," *Cyberpsychology and Behavior* 7, no. 3 (2004): 321–326.

9.   Aaron Ben-Ze'ev, "Envy and Jealousy," *Canadian Journal of Philosophy* 20, no. 4 (1990): 487–516.

10. Alexandra Samuel, "What to Do When Social Media Inspires Envy," *JSTOR Daily*, February 6, 2018, https://daily.jstor.org/what-to-do-when-social -media-inspires-envy/.

11. Bertrand Russell, *The Conquest of Happiness* (New York: Liveright, 1971), 80–81.

12. Samuel, "What to Do."

13. Quoted in Lauren Cassani Davis, "The Flight from Conversation," *Atlantic*, October 7, 2015.

14. Sherry Turkle, *Reclaiming Conversation: The Power of Talk in a Digital Age* (New York: Penguin, 2015), 25.

15. Helen Riess, "The Science of Empathy," *Journal of Patient Experience* 4, no. 2 (2017): 74–77.

16. Irwin Altman and Dalmas A. Taylor, *Social Penetration: The Development of Interpersonal Relationships* (New York: Holy, Rinehart & Winston, 1973). See also, by the same authors, "Communication in Interpersonal Relationships: Social Penetration Processes," in *Interpersonal Processes: New Direc-*

tions in Communication Research, ed. Michael E. Roloff and Gerald R. Miller (Newbury Park, CA: Sage, 1987), 257–277.

17. Irwin Altman et al., "Dialectic Conceptions in Social Psychology: An Application to Social Penetration and Privacy Regulation," *Advances in Experimental Social Psychology* 14 (1981): 107–160.

18. Ibid.

19. Georg Simmel, "The Metropolis and Mental Life," in *The Blackwell City Reader* (Chichester, UK: Blackwell, 2010), 106.

20. See, e.g., Elisabeth Mangrio and Slobodan Zdravkovic, "Crowded Living and Its Association with Mental Ill-Health among Recently-Arrived Migrants in Sweden," *BMC Research Notes* 11 (2018): 609.

21. Adam N. Joinson et al., "Digital Crowding: Privacy, Self-Disclosure, and Technology," in *Privacy Online*, ed. Sabine Trepte and Leonard Reinecke (Berlin: Springer, 2011), 33–45.

22. Ian Bogost, "The Age of Social Media Is Over," *Atlantic*, November 10, 2022.

CHAPTER 6: THE DEMOCRATIZATION FALLACY

1. Reno v. ACLU, 521 U.S. 844 (1997).

2. Francis Fukuyama, "The End of History?," *National Interest*, Summer 1989.

3. Frances Cairncross, *The Death of Distance* (Boston: Harvard Business School Press, 1997), xvi.

4. Douglas Rushkoff, *Open Source Democracy: How Online Communication Is Changing Offline Politics* (London: Demos, 2003).

5. Jeff Jarvis, "Argue with Me," BuzzMachine, November 11, 2004.

6. Joe Trippi, *The Revolution Will Not Be Televised: Democracy, the Internet, and the Overthrow of Everything* (New York: Regan Books, 2004), 235.

7. Jay Rosen, "The People Formerly Known as the Audience," *Huffington Post*, June 30, 2006.

8. Yochai Benkler, *The Wealth of Networks: How Social Production Transforms Markets and Freedom* (New Haven, CT: Yale University Press, 2006). Most of the quotations from the book are drawn from the seventh chapter, "Political Freedom Part 2: Emergence of the Networked Public Square."

9. Cass Sunstein, *Republic.com* (Princeton, NJ: Princeton University Press, 2001), 87.

10. Benkler, *Wealth of Networks*, 465.

11. Walter Lippmann, *U.S. Foreign Policy: Shield of the Republic* (Boston: Little, Brown, 1943), ix.

12. Quoted in Ronald Steel, *Walter Lippmann and the American Century* (Boston: Little, Brown, 1980), 88.

13. Ibid., 148.

14. Ibid., 154.

15. George Creel, *How We Advertised America: The First Telling of the Amazing Story of the Committee on Public Information That Carried the Gospel of*

Americanism to Every Corner of the Globe (New York: Harper & Brothers, 1920), 5.

16. John Brown, "Janus-Faced Diplomacy: Creel and Lippmann during the Great War," in *Nontraditional U.S. Public Diplomacy: Past, Present, and Future*, ed. Deborah L. Trent (Washington, DC: Public Diplomacy Council, 2016), chap. 3.

17. Walter Lippmann, "The Basic Problem of Democracy," *Atlantic Monthly*, November 1919.

18. James W. Carey, *Communication as Culture: Essays on Media and Society* (Boston: Unwin Hyman, 1989), 75.

19. Ibid., 76.

20. Walter Lippmann, *Public Opinion* (New York: Macmillan, 1922), 11–16.

21. Ibid., 53–62.

22. Walter Lippmann, *The Phantom Public* (New York: Macmillan, 1927), 10–11.

23. Michael Schudson, "The 'Lippmann–Dewey Debate' and the Invention of Walter Lippmann as an Anti-Democrat 1986–1996," *International Journal of Communication* 2 (2008): 1031–1042.

24. Lippmann, *Phantom Public*, 29.

25. The articles are collected in Herbert A. Simon, *Models of Man* (New York: Wiley, 1957). See in particular pp. 196–273.

26. Herbert A. Simon, "Human Nature in Politics: The Dialogue of Psychology with Political Science," *American Political Science Review* 79, no. 2 (1985): 293–304.

27. Christopher H. Achen and Larry M. Bartels, *Democracy for Realists: Why Elections Do Not Produce Responsive Government* (Princeton, NJ: Princeton University Press, 2016), 7–12.

28. Zac Gershberg and Sean Illing, *The Paradox of Democracy: Free Speech, Open Media, and Perilous Persuasion* (Chicago: University of Chicago Press, 2022), 256.

29. Daniel Yudkin et al., *The Perception Gap: How False Impressions Are Pulling Americans Apart* (New York: More in Common, 2019).

30. Donald R. Kinder and Nathan P. Kalmoe, *Neither Liberal nor Conservative: Ideological Innocence in the American Public* (Chicago: University of Chicago Press, 2017), 41.

31. Susan Blackmore, "Imitation Makes Us Human," in *What Makes Us Human?*, ed. Charles Pasternak (Oxford: Oneworld, 2007), 1. Aristotle was perhaps the first to recognize the distinctive human talent for mimicry. "Imitation is natural to man from childhood," the philosopher wrote in his *Poetics*, "one of his advantages over the lower animals being this, that he is the most imitative creature in the world, and learns at first by imitation."

32. See, e.g., Timur Kuran and Cass R. Sunstein, "Availability Cascades and Risk Regulation," *Stanford Law Review* 51, no. 683 (1999): 683–768.

33. Sunstein, *Republic.com*, 80–84. See also Cass Sunstein's "Law of Group Polarization," *Journal of Political Philosophy* 10, no. 2 (2002): 175–195.

34. Lynn Hasher et al., "Frequency and the Conference of Referential Validity," *Journal of Verbal Learning and Verbal Behavior* 16, no. 1 (1977): 107–112.

35. Valentina Vellani et al., "The Illusory Truth Effect Leads to the Spread of Misinformation," *Cognition* 236 (July 2023): 105421.

36. Victor Klemperer, *The Language of the Third Reich*, trans. Martin Brady (London: Continuum, 2006), 28.

37. Alex Kantrowitz, "The Man Who Built the Retweet: 'We Handed a Loaded Weapon to 4-Year-Olds,'" *BuzzFeed*, July 23, 2019.

38. Alexis C. Madrigal, "The Case Against Retweets," *Atlantic*, April 2018.

39. Andy Baio, "72 Hours of #Gamergate," *Medium*, October 27, 2014.

40. Kantrowitz, "The Man Who Built the Retweet."

41. Soroush Vosoughi, Deb Roy, and Sinan Aral, "The Spread of True and False News Online," *Science* 359, no. 6380 (March 9, 2018): 1146–1151.

42. Steve Rathje et al., "Out-group Animosity Drives Engagement on Social Media," *Proceedings of the National Academy of Sciences USA* 118, no. 26 (2021): e2024292118.

43. Jeff Horwitz and Deepa Seetharaman, "Facebook Executives Shut Down Efforts to Make the Site Less Divisive," *Wall Street Journal*, May 27, 2020.

44. Chris Bail, *Breaking the Social Media Prism: How to Make Our Platforms Less Polarizing* (Princeton, NJ: Princeton University Press, 2021), 31, 39.

45. See Achen and Bartels, *Democracy for Realists*, 213–231.

46. Jan-Werner Müller, "The Myth of Social Media Populism," *Foreign Affairs*, Winter 2024. For a description of how Facebook embeds its staff in political campaigns, see Siva Vaidhyanathan, *Antisocial Media: How Facebook Disconnects Us and Undermines Democracy* (Oxford: Oxford University Press, 2018).

47. Fred Turner, "The Big Picture: Trump on Twitter," *Public Books*, October 16, 2017. Italics are Turner's.

48. Gideon Lewis-Kraus, "How Harmful Is Social Media?," *New Yorker*, June 3, 2022.

49. James Madison, *Federalist*, no. 10, November 22, 1787.

50. Williams: David Streitfeld, "The Internet Is Broken," *New York Times*, May 21, 2017. Palihapitiya: "Former Facebook Exec Says Social Media Is Ripping Apart Society," *Verge*, December 11, 2017. Parker: Mike Allen, "Sean Parker Unloads on Facebook," *Axios*, November 9, 2017. Rosenstein: Paul Lewis, "'Our Minds Can Be Hijacked': The Tech Insiders Who Fear a Smartphone Dystopia," *Guardian*, October 6, 2017. Zuckerberg: Mark Zuckerberg, Facebook post, September 30, 2017.

51. Brooke Auxier, "64% of Americans Say Social Media Have a Mostly Negative Effect on the Way Things Are Going in the U.S. Today," Pew Research, October 15, 2020.

52. Ian Bogost, "The Age of Social Media Is Over," *Atlantic*, November 10, 2022.

53. Jack Dorsey, Twitter, April 2, 2022, https://twitter.com/jack/status/1510314535671922689.

54. Derek Thompson, "America's Teenage Girls Are Not Okay," *Atlantic,* February 16, 2023.

55. Brian L. Ott, "The Digital Mind: How Computers (Re)Structure Human Consciousness," *Philosophies* 8, no. 1 (2023): 4.

56. John Dewey, "Public Opinion," *New Republic,* May 3, 1922.

57. John Dewey, *The Public and Its Problems* (New York: Henry Holt, 1927), 184.

58. Schudson, "The 'Lippmann–Dewey Debate.'"

59. Lippmann, *Public Opinion*, 49. T. S. Eliot was a classmate of Lippmann's at Harvard.

CHAPTER 7: THE DISLOCATED I

1. Andrew Perrin and Sara Atske, "About Three-in-Ten U.S. Adults Say They Are 'Almost Constantly' Online," Pew Research, March 26, 2021; and Emily A. Vogels et al., "Teens, Social Media and Technology 2022," Pew Research, August 10, 2022.

2. Steven Levy, *Facebook: The Inside Story* (New York: Blue Rider, 2020), 181.

3. Patricia Lockwood, *No One Is Talking about This* (New York: Riverhead Books, 2021), 3.

4. For a review of relevant research, see Nicholas Carr, "How Smartphones Hijack Our Minds," *Wall Street Journal,* October 7, 2017.

5. Charles Horton Cooley, *Human Nature and the Social Order* (1902; repr. New York: Schocken, 1964), 184.

6. Ibid., 180.

7. Ibid., 121. Italics are Cooley's.

8. Ibid., 184–185.

9. William James, *The Principles of Psychology*, vol. 1 (New York: Henry Holt, 1890), 294. Italics are James's.

10. Erving Goffman, *The Presentation of Self in Everyday Life* (New York: Anchor, 1959), 208.

11. The term *offstage*, as I use it here, shouldn't be confused with what Goffman calls *back stage*. In Goffman's dramaturgic analogy, the back stage is where individuals prepare, alone or with others, for an upcoming performance of the self. When offstage, by contrast, individuals are relieved of the pressures of performance. They're at a distance from society, alone with their own thoughts.

12. Erving Goffman, *Relations in Public: Microstudies of the Public Order* (New York: Basic Books, 1971), 70.

13. Joshua Meyrowitz, *No Sense of Place: The Impact of Electronic Media on Social Behavior* (New York: Oxford University Press, 1985), 41ff.

14. For a Freudian take on the net's effects, see Mark Edmundson, *The Age of Guilt: The Super-Ego in the Online World* (New Haven, CT: Yale University Press, 2023).

15. Jia Tolentino, *Trick Mirror* (New York: Random House, 2019), 14.

16. Meyrowitz, *No Sense*, 125.

17. Danah Boyd, "None of This Is Real: Identity and Participation in Friendster," in *Structures of Participation in Digital Culture*, ed. Joe Karaganis (New York: Social Science Research Council, 2007), 132–157.

18. Michael Wesch, "YouTube and You: Experiences of Self-Awareness in the Context Collapse of the Recording Webcam," *Explorations in Media Ecology* 8, no. 2 (2009): 19–34.

19. David Kirkpatrick, *The Facebook Effect: The Inside Story of the Company That Is Connecting the World* (New York: Simon & Schuster, 2010), 199.

20. S. Dixon, "Global Social Media Account Ownership from 2013 to 2018," Statista, April 28, 2022.

21. James A. Holstein and Jaber F. Gubrium, *The Self We Live By: Narrative Identity in a Postmodern World* (Oxford: Oxford University Press, 2000), 66.

22. Jean Baudrillard, *The Perfect Crime* (London: Verso, 2008), 28.

23. Dorothy E. Smith, *Texts, Facts, and Femininity: Exploring the Relations of Ruling* (London: Routledge, 1990), 209.

24. Cooley, *Human Nature*, 184.

25. Kwame Anthony Appiah, *The Lies That Bind* (New York: Liveright, 2018), xvi, 3–5. Appiah also offers an illuminating discussion of how identity becomes embodied through a process known as *habitus* (pp. 20–25).

26. Victoria Rideout and Michael B. Robb, *Social Media, Social Life: Teens Reveal Their Experiences* (San Francisco: Common Sense Media, 2018).

27. See Jean M. Twenge, *Generations* (New York: Atria, 2023). See also *Youth Risk Behavior Study Survey, 2011–2021*, Centers for Disease Control and Prevention, 2023. Unless otherwise noted, the figures in this section are drawn from Twenge's book.

28. Twenge, *Generations*, 408–409.

29. Viji Diane Kannan and Peter J. Veazie, "U.S. Trends in Social Isolation, Social Engagement, and Companionship—Nationally and by Age, Sex, Race/Ethnicity, Family Income, and Work Hours, 2003–2020," *SSM–Population Health* 21 (March 2023): 101331.

30. See, e.g., Eric M. Vogelsang, "Social Participation across Mid- and Later-Life: Evidence from a Longitudinal Cohort Study," *Sociological Perspectives* 64, no. 6 (2021): 1187–1205.

31. Twenge, *Generations*, 393–395.

32. Jonathan Haidt, "Social Media Is a Major Cause of the Mental Illness Epidemic in Teen Girls. Here's the Evidence," Substack, February 22, 2023, https://jonathanhaidt.substack.com/p/social-media-mental-illness-epidemic. For a more extensive discussion, see Jonathan Haidt, *The Anxious Generation* (New York: Penguin Press, 2024).

33. Stephani L. Hatch and Michael E. J. Wadsworth, "Does Adolescent Affect Impact Adult Integration? Evidence from the British 1946 Birth Cohort," *Sociology* 42, no. 1 (2008): 155–177.

34. Haidt, "Social Media Is a Major Cause." The italics are Haidt's.

35. Twenge, *Generations*, 384–450.

36. The differences in the adolescent experiences of Gen Z girls and boys come through clearly in the findings of the Millennium Cohort Study, an ongoing study of thousands of U.K. children born between 2000 and 2002. Girls spend substantially more time on social media, are more likely to be involved in online harassment, and are more likely to be dissatisfied with their weight and appearance. See Yvonne Kelly et al., "Social Media Use and Adolescent Mental Health: Findings from the U.K. Millennium Cohort Study," *eClinicalMedicine* 6 (2018): 59-68.

37. The dose-response methodology does have its place in internet research. It's appropriate when examining the effects of technology on facets of individual behavior that don't have a strong social component. For example, a great deal of research, including long-term studies by the Program for International Student Assessment, shows that the more time students spend using their phones and social media apps, the less well they tend to perform in school. For a review, see Derek Thompson, "It Sure Looks Like Phones Are Making Students Dumber," *Atlantic*, December 19, 2023.

38. Kirsten R Müller-Vahl et al., "Stop That! It's Not Tourette's but a New Type of Mass Sociogenic Illness," *Brain* 145, no. 2 (2022): 476–480.

39. John D. Haltigan et al., "Social Media as an Incubator of Personality and Behavioral Psychopathology: Symptom and Disorder Authenticity or Psychosomatic Social Contagion?," *Comprehensive Psychiatry* 121 (February 2023): 152362.

40. Amelia Lester, "Show Our Best Face," *Harvard Crimson*, February 17, 2004. Lester would go on to become a magazine editor at *The New Yorker* and at *Foreign Policy*.

CHAPTER 8: MACHINES WHO SPEAK

1. Quoted in Ann Saddlemyer, *Becoming George: The Life of Mrs. W. B. Yeats* (Oxford: Oxford University Press, 2002), 136.

2. *The Collected Works of W.B. Yeats, Volume IV: Early Essays*, ed. Richard J. Finneran and George Bornstein (New York: Scribner, 2007), 25.

3. William Butler Yeats, *A Vision* (rev ed. 1937; repr. New York: Collier, 1966), 8.

4. *Yeats's Vision Papers*, vol. 2 (Iowa City: University of Iowa, 1992), 269.

5. John Durham Peters, *Speaking into the Air: A History of the Idea of Communication* (Chicago: University of Chicago Press, 1999), 139.

6. Arthur Conan Doyle, *The History of Spiritualism*, vol. 1 (New York: George H. Doran, 1926), vii.

7. Peters, *Speaking*, 94.

8. Andrew Jackson Davis, *The Present Age and Inner Life* (New York: Partridge & Brittan, 1853), 66. Italics are Davis's. See also Jeffrey Sconce, *Haunted*

Media: Electronic Presence from Telegraphy to Television (Durham, NC: Duke University Press, 2000).

9. "Pause Giant AI Experiments: An Open Letter," Future of Life Institute, March 22, 2023, https://futureoflife.org/open-letter/pause-giant-ai-experiments/. Musk made his comment about "civilization destruction" during a Fox News interview with Tucker Carlson on April 17, 2023.

10. "Statement on AI Risk," Center for AI Safety, May 30, 2023, https://www.safe.ai/statement-on-ai-risk.

11. Cade Metz, "He's Not Worried, But He Knows You Are," *New York Times*, April 2, 2023.

12. Yann LeCun, Twitter, April 1, 2023, https://twitter.com/ylecun/status/1642205736678637572.

13. Ross Andersen, "Inside the Revolution at OpenAI," *Atlantic*, September 2023.

14. Stephen Wolfram, "What Is ChatGPT Doing . . . and Why Does It Work?," February 14, 2023, https://writings.stephenwolfram.com/2023/02/what-is-chatgpt-doing-and-why-does-it-work/.

15. Ted Chiang, "ChatGPT Is a Blurry JPEG of the Web," *New Yorker*, February 9, 2023.

16. Wolfram, "What Is ChatGPT Doing?"

17. Chiang, "ChatGPT Is a Blurry JPEG."

18. Vauhini Vara, "Ghosts," *Believer*, August 9, 2021. The essay subsequently became the basis of a *This American Life* episode.

19. Santosh Janardhan, "Reimagining Meta's Infrastructure for the AI Age," Meta, May 18, 2023.

20. Bill Gates, "The Age of AI Has Begun," GatesNotes, March 21, 2023, https://www.gatesnotes.com/The-Age-of-AI-Has-Begun.

21. Hannah H. Kim, "If Pinocchio Doesn't Freak You Out, Sydney Shouldn't Either," *Wired*, June 4, 2023.

22. Sangeeta Singh-Kurtz, "The Man of Your Dreams," *Cut*, March 10, 2023.

23. Andersen, "Inside the Revolution."

24. Jonas Bendiksen, *The Book of Veles* (London: Gost, 2022).

25. Jade Chao, "The Book of Veles," Magnum Photos, September 17, 2021, https://www.magnumphotos.com/arts-culture/society-arts-culture/book-veles-jonas-bendiksen-hoodwinked-photography-industry/. See also Tom Simonite, "A True Story about Bogus Photos of People Making Fake News," *Wired*, October 6, 2021.

26. Susan Sontag, *On Photography* (New York: Farrar, Straus and Giroux, 1977), 5.

27. See Walter J. Scheirer, *A History of Fake Things on the Internet* (Stanford, CA: Stanford University Press, 2024), 59–87.

28. Luc Cohen, "Taylor Swift Searches Blocked on X after Fake Explicit Images Spread," Reuters, January 29, 2024.

29. GOP, "Beat Biden," YouTube, April 25, 2023, https://www.youtube.com/watch?v=kLMMxgtxQ1Y&t=1s.

30. Matteo Wong, "We Haven't Seen the Worst of Fake News," *Atlantic*, December 20, 2022.

31. Sam Altman, X, August 3, 2023, https://twitter.com/sama/status/1687236201496064000.

32. Noah Giansiracusa, *How Algorithms Create and Prevent Fake News* (New York: Apress, 2021), 41.

33. Bobby Chesney and Danielle Citron, "Deep Fakes: A Looming Challenge for Privacy, Democracy, and National Security," *California Law Review* 107 (2019): 1753–1819.

34. See Konstantin Sheiko and Stephen Brown, *History as Therapy: Alternative History and Nationalist Imaginings in Russia, 1991–2014* (Stuttgart: Ibidem-Verlag, 2014), 83–85.

35. "A Dialogue—Marshall McLuhan and Gerald Emanuel Stearn," in *McLuhan: Hot and Cool*, ed. Gerald E. Stearn (New York: Dial, 1967), 280.

36. See, among many other press reports, Abby Ohlheiser, "Trolls Turned Tay, Microsoft's Fun Millennial Bot, into a Genocidal Maniac," *Washington Post*, May 25, 2016.

37. Peter Lee, "Learning from Tay's Introduction," Official Microsoft Blog, March 25, 2016, https://blogs.microsoft.com/blog/2016/03/25/learning-tays-introduction/.

38. Andersen, "Inside the Revolution."

39. "DALL-E Pre-Training Mitigations," OpenAI, June 28, 2022, https://openai.com/research/dall-e-2-pre-training-mitigations.

40. Tom Warren, "Google Pauses Gemini's Ability to Generate AI Images of People after Diversity Errors," *Verge*, February 22, 2024.

41. Prabhakar Raghavan, "Gemini Image Generator Got It Wrong. We'll Do Better," Google Blog, February 23, 2024, https://blog.google/products/gemini/gemini-image-generation-issue/.

42. Andersen, "Inside the Revolution."

43. Elon Musk, X, November 28, 2022, https://twitter.com/elonmusk/status/1597405399040217088.

44. Angel Eduardo, "Twitter Is No Free Speech Haven under Elon Musk," FIRE, April 12, 2023. See also Thomas Germain, "Elon Musk, King of Censorship," *Gizmodo,* July 13, 2023.

45. Georgia Wells et al., "Musk's Impulses Remake Twitter," *Wall Street Journal*, September 8, 2023.

CHAPTER 9: WORLD WITHOUT WORLD

1. Marc Andreessen, "Why Software Is Eating the World," *Wall Street Journal*, August 20, 2011.

2. Marc Andreessen, "Why AI Will Save the World," Andreessen Horowitz, June 6, 2023, https://a16z.com/2023/06/06/ai-will-save-the-world/.

3. Niccolo Soldo, "The Dubrovnik Interviews: Marc Andreessen—Interviewed by a Retard," Substack, May 31, 2021, https://niccolo.substack.com/p/the-dubrovnik-interviews-marc-andreessen. When the freewheeling interview appeared, many wondered whether it was a fake. An Andreessen spokesperson confirmed it was genuine.

4. Iris Murdoch, "Metaphysics and Ethics," in *Existentialists and Mystics*, ed. Peter Conradi (New York: Penguin, 1999), 75.

5. Nathan Jurgenson, *The Social Photo* (London: Verso, 2019), 35.

6. Annelyse Gelman, *Vexations* (Chicago: University of Chicago Press, 2023).

7. Jean Baudrillard, *Cool Memories*, trans. Chris Turner (London: Verso, 1990), 22.

8. Jean Baudrillard, *Symbolic Exchange and Death*, trans. Iain Hamilton Grant (London: Sage, 1993), 2, 76. Italics are Baudrillard's.

9. Jaak Panksepp, *Affective Neuroscience* (New York: Oxford University Press, 1998), 145.

10. Jean Baudrillard, *The Ecstasy of Communication*, trans. Bernard Schütze and Caroline Schütze (Los Angeles: Semiotext(e), 2012), 20.

11. Caroline Mimbs Nyce, "TikTok Is Opening a Parallel Dimension in Europe," *Atlantic*, August 16, 2023.

12. Jean Baudrillard, *The Vital Illusion* (New York: Columbia University Press, 2000), 66.

13. Jane McGonigal, *Reality Is Broken* (New York: Penguin, 2011), 3.

14. Christopher Mims, "You Can't Look Away from Work," *Wall Street Journal*, February 10, 2024.

15. Antón Barba-Kay, *A Web of Our Own Making* (Cambridge: Cambridge University Press, 2023), 22–23.

16. John Dewey, *The Public and Its Problems* (New York: Henry Holt, 1927), 214.

CHAPTER 10: DR. JOHNSON'S ROCK

1. Anonymous, "Obviously Self-Defense," *New York Times*, October 21, 1952; and Jack Gould, "An Irate Video Owner Has Come Up with an Unusual Solution to Your Chief TV Bete Noir," *New York Times*, October 22, 1952.

2. See Jeffrey Sconce, *Haunted Media* (Durham, NC: Duke University Press, 2000).

3. Tim Wu, "The Google Antitrust Trial Is Really about the Future of AI," *New York Times*, September 19, 2023.

4. Brett Frischmann and Susan Benesch, "Friction-in-Design Regulation as 21st Century Time, Place, and Manner Restriction," *Yale Journal of Law and Technology* 25 (2023): 376–447. For philosophical background, also see Brett Frischmann and Evan Selinger, *Re-engineering Humanity* (Cambridge: Cambridge University Press, 2018).

5. See the June 1, 2022, blog post "How Twitter Is Nudging Users to Have Healthier Conversations": https://blog.twitter.com/common-thread/en/topics/stories/2022/how-twitter-is-nudging-users-healthier-conversations.

6. Julie Jargon, "New Tech That Asks 'Are You Sure about Sending a Nude Photo?,'" *Wall Street Journal*, April 11, 2024.

7. Thomas P. Hughes, "Technological Momentum," in *Does Technology Drive History?*, ed. Merritt Roe Smith and Leo Marx (Cambridge, MA: MIT Press, 1994), 101–113.

8. James Boswell, *The Life of Johnson* (Harmondsworth, UK: Penguin Press, 1979), 122.

9. Quoted in Glenn Zorpette, "Just Calm Down about GPT4 Already," *IEEE Spectrum*, May 17, 2023.

10. Rodney A. Brooks, "Elephants Don't Play Chess," *Robotics and Autonomous Systems* 6 (1990): 3–15. For an expansive discussion of this theme, see Matthew B. Crawford, *The World Beyond Your Head* (New York: Farrar, Straus and Giroux, 2015).

INDEX